Vol. XII

No. 4

Bible Expositor and Illuminator

Large-Print Edition

FALL QUARTER

September, October, November 2021

Faith on Trial

UNIT I: Learning God's Holiness

UNIT II: Seeing God's Faithfulness

UNIT III: Taking God Seriously

Editor in Chief: Kenneth Sponsler

Union **G**ospel **P**ress

Edited and published quarterly by
THE INCORPORATED TRUSTEES C
GOSPEL WORKER SOCIETY
UNION GOSPEL PRESS DIVISI
Rev. W. B. Musselman, Found
Price: $8.50 per quarter*
$34.00 per year*
*shipping and handling extra
ISBN 978-1-64495-165-1

LOOKING AHEAD

This quarter we are going to embark on an exciting journey that will cover many miles of territory over a period of nearly four decades. Where else can you cover forty years in thirteen weeks besides in Sunday school?

Unit I centers on the holiness of God, as God establishes His holiness before the Israelites after He brought them out of Egypt. Lesson 1 covers the ordination of Aaron and his sons as the priests under God's covenant with Israel. Lesson 2 deals with the sudden deaths of two of Aaron's sons, Nadab and Abihu, because they failed to treat God as holy.

In lesson 3, the Day of Atonement is described and established as the holiest day on the Hebrew calendar, with specific instructions for how the high priest was to conduct his duties. Lesson 4 discusses the consequences for blaspheming against God's name.

The second unit deals with seeing God's faithfulness. The lessons here teach us that God is faithful even when we are not. In lesson 5, we find the people complaining about the manna, the special food God faithfully provided for them during their wilderness travels. In lesson 6, we see that the attitudes of the people did not improve. When they would not stop complaining, God sent them quail in abundance to eat, but this blessing quickly turned into a plague among the people.

Lesson 7 recounts that Miriam and Aaron joined in the complaining against Moses. They attempted to usurp his authority until they faced dire consequences. Lesson 8 concludes the second unit with a study about the mission of the twelve spies Moses sent out into Canaan to inspect the land.

In unit III, we see the importance of taking God seriously at all times. The rebellion of the people against the will of God is detailed in lesson 9, as the Israelites believed a negative report and refused to enter the Promised Land.

Lesson 10 covers Moses' intercessory prayer for the people and shows the merciful nature of God while not compromising His holiness. Lesson 11 shows us that God will not long tolerate rebellion from people and that it is never wise to challenge the authority of God or those whom He calls into leadership.

Lesson 12 explains how judgment fell on those who rebelled against God, and lesson 13 teaches that even those who are in positions of authority are not above doing as the Lord commands.

—*Robert Ferguson, Jr.*

EDITORIALS

How Does God Deal with Our Failures?

JEFFERY J. VANGOETHEM

For our study and edification this quarter we have before us a series of lessons that feature numerous failures of Israel as the nation struggled to be faithful to God in the days after the Exodus from Egypt. Sadly, there were moments of blasphemy, disobedience, rebellion, weakness, and complaining, among other shortcomings. How did God deal with such failures and sins?

God's response was not the same in every instance. Sometimes there was rebuke, sometimes discipline, and sometimes judgment. But one thing was a constant. God kept ministering to His people, no matter what they did wrong. We can see this best perhaps from the description of God's character in Numbers 14:18: "The Lord is longsuffering, and of great mercy, forgiving iniquity and transgression, and by no means clearing the guilty." Yes, God brought discipline and even stern judgment when needed, but He still remained patient and forgiving toward His people.

We are all well aware of our own failures in the Christian life: seasons of apathy, moments of disobedience, occasions of sin, and blunders of word and deed. Even more, we sin repeatedly against God in our hearts, holding up idols in place of Him. How does God deal with such failures? The biblical answer to that question as we review the story of Israel is this: God is merciful, patient, kind, and gracious regarding our shortcomings, sins, and failures.

God knows that it takes time for us to learn His ways. Even those of us steeped in the faith from our youth continue to have much to learn and much growing to do. And many of us who came to the faith from more difficult backgrounds have a lot of rough edges that need to be made smooth. It takes time. God knows this. There is grace for our failures.

God's love for us is larger than our failures. The first point we need to understand about this is that our sins do not defeat God's holy purpose for our lives. The book of Philippians says it so powerfully: "Being confident of this very thing, that he which hath begun a good work in you will perform it until the day of Jesus Christ" (1:6). Let that truth sink in. God is determined to bring His children to holiness and complete redemption. We are saved and kept by grace.

As we journey through this difficult world, we must never lose sight of that. We may blow it at times, but if we have received the Lord Jesus Christ as Saviour, we never completely fall out of favor with God. He stays with us, and despite our failures, no matter how serious, our relationship with God remains intact. We are precious to Him. The Lord Jesus paid a steep price to bring us into God's family, and He intends to keep us. That is amazing news!

That leads to a second point. What do we do when we fail? Do we remember when Abraham left the Promised Land shortly after being sent there (Gen. 12:10—13:4)? He ended up in Egypt. It was an ill-advised trip. Nothing good happened there. When Pharaoh found out that Abraham had lied to him, telling him that his wife was his sister, he rebuked Abraham

(Editorials continued on page 186)

SCRIPTURE LESSON TEXT

LEV. 8:1 And the LORD spake unto Moses, saying,

2 Take Aaron and his sons with him, and the garments, and the anointing oil, and a bullock for the sin offering, and two rams, and a basket of unleavened bread;

3 And gather thou all the congregation together unto the door of the tabernacle of the congregation.

4 And Moses did as the LORD commanded him; and the assembly was gathered together unto the door of the tabernacle of the congregation.

5 And Moses said unto the congregation, This is the thing which the LORD commanded to be done.

6 And Moses brought Aaron and his sons, and washed them with water.

7 And he put upon him the coat, and girded him with the girdle, and clothed him with the robe, and put the ephod upon him, and he girded him with the curious girdle of the ephod, and bound it unto him therewith.

8 And he put the breastplate upon him: also he put in the breastplate the Urim and the Thummim.

9 And he put the mitre upon his head; also upon the mitre, even upon his forefront, did he put the golden plate, the holy crown; as the LORD commanded Moses.

10 And Moses took the anointing oil, and anointed the tabernacle and all that was therein, and sanctified them.

11 And he sprinkled thereof upon the altar seven times, and anointed the altar and all his vessels, both the laver and his foot, to sanctify them.

12 And he poured of the anointing oil upon Aaron's head, and anointed him, to sanctify him.

13 And Moses brought Aaron's sons, and put coats upon them, and girded them with girdles, and put bonnets upon them; as the LORD commanded Moses.

NOTES

Ordination of Aaron and His Sons

Lesson Text: Leviticus 8:1-13

Related Scriptures: Exodus 29:1-37; Hebrews 10:19-25; Acts 22:14-16

TIME: about 1445 B.C.   PLACE: Mount Sinai

GOLDEN TEXT—"Let us draw near with a true heart in full assurance of faith, having our hearts sprinkled from an evil conscience, and our bodies washed with pure water" (Hebrews 10:22).

Introduction

One of the most overlooked characteristics of God in modern biblical and theological teaching is His holiness. The word "holiness" speaks of separation. God is holy in that He is separate from the world He created. He is separate from the evil world system that dominates and controls fallen human thought. Since humans are created in the image of God, God calls us to be holy as well, just as He is holy (cf. Lev. 11:44; I Pet. 1:15-16).

The perfect holiness of God suggests that He pays attention to details. Even what seem like little things to us are important to the Lord.

This week's lesson shows that God calls us to be holy, but He does not require us to manufacture holiness in ourselves. As we will see, He has anointed us with the Holy Spirit to produce the fruit of the Spirit in our lives.

LESSON OUTLINE

I. **CALLED BY THE LORD—**
   Lev. 8:1-4

II. **PREPARED BY THE LORD—**
    Lev. 8:5-9

III. **ORDAINED BY THE LORD—**
     Lev. 8:10-13

Exposition: Verse by Verse

CALLED BY THE LORD

LEV. 8:1 And the LORD spake unto Moses, saying,

2 Take Aaron and his sons with him, and the garments, and the anointing oil, and a bullock for the sin offering, and two rams, and a basket of unleavened bread;

3 And gather thou all the congregation together unto the door of the

tabernacle of the congregation.

4 And Moses did as the Lord commanded him; and the assembly was gathered together unto the door of the tabernacle of the congregation.

God calls for Aaron and his sons (Lev. 8:1-2). One of the greatest problems humans face is that we are sinful and God is holy. Sinful humans cannot approach a holy God on their own but must have someone to represent them. In order to come to God, we must have a representative to appear before Him on our behalf. God's answer to this predicament for His Old Testament people was the priesthood.

Today, because of the death and resurrection of Jesus, Christ is our Great High Priest and represents all believers before God (cf. Heb. 4:14-16). Before Christ came, however, God chose Aaron and his sons to serve as priests under the old covenant established through Moses.

Since Aaron and his sons were also guilty of sin, they had to be cleansed, or ritually made holy, if they were going to serve as priests between people and God. They were specifically chosen by God for a unique service. This did not make them better than anyone else, and it did not absolve them of their own personal sins. It did, however, require specific rituals to consecrate them, or set them apart, for their service to the Lord.

{God began by telling Moses to call Aaron and his sons together.}Q1 He then instructed Moses to take certain garments, anointing oil, a bull for a sin offering, two rams, and a basket of unleavened bread. All these elements were necessary to fulfill the requirements for the ordination of priests as set forth in Exodus 29.

A public ceremony (Lev. 8:3-4). Moses set Aaron and his sons before the entire assembly at the entrance of the tabernacle. {The ceremony was designed to be in a public setting, not a private space. The people were to see who their priests were and that God had designated them for this office.}Q2 The priesthood was not an office to be aspired to but one for which the individual was chosen. Future priests had to be descendants of Aaron in order to qualify.

Moses did as God had directed, and the people were gathered at the tabernacle for the ordination of their priests. While the ceremony did not mean the priests suddenly became superhuman and would no longer sin, it did show publicly that God had chosen these specific men for this unique role, and as such, they were to be respected by the people.

PREPARED BY THE LORD

5 And Moses said unto the congregation, This is the thing which the Lord commanded to be done.

6 And Moses brought Aaron and his sons, and washed them with water.

7 And he put upon him the coat, and girded him with the girdle, and clothed him with the robe, and put the ephod upon him, and he girded him with the curious girdle of the ephod, and bound it unto him therewith.

8 And he put the breastplate upon him: also he put in the breastplate the Urim and the Thummim.

9 And he put the mitre upon his head; also upon the mitre, even upon his forefront, did he put the golden plate, the holy crown; as the Lord commanded Moses.

The commandment of the Lord (Lev. 8:5). When the people had gathered at the entrance of the tabernacle, Moses declared to them that the following ceremony had been commanded by God. Aaron was not chosen by Moses as a result of nepotism; rather, he was chosen by God. Moses had nothing to do with Aaron's appointment to serve as the first high priest.

The people needed to understand at the outset that God had ordained not only those who would serve as priests but also the priesthood itself. Again, this was not Moses' idea of the best way for the people to come to God. He was only following the directives he received from the Lord, including the institution of the priesthood under the covenant and those who would serve in this capacity.

The washing of the priests (Lev. 8:6). The first act in this ceremony was the washing, or cleansing, of Aaron and his sons. In a very humbling action, Aaron and his sons had their bodies washed by Moses before the gathered assembly. {The fact that Moses washed them illustrated that they could not cleanse themselves of their own personal sin but had to be cleansed by another.}Q3 Since Moses was the mediator of the old covenant, this duty fell on him.

The modern significance of this act is that we too cannot cleanse ourselves of our personal sin. We have to be washed by Someone else, namely Christ. {We are cleansed not by water but by the perfect blood of Jesus (cf. I Pet. 1:18-19). Our sins have been washed away by the Mediator of the new covenant we now live under, which was ushered in by Christ Himself.}Q4 Having been cleansed of sin, we are to publicly profess Jesus as our Lord and risen Saviour.

Under the new covenant, all Christians are priests before God (cf. I Pet. 2:9-10; Rev. 5:9-10), even as Christ is our Great High Priest in heaven. We have been chosen and cleansed by God to serve Him in loving obedience, representing Him to the world in which we live. Just as this washing of Aaron and his sons was a one-time event, our sins are washed away by the blood of Christ once and for all.

Jesus washed the disciples' feet and stated that because they had already been washed completely, they needed only to have their feet washed (John 13:1-10). He was distinguishing between the one-time event of justification (whereby God declares us righteous through faith) and the ongoing process of sanctification (pictured by the washing of the disciples' feet). That process is a continual exercise of being conformed daily to the image of Christ.

Jesus washed the disciples' feet because they got dirty from the dusty roads they traveled. Likewise, we get dirty from sin we commit each day. This does not negate our initial cleansing, however. We confess our sins to God so we can experience restoration and renewal, but our initial cleansing is permanent.

Priestly garments and the ephod (Lev. 8:7). After Aaron and his sons were washed, the next step was to clothe Aaron with the priestly garments (cf. Ex. 28:4-36). The purpose of these garments was not just to cover his nakedness but to invest the worship of the Lord with beauty and to elevate the role and office of the high priest (cf. vs. 2). Additionally, they would clearly identify the high priest to the people.

An interesting element to all the priestly garments is that neither Aaron nor his sons had anything to do with making them. They were already made and ready to be worn for the first time on this occasion. In other words, this was not a haphazard event that was quickly thrown together. Great preparations had been made for quite some time so the garments would be ready. It was because of the work of skilled craftsmen that Aaron and his sons were able to don the special garments of priests.

The high priest's "coat" (Lev. 8:7) was a tunic that was worn next to the skin and reached to the feet. It was tied with a "girdle," or sash, around the waist to hold it close to the body. A robe, an outer garment, was worn over the coat. {It was made of a beautiful combination of blue, purple, and scarlet materials with golden bells on the hem.}Q5

{The "ephod," which was worn over the robe, was a special article of clothing that was similar in appearance to an apron. It was made of two pieces joined at the shoulders and was open on both sides.}Q6 The ephod was made of gold, blue, purple, and scarlet threads. These threads were skillfully woven together by craftsmen who were gifted and equipped by God for such a purpose.

Two onyx stones were set on the shoulder pieces of the ephod, and each stone was to have the names of six of the tribes of Israel engraved on it. This showed that the high priest bore Israel on his shoulders, a place of work. The duties of the priest were not easy and included great labor on behalf of the people.

The "curious girdle" was made of the same material as the ephod. It was a belt that held the ephod to the body at the waist.

The breastplate (Lev. 8:8-9). The breastplate was then placed upon the high priest, Aaron. The square breastplate was made of woven material and rested on the front of the ephod. Like the other priestly garments, it was to be skillfully made and consisted of gold, blue, purple, and scarlet threads. The specifications given in Exodus 28:15-29 concerning the making of the breastplate show that details are important to God. The office of the high priest, as well as that of the priests, was not to be seen as something common, and the garments reflected that fact.

{Attached to the breastplate were twelve precious stones, each one engraved with the name of a tribe of Israel.}Q7 God no doubt used precious stones because His people are precious to Him. Similar stones will also be prominent in the New Jerusalem, the future eternal home of every child of God (cf. Rev. 21:19-20).

{The breastplate was identified with judgment (cf. Ex. 28:15).}Q7 The high priest wore the breastplate as he entered God's presence and sought deliverance from God's judgment on behalf of the people.

The Urim and Thummim were then placed inside the breastplate. The text in Leviticus does not reveal their size, shape, number, or even function, so they have engendered much speculation and debate. {They are often thought to have been dice-like stones, but they were somehow used on occasion to determine the will of God in certain situations.}Q8 There is no mention of them in the New Testament, so their association is exclusively with the old covenant. We now have the Holy Spirit and Scripture to direct us in determining the will of God.

The "mitre" (Lev. 8:9), or turban, that was placed on the head of the high priest was similar to a crown. Fastened to the front of it was a plate of pure gold that had the words "Holiness to the Lord" engraved on it (Ex. 28:36). The high priest in his glorious garments was quite a sight to see for the people of Israel, and his responsibilities were great. He was the one who stood between the people and God.

ORDAINED BY THE LORD

10 And Moses took the anointing oil, and anointed the tabernacle and all that was therein, and sanctified them.

11 And he sprinkled thereof upon the altar seven times, and anointed the altar and all his vessels, both the laver and his foot, to sanctify them.

12 And he poured of the anointing oil upon Aaron's head, and anointed him, to sanctify him.

13 And Moses brought Aaron's sons, and put coats upon them, and girded them with girdles, and put bonnets upon them; as the Lord commanded Moses.

Anointing of objects (Lev. 8:10-11). While the ordination of Israel's first priests might bear some similarities to the modern ordination of individuals to pastoral ministry, there is also much in Leviticus 8 that was unique. Contemporary ordination services focus on the person being ordained. The ordination of Aaron and his sons, however, also included the consecration of the tabernacle, the altar, and all the utensils and instruments the priests would be using.

The anointing with oil showed the people that these items had been set apart for service to the Lord, or "sanctified." Nothing was left out, and nothing was overlooked.

Anointing of the priests (Lev. 8:12-13). After anointing the tabernacle and the items in it, Moses then poured oil on Aaron's head to anoint him for service as high priest. {Oil is sometimes a symbol of the Holy Spirit in Scripture,}[Q9] and the anointing here likely pictures the Holy Spirit being poured upon Aaron, empowering him for his high priestly service. Aaron could not fulfill his duties in his own power. He needed a special infusion of God's help.

{That the oil was poured on Aaron's head and allowed to run down shows that the Spirit is given without measure. There was no concern for wasting oil here. Objects such as the altar were sprinkled with oil, but God's chosen servant had oil poured on him.}[Q10]

God gives us His Spirit without measure to empower, equip, guide, instruct, and convict us.

Moses then called for Aaron's sons to come forward, and he clothed them with their priestly garments. The garments worn by the priests were simpler than that of the high priest and were all white (cf. Ex. 28:40-43). Their clothing also made them easily identifiable as priests.

Throughout the ordination process, Moses did what he was commanded by God. At no point did God consult with Moses, and at no point did Moses challenge God or try to give his input. As great a leader as Moses was, he was still a mere human being. He was not divine or even semi-divine. He was just a man who had been called by God for a specific purpose.

God cares about you and the details of your life. He has called you into a particular realm of service and wants to equip you for that role. He has anointed you with His Holy Spirit to accomplish His will in your life. Have you surrendered to this calling? The only way to do anything of eternal value is to yield to the will of God.

—Robert Ferguson, Jr.

QUESTIONS

1. What did God instruct Moses to do with Aaron and his sons?
2. Why was it important for this ceremony to be public?
3. What was the significance of the washing of Aaron and his sons?
4. How are we cleansed under the new covenant?
5. What colors were used in the priestly garments?
6. What was the ephod, and what was included in its composition?
7. What was attached to the breastplate of the high priest, and with what was the breastplate associated?
8. What purpose did the Urim and Thummim serve?
9. What does oil sometimes represent in Scripture?
10. How did the consecration of the tabernacle utensils differ from how Aaron was anointed?

—Robert Ferguson, Jr.

Preparing to Teach the Lesson

We are beginning a series of lessons in the books of Leviticus and Numbers that will focus on the importance of living out our faith, especially in difficult times. All of us have encountered moments of distress that have tested our faith, or we know someone who has experienced such trials. In these stressful moments, we find out what we are really made of.

As we read the pages of Scripture, we realize that God has designed us to prevail through all situations, good and bad. Our study this quarter in Leviticus and Numbers will help us build our faith so that when it is tested, we will be found faithful. An enduring, unwavering faith must grasp the holiness of God.

TODAY'S AIM

Facts: to observe three very important aspects of God's holiness.

Principle: to emphasize that God's children are to reflect the holiness of their Heavenly Father.

Application: to investigate our personal lives with a goal of becoming more consistent in our personal holiness.

INTRODUCING THE LESSON

The first five books of the Bible (also known as the Pentateuch) comprise the historical record of many beginnings. Genesis 1—3 recounts the beginning of all creation, and Genesis 12 tells of the beginning of God's people through the patriarch Abraham. Exodus 1—14 depicts the beginning of the nation of Israel, while the remainder of Exodus records the beginning of Israel's journey to Canaan.

The book of Leviticus continues the narrative of beginnings. Here we find God beginning to develop in greater detail what it means to have a relationship with the Creator. Such a relationship demands that God's people deeply understand the concept of true holiness.

In Leviticus 8:1-13, we read of the consecration of Moses' brother, Aaron, and Aaron's sons. The ordination of Aaron and his sons to the priesthood presents interesting aspects of God's holiness (cf. Ex. 29:1-37; Heb. 10:19-25). Biblical holiness is on display in a number of ways in our lesson text.

DEVELOPING THE LESSON

There are three requirements of biblical holiness that can be clearly discerned from Leviticus 8:1-13.

1. A thorough understanding of that which God requires (Lev. 8:1-3). Notice here that Aaron's sanctification took much more than well-meaning effort. The Lord had very specific requirements that He demanded be met. For Aaron, the sanctification process required "the garments, and the anointing oil, and a bullock for the sin offering, and two rams, and a basket of unleavened bread." While these elements have symbolic meaning, they all point to the fact that sanctification, becoming holy, is not a process of our own design. We must know and submit to God's requirements.

2. A clear determination to give God the glory (Lev. 8:4-5). Not only is it insufficient to try to be holy on our own terms, but it is also insufficient to seek holiness with the wrong intentions. In verses 4-5, we see Moses' desire to give all the glory to God, not himself. Moses' own words reveal his intention, as he said to the congregation, "This is the thing which the Lord commanded to be done." Moses did not claim to be extraordinarily wise or religious. Rather, he simply wanted to be completely obedient to the Lord and to publicly express the importance of obeying and honoring a holy God.

3. Complete obedience in following God's instructions (8:6-13). After one has clearly understood God's requirements for holiness and has demonstrated the right motives, there is still an important step remaining: the believer must follow through completely by diligently following God's instructions. A close reading of Leviticus 8:6-13 reveals Moses' meticulous attention to detail in following through on the commands God gave him in relation to the sanctification of Aaron and his sons.

The clear responsibility we have as believers is to closely follow Moses' example in principle. Whether the Lord's commands relating to our personal holiness make sense to us or not, we must completely obey those commands if we are to grow in holiness and Christlikeness.

Biblical holiness finds its source in the Lord Himself as communicated through His Word and His commands. Biblical holiness thus has very little to do with what we want and very much to do with what the Lord desires for us.

We might illustrate this spiritual concept by the very common situation of entering another country. Typically, countries require the documentation of a passport for a person to gain entry into their jurisdiction. It does not matter if the traveler has numerous other identification documents; if he or she does not possess a valid passport, entry into another country will be denied. Regardless of how sincere and well-meaning the traveler might be, and regardless of how much the traveler might be trusting in the validity of other documents he or she might be carrying, the absence of a valid passport is insurmountable. Likewise, biblical holiness is determined by the Lord's standard, not ours. Seeking our own way brings glory only to ourselves and produces self-righteousness. Following the Lord's standards produces biblical holiness, which glorifies Him.

ILLUSTRATING THE LESSON

The visual aid summarizes a basic principle we can draw from the lesson text. Following our own standards through our own efforts leads to sinful self-righteousness. Following the standards set forth in God's Word humbles us and leads to true holiness and Christlikeness.

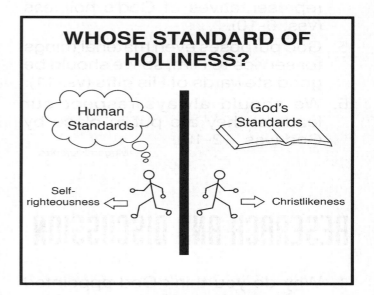

WHOSE STANDARD OF HOLINESS?

Human Standards

God's Standards

Self-righteousness

Christlikeness

CONCLUDING THE LESSON

Leviticus 8:1-13 communicates a number of very important concepts related to biblical sanctification, or growth in holiness. We have seen that biblical holiness requires a thorough understanding of God's requirements, the right motives on the part of the believer, and complete obedience in following God's instructions.

ANTICIPATING THE NEXT LESSON

The central theme of our next lesson is also God's holiness, but it has a very different feel, as it examines the death of Nadab and Abihu (Lev. 10:1-7).

—*Nigel C. Black.*

PRACTICAL POINTS

1. We should never be irreverent when we speak to God; we should fear and obey Him (Lev. 8:1-2).
2. Always try to display the Lord's attributes to others (vss. 3-4).
3. We should always be able to point to the Lord's authority over whatever we do. If we cannot, it is not worth doing (Lev. 8:5; Rom. 14:23).
4. As Christians, we should clothe ourselves in righteousness as representatives of God's holiness (vss. 6-10).
5. God purposes even material things for service to Him, so we should be good stewards of His gifts (vs. 11).
6. We should always respect our leaders; they are put in place by God (vss. 12-13).

—*Megan Hickman.*

RESEARCH AND DISCUSSION

1. Why do you think God appointed priests instead of just approaching the people directly?
2. In what ways do some churches belittle God's holiness?
3. Why did God want Israel to see the anointing of the priests (Lev. 8:3)?
4. Outer holiness should reflect inner holiness. How can we maintain integrity as believers (Matt. 23:27-28; I John 1:7; Rev. 4:17)?
5. Even though we have been made righteous by the blood of Jesus (Heb. 10:19), why is it still crucial for us to pursue holiness (9:14)?
6. How can we encourage others not to waver on God's Word?

—*Megan Hickman.*

ILLUSTRATED HIGH POINTS

As the Lord commanded (Lev. 8:4)

When I was little, I liked to help my mom make food for my whole family. Because I was so young, she only let me do simple tasks, such as washing the vegetables or stirring the cake batter. She would not let me do anything where I could potentially hurt myself, such as using a knife or the stove top burners.

On one occasion, I was baking brownies with my mom. She warned me to stay away from the oven because it was very hot. She put the brownies into the oven, and I wanted to watch them bake. I tried to look inside the oven, but I could not get a good look through the oven window. I decided I would be able to see the brownies much better if I were to open the oven door. I pulled on the oven door handle as hard as I could. The noise from the door made my mom turn around.

Thankfully, I was not hurt, but she was not happy. She tried to explain to me that the oven was hot even though we had just put the brownies inside and that I could have hurt myself. Just as my mom's rules were for my benefit, the Lord's commands are also for the benefit of His covenant people.

He put upon him the coat (vs. 7)

A wedding day is an exciting time for families, but it can also be very hectic and stressful.

Attire is an important aspect of a wedding. A groom has to put on his suit or tuxedo to prepare to get married and the bride has a special dress.

Similar to a bride and groom in a wedding, Aaron also took his time to prepare for his role as the high priest with his sanctified garb. This signified God's new relationship with Israel as His chosen people.

—*Chelsea Villaseñor.*

Golden Text Illuminated

"Let us draw near with a true heart in full assurance of faith, having our hearts sprinkled from an evil conscience, and our bodies washed with pure water" (Hebrews 10:22).

Our golden text for this week is not taken from this week's lesson text. In fact, it starkly contrasts with its subject matter! Throughout the epistle to the Hebrews, the writer draws a sharp disparity between the Old Testament Aaronic priesthood and the supreme priesthood of Jesus Christ.

Our lesson text (Lev. 8:1-13) recounts the public ordination and sanctification of Aaron and his sons as the exclusive, divinely designated order of priests for Yahweh's tabernacle (and later, His temple) and its sacrifices. It was a supremely solemn and holy occasion, directly commanded by Yahweh through His servant Moses.

Before the entrance to the holy tabernacle, in the sight of the gathering of the congregation of Israel, Moses took pure water and washed Aaron and his sons with it. Thus ceremonially cleansed, Aaron was clothed with the tunic, sash, priestly robe, and the ephod, a priestly cape or mantle. The ephod was bound to Aaron with a girdle said to be of ingenious craftmanship.

Aaron was then adorned with the priestly breastplate bearing the twelve jewels representing the tribes of Israel. The Urim and the Thummim (literally the "lights" and the "perfection"), two gemstones for discerning the will of Yahweh in specific cases, were stored in a compartment of the breastplate. Finally, He was crowned with the priestly "mitre," or turban, bearing a diadem of gold inscribed with the words, "Holy to the Lord" (Ex. 28:36).

Whereas Aaron's priesthood was one of temporary appeasement of God's wrath toward the people's sins through animal sacrifices that had to be repeated regularly, Jesus' sacrifice provides complete and permanent atonement for all the sins of everyone who trusts in Him.

This is the background of our golden text's admonition to "draw near." In the context of the epistle to the Hebrews, what we are encouraged to draw near to is the "holiest" (10:19). This is a reference to the holiest place in Yahweh's temple in the heavenly realm, the very throne of Yahweh Himself!

In contrast to Aaron and his sons, we have been sprinkled not with mere oil but with the Holy Spirit, who has cleared our consciences once and for all from the guilt of our sins. We have been washed not by mere water but with the pure, living water of the Holy Spirit's sanctifying, indwelling presence through the atoning blood of our Lord and Saviour, Jesus Christ.

These things are meant to give us full assurance of faith, enabling us to boldly approach God's throne in confident supplication. As the writer of Hebrews wrote, "Seeing then that we have a great high priest, that is passed into the heavens, Jesus the Son of God, let us hold fast our profession. For we have not an high priest which cannot be touched with the feeling of our infirmities; but was in all points tempted like as we are, yet without sin. Let us therefore come boldly unto the throne of grace, that we may obtain mercy, and find grace to help in time of need" (4:14-16).

—*John Lody.*

Heart of the Lesson

The salvation that God gives is a miraculous thing. In the story of the Exodus, the Lord saved the Israelite people from bondage. But their salvation was just the beginning of their story as God's chosen people.

As faithful Christians, we must continually learn how to treasure, worship, trust, and obey the Lord. It is a long and difficult process—but it is well worth it. The Israelites had to learn how to respond to God as well.

The establishment of Aaron and his sons as priests—mediators between God and the people—reminds us of a very important attribute of God: He is completely holy. We can see from the description of their consecration that this was a very high calling.

Moses displays God's holiness (Lev. 8:1-4). The consecration of Aaron and his sons gives us an idea of how serious God really is about His holiness. Not only is He completely holy, He also requires holiness of us (Lev. 11:44-45). He calls all His servants to be set apart, or consecrated, but in the ordination of the priesthood this would be on display for the people. Moses was to bring Aaron and his sons before the people to show them the purity that the Lord required of them. The need for priests as mediators also made clear the depth of their sin.

Moses cleanses the priests (Lev. 8:5-9). Moses made sure the people knew he was about to perform the Lord's explicit instructions. He then proceeded to wash the priests, clothe them in majestic garb, and crown them.

The Lord had a distinct purpose in commanding these things. God was not only showing the people His holiness; He was also initiating traditions that would point forward to the ultimate redemption of His people through His Son. All of the ordination details point forward to our ultimate consecration through Christ's atoning sacrifice. We must be washed by His blood (Heb. 10:22; 9:22). In the end, He will give us robes of righteousness (Isa. 61:10; II Cor. 5:21), and we will be crowned in glory (I Pet. 1:4).

Moses anoints the altar (Lev. 8:10-13). After the purification process, Moses anointed the altar and the priests. Once consecrated, the altar too was considered holy, along with anything that touched it (Ex. 29:37). These things were set apart for God's work. In the same way, Jesus Christ makes us holy when we trust in Him as our Saviour, and we are also set apart for the works He has called us to.

Our relationship with God through His Son is a new gift of grace. God is still completely holy, and His wrath toward sin did not disappear. But instead of requiring repeated sacrifices for our sins, Christ took our full punishment and gave us His righteousness. We can now come boldly, though still reverently, before God's throne (Heb. 4:16).

How often do we take time to meditate on God's holiness? God gave us the Law so we could reflect on the entirety of the gospel. Apart from the reality of God's holiness and our own sin, there would be no purpose for the sacrifice of Jesus. Just as the consecration and ordination of Aaron and his sons put God's holiness and the people's sin on display, Jesus was displayed on a cross for us. God's holiness is essential to the gospel message; let us grow in awareness of His holiness and revere Him for His mercy all the more.

—*Megan Hickman.*

World Missions

When God sets apart individual men and women for His service, much is required of them. God promises to provide all their needs, but He does not promise luxury, comfort, or even safety. Rather, believers are called to suffer alongside Christ, to die to themselves so that others might live.

Few answer the call, but oh, the joy of those who do!

Pastor M_____, currently serving in Pakistan, is no stranger to suffering. For him, serving God is far from a safe occupation. And yet, by offering himself as a holy sacrifice to God, he gets to see God do miraculous things in people's lives.

Here is just one story he relates:

I received a phone call from an unknown number. . . . The voice said, '. . . you are a preacher of the Gospel of Christ.' I said, 'Yes, I am.' Then he threatened my life and cut off the phone call. I prayed to the Lord for his soul and for the protection of my life and my family. Then I slept.

A few days later, some people came and kidnapped me when I was coming from a village after preaching. They tied my eyes with a cloth and said for me to keep quiet. After four or five hours, they reached a place that was in the mountains. When they took the cloth from my eyes, I saw many men with guns in their hands. I guessed they were Talibans. One of them asked me to explain the Gospel of Christ to them. I was much afraid because I knew that they were going to torture me and then they would kill me. But I prayed to the Lord Jesus Christ and He spoke into my heart, I *am with you always, even unto the end of the world.*

I explained the Gospel of our Lord Jesus Christ to them with verses like John 3:16. I told them Jesus is life. He is salvation, and He will come for the judgment of the world. I explained about His love, grace, crucifixion, resurrection from the dead, and ascension.

Then they beat me and threw me beside the road. . . . Someone found me there and when I opened my eyes I was in a hospital. . . .

A few months later, I received a call and the person said he wanted to meet me and learn more about Jesus and His Gospel. I . . . met with him in a hotel and he. . . . said that he is a Taliban and he was the one who called last time. He was the one who kidnapped me, who asked me to explain the Gospel of Christ, who beat me, and asked me to stop preaching Christ and His Gospel.

He said God has changed his life by His Gospel. He told me that he has been reading the Bible and the books, *New Life in Christ* and *Practical Christian Living*, which he found in my bag that I left behind. The other Talibans beat him, put him on ice for many hours, and then they threw him to die, but he told me that nothing could part him from the love of Christ, not even death. The Gospel transformed him from a Taliban to a Disciple of Jesus Christ! (*Reaper*, Spring 2016, Source of Light)

Pastor M_____ lives for Christ. Someday, he may die for Christ. One thing is sure—he will die without regrets for how he spent his life.

—Kimberly Rae.

The Jewish Aspect

Scientists have discovered a gene that can be traced from Aaron to a segment of the Jewish population that even today carries the priestly lineage (Berkowitz, "DNA Studies Trace Jewish Priestly Lineage from Biblical Times," breakingisraelnews.com). Aaron, a Levite and the elder son of Amram and Jochebed, played an important part in the history of the Jewish nation and helped shape Jewish religion.

The Bible records that Aaron was the first high priest. God intended all of the firstborn of Israel to serve Him after He saved them from the last plague in Egypt. However, many of the firstborn Israelites took part in worshipping the golden calf; this act disqualified them from serving in the soon-to-be-constructed tabernacle. The tribe of the Levites refrained from the sin, so they took the place of all the firstborn in the tabernacle (and later the temple) service.

Even before God chose him for his priestly role, Aaron was important to Judaism. The Bible records that Aaron served as a mouthpiece for his brother Moses. Jewish writings claim that he possessed eloquent and persuasive speech.

The Scriptures state it was Aaron, not Moses, who stretched his rod to bring on the first three plagues (Ex. 7:19; 8:5, 17). In addition, it was Aaron whose staff turned into a serpent (7:9-10). Finally, the Bible records it was Aaron, with Hur, who supported Moses' hands so Israel could defeat the Amalekites (17:10-13). Aaron was being actively used by God.

Some scholars maintain that Aaron's most notable personal quality was that of being a peacemaker. According to Jewish legend, when Aaron heard that two people were arguing, he would go to each of them and state how much the other regretted his actions. The people would then agree to meet as friends ("Moses, Aaron and Miriam," jewfaq.org).

Though that method might seem ethically questionable to modern Christians, Jews believe Aaron personified kindness. The Mishnah encourages Jews to strive to be "students of Aaron" by acting lovingly themselves and pursuing peace.

Jews also describe Aaron as being very humble. They write that his humility was evident in the fact that he let his younger brother take center stage as Moses became the leader of the Israelites (Adelman, "Aaron of the Bible," chabad.org).

This week's Scripture lesson covers the ordination of Aaron and his sons for the priesthood. Perhaps it was Aaron's positive traits that factored into God's choice to put him in this important role.

But Aaron was not without fault. He was the one who, while Moses was meeting with God, bent under the pressure of the people and told them to remove their golden rings so he could make them an idol. Still, despite Aaron's failure, God established the priesthood through his lineage.

Even with his flaws, Jews describe Aaron as an extraordinary man. They record that he was a man characterized by his willingness to love.

The Bible tells us that as Christians we have a High Priest. In Hebrews 4:14, the Bible calls Jesus our "great high priest." Aaron may have been characterized by love, but Jesus was characterized by an even greater love—a love in which He would lay down his life for the world.

When Aaron, the first high priest, faced temptation, he sinned. Jesus, our High Priest, never sinned. Instead, Jesus offered His own life as our sinless sacrifice.

—Robin Fitzgerald.

Guiding the Superintendent

Beginning with Creation, God has pursued a relationship with mankind grounded in love and holiness. His desire to dwell with mankind is evident from the first chapter of Genesis; His demand for mankind's holiness is apparent in the expulsion from the Garden. God went to great lengths to show us His holiness and His expectation for our holiness.

In these first few lessons, we will consider the holiness of God as seen through His requirements for people who are in service to Him and will note the dire consequences of disobeying or neglecting those requirements. God's foremost desire for us is that we be made holy so that we might abide with Him for all eternity. We will discover that Jesus Christ embodies God's fulfillment of that holy purpose.

DEVOTIONAL OUTLINE

1. The ordination of Aaron (Lev. 8:1-9). After detailing the requirements of the law pertaining to offerings for sin and guilt, the text explains how Moses was to prepare Aaron and his sons to be priests in service to the tabernacle. The ritual of this preparation is comprehensive, with the complex dress for the high priest described in detail. Each piece is imbued with symbolic significance, and each represents a mark of separation between a holy God and His sinful people.

2. The anointing of Aaron (Lev. 8:10-13). Once adorned and anointed by Moses, Aaron and his sons were ready to receive the sacrifice for their sins. Atonement for sin always requires the shedding of blood. For Aaron and his sons to be the holy priests for the people of Israel, they first had to undergo this ritual anointing in order to be fit for God's service.

As Christians, we know that our own forgiveness also comes at the shedding of blood—that of a priest greater than Aaron and one who had no need of purification for Himself. The New Testament tells us of the good news of our salvation through the sacrifice of the Son of God. It tells us of the breaking down of the wall of separation between God and His people. No longer are we separated by degrees of holiness; we now have full access to God's throne directly.

Two related Scriptures for this lesson (Heb. 10:19-25; Acts 22:14-16) tell us that we can now directly enter the presence of the Lord and proceed to the holiest place inside the tabernacle. God is now with us, granting us immediate access to Himself.

We have this confidence when we draw near in faith and call on Jesus' name for salvation. It is only then that we proceed to encourage each other to manifest love and good works out of gratefulness for the gift of salvation. These texts teach us that the way through the temple veil has been opened to all who approach by faith in Christ. No longer are rituals and purification rites necessary. God has tabernacled with us eternally through the incarnation and sacrifice of Jesus Christ and the indwelling of the Holy Spirit.

CHILDREN'S CORNER

Children often cannot see the forest for the trees. They may be fascinated by the details of Aaron's finery, especially his golden crown and his jeweled breastplate. Direct their attention to the way in which all this finery symbolized the perfect holiness of God and how Aaron had to be made holy in God's sight in order to serve in His presence as His high priest.

—*Mike Spencer.*

Scripture Lesson Text

LEV. 10:1 And Nadab and Abihu, the sons of Aaron, took either of them his censer, and put fire therein, and put incense thereon, and offered strange fire before the Lord, which he commanded them not.

2 And there went out fire from the Lord, and devoured them, and they died before the Lord.

3 Then Moses said unto Aaron, This *is it* that the Lord spake, saying, I will be sanctified in them that come nigh me, and before all the people I will be glorified. And Aaron held his peace.

4 And Moses called Mishael and Elzaphan, the sons of Uzziel the uncle of Aaron, and said unto them, Come near, carry your brethren from before the sanctuary out of the camp.

5 So they went near, and carried them in their coats out of the camp; as Moses had said.

6 And Moses said unto Aaron, and unto Eleazar and unto Ithamar, his sons, Uncover not your heads, neither rend your clothes; lest ye die, and lest wrath come upon all the people: but let your brethren, the whole house of Israel, bewail the burning which the Lord hath kindled.

7 And ye shall not go out from the door of the tabernacle of the congregation, lest ye die: for the anointing oil of the Lord *is* upon you. And they did according to the word of Moses.

NOTES

18

Death of Nadab and Abihu

Lesson Text: Leviticus 10:1-7

Related Scriptures: I Samuel 2:12-17; Joshua 7:1-20;
Acts 5:1-11; Psalm 2:10-12

TIME: 1445 B.C.   PLACE: plain before Mount Sinai

GOLDEN TEXT—"Serve the Lord with fear, and rejoice with trembling" (Psalm 2:11).

Introduction

Many people fail to fully grasp how seriously God takes sin. He expects us to obey Him at all times in all situations. The commands of God should not be seen as arbitrary or simply as a random list of rules. God did not give us the Bible so we would have a religious rule book but rather so that we could know how to know and love Him.

God calls us into His service, and He knows what is best for us. He wants us to serve Him and Him alone. The result of this is that we are bound to look different from the world we live in. We might appear to be strange and peculiar to those around us, and they may consider our worship of the Lord to be bizarre. But we must keep in mind that God does not delight in putting us in circumstances where we appear to be odd. It is just that He has a different set of priorities than the world does.

This week's lesson shows the danger of trying to circumvent God's purposes. Some people want to serve God, but they want to do so in their own way. This will never work. God knows what is best, and He calls for us to serve Him in faithful obedience.

LESSON OUTLINE

I. **THE FIRE OF THE LORD—**
    Lev. 10:1-3

II. **OUR SERVICE TO THE LORD—**
    Lev. 10:4-5

III. **THE CALL OF THE LORD—**
     Lev. 10:6-7

Exposition: Verse by Verse

THE FIRE OF THE LORD

LEV. 10:1 And Nadab and Abihu, the sons of Aaron, took either of them his censer, and put fire therein, and put incense thereon, and of-fered strange fire before the Lord, which he commanded them not.

2 And there went out fire from the Lord, and devoured them, and they died before the Lord.

3 Then Moses said unto Aaron, This is it that the Lord spake, saying, I will be sanctified in them that come nigh me, and before all the people I will be glorified. And Aaron held his peace.

Death of Aaron's sons (Lev. 10:1-2). In last week's lesson, we studied the ordination of Aaron and his sons as priests of Israel, establishing the Aaronic priesthood under the Mosaic covenant. God showed His approval by accepting Aaron's first sacrifice, as recorded in chapter 9.

When God supernaturally consumed Aaron's sacrifice with fire (9:24), it indicated that the torch had been passed from Moses to Aaron. Aaron, the high priest, along with the other priests, would now serve as mediators between God and the people. Moses would continue to intercede when necessary, but he was primarily occupied with leading the people. The priests, therefore, now took on a new responsibility with the nation.

To show the complete harmony between Moses and Aaron, the two went into and came out of the tabernacle together and blessed the people. It was then that the glory of the Lord appeared and fire came forth to consume the sacrifice (vss. 22-24).

What happened next, however, became a national tragedy witnessed by many. Two of Aaron's four sons who had just been ordained as priests, Nadab and Abihu, took their own censers, put incense in them, and offered "strange," or unauthorized, fire to the Lord (10:1). Their actions were not something God had commanded or mandated.

{The strange fire offered by Nadab and Abihu apparently did not come from the altar where the burnt offering had been made (cf. 16:12). It had no association with atonement or sacrifice and was therefore profane to God, making it unacceptable.}Q1 They tried to come to God their own way and were struck dead as a result.

Some have speculated that the fact that they brought the unauthorized fire "before the Lord" (10:1) may mean they actually entered the Holy of Holies, going beyond the veil into a place that was off limits to them. God's warning to Aaron not to enter the tabernacle after drinking alcohol (vss. 8-9) may suggest that they were guilty of this as well.

God is very clear in His Word that He is no respecter of persons (cf. Acts 10:34). It does not matter if we were saved five minutes ago or if we have been saved for many decades: we must come to the Lord in reverence. Ignorance, tradition, or firmly held ideas are not excuses for improper worship. God does not allow us to be renegades who set the terms of our own individual worship.

God responded with swift and severe action. Just as fire came from the Lord and consumed Aaron's sacrifice, fire came forth and consumed Aaron's sons when they acted in a manner that was not consistent with the holiness of God. This should not be seen as an overreaction on God's part to a minor offense. His holiness cannot be violated with impunity.

Nadab and Abihu were without excuse. They could not claim ignorance because they had been fully instructed as to what God wanted. They had accompanied the seventy elders who climbed Mount Sinai with Moses and Aaron to meet with God for a very intimate time of fellowship (cf. Ex. 24:9-11). They were no strangers to the holiness and glory of God. They had witnessed it many times before.

Aaron's silence before the Lord (Lev. 10:3). {God spoke to Moses next, telling him to remind Aaron that He would be glorified before all the people.}Q2 Had Nadab and Abihu not been punished, God's glory would have been diminished. Of all people, those chosen to come near Him as priests must come in a holy manner that reflected His own holiness.

We cannot think that past success or privilege means we can treat our holy God however we please. We cannot dismiss His commands and demean His character. He loves us and calls us to Himself into a loving relationship, but we must understand that God is holy and must be served and worshipped accordingly.

{After listening to Moses' words, Aaron remained silent. He did not dare to speak a word against the Lord in protest or dispute.}Q3

God had accepted Aaron's sacrifice with a fire of glory, but He condemned Aaron's sons with a fire of judgment. His judgment is always righteous, and God has every right to judge those who sin against Him.

When we come to God in our own way according to our own plan, we are putting ourselves ahead of Him. As worshippers of the Lord, our focus must be on Him, not ourselves. This is a battle many of us wrestle with, but we must take every precaution not to place our own wants and desires ahead of the Lord.

OUR SERVICE TO THE LORD

4 And Moses called Mishael and Elzaphan, the sons of Uzziel the uncle of Aaron, and said unto them, Come near, carry your brethren from before the sanctuary out of the camp.

5 So they went near, and carried them in their coats out of the camp; as Moses had said.

Called to serve the Lord (Lev. 10:4). No one ever said that service to the Lord is easy, and it certainly is not glamorous. Unfortunately, it seems that many people's perception of ministers is limited to what they see from their pastor in the pulpit. He is typically a well-dressed man who gives a nice speech that lasts on average about thirty minutes. Afterward, people file out of the sanctuary, shaking his hand and complimenting him on a nice sermon. Sadly, some people think this is the extent of what it means to serve the Lord.

God often calls us to do things that are unappealing, unappreciated, unnoticed, and emotionally difficult. Service to the Lord is not only for preachers, pastors, deacons, and missionaries. Everyone who is a follower of Jesus Christ is called to serve Him in whatever capacity the Lord desires. {This was the case for Mishael and Elzaphan. These two men were the sons of Moses and Aaron's uncle Uzziel, making them first cousins of Israel's two primary leaders.}Q4

Under the law, anyone who touched a corpse became ceremonially unclean for seven days (Num. 19:11). For Aaron and his two remaining sons, this would mean being unable to perform their priestly duties during that time. {Therefore, Moses called on his relatives who were not from the priestly family to come and remove the bodies of Nadab and Abihu from the sanctuary and bury them outside the camp.}Q4

Obedient servanthood (Lev. 10:5). Our devotion to the Lord is proved by our faithful, obedient service to Him. We should consider it a privilege to do anything God calls us to do, regardless of how demeaning others may consider it.

What area of ministry has God called you into? You may not think that what you are doing is very significant, but if God gave you the assignment you have, then it is worthwhile and a valuable means of honoring the Lord no matter what anyone else may think. It is a joy to serve God and His people in any capacity. No job is unimportant in the church. Some, such as cleaning the church building and taking care of the grounds, are not as visible as preaching, singing, or teaching, but janitorial work is just as important.

Do not make the mistake of seeking approval or recognition for serving Christ. The accolades we receive from other people are momentary and fleeting. Plaques gather dust and trophies tarnish, but pleasing the Lord lasts for eternity. God may not call you to be a leader like Moses or a priest like Aaron. He may call you to do the dirty work like He did Mishael and Elzaphan. The question is, will you do it?

When Moses called on Mishael and Elzaphan to remove the dead bodies of Nadab and Abihu, they simply came forward and did what was expected of them. There was no protest or complaint on their part, and there was certainly no applause from others. This was a very somber occasion that required someone to simply step up and do what needed to be done.

Times of tragedy call for faithful people to step up and serve. With the sudden deaths of two of Israel's first priests, the people were undoubtedly in shock. Priests would naturally be considered the holiest people in the community, so to see two of them killed instantly was unsettling to say the least. Their remains had to be removed, so this was a very important job even if it was not one that likely would have garnered many volunteers.

While we do not want to overstate the importance of what Mishael and Elzaphan did, we do not want to overlook it either. The work they did receives very little attention in commentaries, but removing the bodies of these two fallen priests was extremely significant at the time. That the two men obeyed when called on is worth mentioning, and there is something we can learn from their example of faithful obedience to the unheralded work the Lord called them to do.

THE CALL OF THE LORD

6 And Moses said unto Aaron, and unto Eleazar and unto Ithamar, his sons, Uncover not your heads, neither rend your clothes; lest ye die, and lest wrath come upon all the people: but let your brethren, the whole house of Israel, bewail the burning which the Lord hath kindled.

7 And ye shall not go out from the door of the tabernacle of the congregation, lest ye die: for the anointing oil of the Lord is upon you. And they did according to the word of Moses.

As we have seen, God's call on those who follow Him is seldom easy, and at times it is quite difficult. {This was especially true for Aaron in this situation, as he was not allowed to publicly grieve the loss of his sons.}[Q5] Any complaint on his part would have been considered further rebellion against the righteousness of God. Any type of public mourning would have actually shown sympathy to those who rebelled against God and incurred His just wrath.

How agonizing it must have been for Aaron, on the worst day of his life, to not be able to mourn the deaths of two of his sons. To do so may have given the impression that God was wrong in bringing about the deaths of the two rebellious priests, and this would have invited further wrath. Nothing, not even what we might see as understandable grieving on the part of a heartbroken father, was an excuse for challenging God's holiness.

Some may be asking whether this means it is wrong to publicly grieve the loss of a loved one today, and the answer is an emphatic no. {Grieving the death of someone close to us is natural and is to be expected. God in no way will punish anyone for mourning a death.}[Q6] In this instance, however, the Lord was establishing a new nation He had called out of Egyptian bondage to be a people separated from the world to Himself.

The people of Israel needed to understand that God is uncompromisingly holy in His very nature. This meant that in times of extreme difficulty and hardship, they had to persevere in faith and obedience regardless of the circumstances. {God was not unsympathetic to Aaron, but Aaron had to demonstrate the importance of revering God regardless of personal struggles and loss.}Q7

Those who serve the Lord as spiritual leaders and teachers bear great accountability to Him (cf. Jas. 3:1). They are entrusted with great responsibility but given the indwelling Holy Spirit to empower them to live differently from those around them and be examples to God's people. Since Aaron and his surviving sons had been anointed with the oil of the Lord (again, a picture of the Holy Spirit) as Israel's priests, they were not able to join the rest of the people in mourning.

The people had just endured a terrible tragedy, {but the work of the high priest (Aaron) and the priests (his two living sons, Eleazar and Ithamar) could not be laid aside. They still had priestly duties that had to be conducted (cf. Lev. 10:12-15).}Q8 The work of the Lord was not going to stop because of two rebellious priests. The remaining priests were still under the anointing of God and had to conduct themselves accordingly.

It must be noted here that although the command that prevented Aaron from publicly mourning his sons and that commanded him to continue to serve as priest between God and the people was grueling from a human standpoint, {the anointing of the Lord was still on Aaron. In other words, God was still with him.}Q9 The anointing had not left. God knew Aaron would not be able to continue on his own, and the Lord never abandoned him.

{God may call us to an arduous task, but He will equip and empower us for whatever service He calls us to. He will not leave us alone. Even in the midst of the worst tragedies of life, He will be with us. As such, God expects us to be diligent in service and faithful to Him at all times.}Q10

Nadab and Abihu failed to respect the holiness of God. They tried to worship Him the way they wanted, and it cost them their lives. As followers of Jesus Christ, we are His servants. It is essential that we serve Him humbly, yielding always to His authority. God is holy and is to be treated as such.

—Robert Ferguson, Jr.

QUESTIONS

1. What was unacceptable about the fire that the two sons of Aaron brought before the Lord?

2. What did Moses immediately tell Aaron after the deaths of his two sons?

3. How did Aaron respond to Moses' words?

4. Who did Moses call on to remove the corpses of Nadab and Abihu, and why did he choose these men?

5. What was Aaron forbidden to do under these circumstances?

6. Is it improper to grieve the death of a loved one? Explain.

7. What was God teaching through the limits on Aaron and his sons?

8. Why could Aaron, Eleazar, and Ithamar not leave the tabernacle?

9. What did the anointing of Aaron and his sons indicate?

10. What lessons does this incident have for us?

—Robert Ferguson, Jr.

Preparing to Teach the Lesson

Last week, we learned about God's holiness from Leviticus 8:1-13. We discovered that biblical holiness requires a thorough understanding of God's requirements, the right motives on behalf of the believer, and complete obedience in following God's instructions.

Today, we are turning to a much different story that presents important insight on God's holiness through the deaths of Nadab and Abihu (Lev. 10:1-7). As disturbing as this episode in Israel's history is, we will find amazingly relevant theological truth that we can carry into our everyday lives.

TODAY'S AIM

Facts: to learn important aspects of God's holiness from the negative example of Aaron's sons.

Principle: to note numerous potential consequences of disregarding God's holiness and failing to obey His commands.

Application: to ensure that our personal holiness is in complete alignment with the principles of Scripture and that we are serving the Lord in a manner that He desires.

INTRODUCING THE LESSON

The early portions of Scripture present a historical account of God's dealings with the nation of Israel. There are many dissimilarities between the nation of Israel and the church. God required the Israelites to follow the Mosaic Law, whereas the church is not bound by this Law (Rom. 6:14-15; Gal. 3:23-25). Israel was designated to occupy a geographic location known as the land of Canaan, whereas the church is scattered throughout the world among Jews and Gentiles, with each individual believer indwelt by Christ (Col. 1:27).

Yet amidst the dissimilarities, striking similarities between Israel and the church cannot be ignored. Just as Israel was God's people in the Old Testament era and the primary vehicle God was using in the world, the church is God's people today and is the primary vehicle God is using at this time. Also, New Testament believers find that the written text of the Old Testament is relevant to living life God's way.

In Leviticus 10:1-7, the account of the deaths of Nadab and Abihu serves as an informative text on God's holiness in general and the consequences of not following God's holiness commands.

DEVELOPING THE LESSON

Leviticus 10:1-7 stands in sad contrast to 8:1-13 and teaches, through negative example, important aspects of God's holiness. The lesson text sets forth the consequences of disregarding God's holiness and disobeying His holiness commands. However, there are three underlying concepts related to God's holiness that can be discerned from the text as well: biblical holiness is clearly communicated, necessary to serve God, and unrelenting in nature.

Large portions of the books of Exodus and Leviticus communicate the biblical concept of holiness, primarily through the laws God gave through Moses.

Holiness is necessary in order to serve God. Nadab and Abihu were not only the sons of Aaron, but both were also legitimate priests, authorized to execute the priestly duties of the tabernacle. Yet, regardless of their lineage or vocational credentials, Nadab and Abihu were still expected to abide completely by the Mosaic Law, and their failure to do so not only disqualified them from serving God as priests, but resulted in their demise.

Another concept of holiness found in Leviticus 10:1-7 is that biblical holiness is unrelenting in nature. When Aaron's sons made the decision to alter the Mosaic formula, God's holiness did not make any concessions for them; instead, it demanded their judgment. With these underlying principles in mind as we approach the lesson text, we can observe three noteworthy results from disobeying God's commands regarding His holiness.

1. God's judgment (Lev. 10:1-3). The judgment of God rests on those who violate His holiness. Nadab and Abihu learned this the hard way as they ignored God's instructions concerning the incense offering in the tabernacle. Their act brought their immediate deaths by supernatural means. In fact, the Lord's response to Aaron's sons' indiscretion is summed up succinctly by the Lord's words, spoken by Moses: "I will be sanctified in them that come nigh me."

2. God's wrath affects others (Lev. 10:4-5). A second result of disobeying God's holiness standard is that God's righteous wrath will have an effect on others connected to the situation. Nadab and Abihu were consumed in flames. Family members were charged with carrying their smoldering, dead bodies from the tabernacle. This is a reminder that disobedience often brings forth consequences that affect more than the offending party alone.

3. Negative examples (Lev. 10:6-7). A third result of violating God's holiness is that those who do so become examples of what not to do. In the case of Aaron's sons, their family was told, "Uncover not your heads, neither rend your clothes; lest ye die, and lest wrath come upon all the people." Here the Lord commands Aaron's family not to grieve. An important lesson was being taught.

God's holiness and the consequences that ensue from disobedience are reaffirmed in the psalmist's injunction to "serve the Lord with fear, and rejoice with trembling" (Ps. 2:11).

ILLUSTRATING THE LESSON

Those who disregard or treat lightly the Lord's holiness place themselves on a downward path to judgment. Those who acknowledge His holiness will seek to humbly obey God.

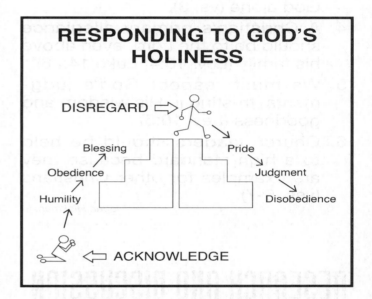

CONCLUDING THE LESSON

Leviticus 10:1-7 demonstrates that biblical holiness is clearly communicated, necessary to serve God, and unrelenting in nature. This passage also draws our attention to a number of the results of disobedience, including the reality of God's judgment, the consequences borne by others, and the negative example one becomes when he goes against God's holiness.

ANTICIPATING THE NEXT LESSON

The grim story of the sin and death of Aaron's sons is followed by a lesson on instructions concerning the great Day of Atonement, which points to the solution for sin.

—*Nigel C. Black.*

PRACTICAL POINTS

1. We should follow the Lord's leading, not expect Him to follow us (Lev. 10:1).
2. God's judgment may not be immediate, but we will have to give an account of ourselves, so we should never use grace as license to sin (vs. 2).
3. Do not steal glory; it belongs to God alone (vs. 3).
4. A Christian's primary allegiance should be to the Lord, even above his family (Lev. 10:4; Luke 14:26).
5. We must respect God's judgments, trusting in His wisdom and goodness (Lev. 10:5).
6. Church leaders should be held to a high standard because they are examples for other Christians (vss. 6-7).

—Megan Hickman.

RESEARCH AND DISCUSSION

1. How should you respond when someone professes to be a believer but neglects His commands (Lev. 10:1)?
2. Why does God have mercy on some people but not on others?
3. In what way is God a "consuming fire" (Heb. 12:29; Lev. 10:2)?
4. Why does God's desire for glory not make Him an egomaniac (Lev. 10:3)?
5. How does knowing when to submit to authorities (especially to the Lord) show spiritual maturity (vs. 3)?
6. Why should Christians react differently from unbelievers to the trials of life (cf. Eph. 4:1)?

—Megan Hickman.

ILLUSTRATED HIGH POINTS

He commanded them not (Lev. 10:1)

A trip to a farm can be both exciting and informative for almost everyone, but a farm is not completely safe. There are animals with various temperaments and there is equipment on a farm that could be dangerous. Most farmers notify their guests of the potential hazards. If a guest were to ignore the farmer's warnings, he or she could be hurt.

Aaron's sons were also commanded not do certain things. If they disobeyed the Lord's commands, they would also be in danger.

Carry your brethren (vs. 4)

My grandfather was a veteran, so during his funeral, an American flag was draped over his casket for his service. A couple Navy soldiers folded the flag carefully and gave it to my family. My grandfather and the Navy soldiers may not have served during the same generation, but they still were brothers in service to their country and to one another.

Nadab and Abihu's family was responsible for removing their dead bodies from the camp. But in contrast to the honorable funeral of my grandfather, it was a somber and shameful occasion for this family.

Ye shall not go out from the door (vs. 7)

There are many vocations in which it would be considered unprofessional and inappropriate to portray one's self in an overly emotional manner.

Professionals are expected to conduct themselves professionally. As the high priest, Aaron was not allowed to leave the tabernacle to mourn his sons. His official service to God had to remain his paramount priority.

—Chelsea Villaseñor.

Golden Text Illuminated

"Serve the Lord with fear, and rejoice with trembling" (Psalm 2:11).

Our golden text for this week touches on a neglected aspect of the Christian life: the fear of the Lord. Although this is far from a popular facet of the Christian experience, it is precisely for this reason that we need to pay more careful attention to it.

The writer of Hebrews warns us, "It is a fearful thing to fall into the hands of the living God" (10:31), and again, "serve God acceptably with reverence and godly fear: for our God is a consuming fire" (12:28-29). It has become fashionable nowadays for preachers and teachers to enfeeble these warnings of inspired holy Scripture by reassuring their audiences that what is really meant by "fear" is merely respect and by no means indicates that we should actually be afraid of God. But is this modern emphasis correct?

Those who claim this usually support it by citing two verses in particular: "For God hath not given us the spirit of fear; but of power, and of love, and of a sound mind" (II Tim. 1:7), and "There is no fear in love; but perfect love casteth out fear: because fear hath torment. He that feareth is not made perfect in love" (I John 4:18). But how do these verses actually apply to the issue of fearing God?

First, II Timothy 1:7 is used entirely out of context in this purpose, since Paul is specifically addressing fear as it concerns being a witness for the gospel before an unbelieving world. It does not apply at all to fearing the Lord.

Second, I John 4:18 is dealing with the issue of a guilty conscience because of sin. This also has nothing to do with fearing the Lord in the sense meant in Psalm 2:11, Hebrews 10:31, and Hebrews 12:28-29. John is writing about the fear and guilt of someone who has not come to full assurance that his sins are forgiven in Christ. It is a fear caused by a lack of faith.

It is essential that we come to a Scriptural understanding of the fear of the Lord, for it is neither only respect nor is it an abject fear of punishment for sins. For as Solomon tells us, "The fear of the Lord is the beginning of wisdom: and the knowledge of the holy is understanding" (Prov. 9:10).

In C.S. Lewis's *The Lion, the Witch, and the Wardrobe*, there is a conversation between Susan, Lucy, and Mrs. Beaver about the nature of Aslan, the great lion. Mrs. Beaver explains that meeting Aslan is no joke.

When Lucy asks if Aslan is safe to meet, Mr. Beaver responds, "Who said anything about safe? 'Course he isn't safe. But he's good. He's the King, I tell you."

Fearing God comes from truly realizing who He is. When we know that He is good but not necessarily safe, that He has all power, and that He gives us every breath and heartbeat we have, we will truly understand what it means to fear God appropriately. If you claim to know who God is and you still do not fear Him, then you do not truly know Him! It is just as simple and as complicated as that.

—John Lody.

Heart of the Lesson

When we read passages like today's lesson, there is no question that the Lord cares how we worship Him. Our corrupt hearts frequently make worship more about ourselves than about God's glory. That is essentially what the sons of Aaron did.

Worship the right way (Lev. 10:1-2). We do not know why Aaron's sons offered unauthorized fire to the Lord and can only speculate why it was considered "strange," but it is clear that Nadab and Abihu's worship was tainted. They had been given specific instructions for worship, and whether it was due to laziness, lack of respect, or a cavalier approach to God's commands, these men disrespected His holiness, and He struck them dead.

We probably give God less than our best worship on a daily basis. We therefore need Jesus' righteousness, and God knew this from the beginning. Nadab and Abihu's punishment seems harsh, but we must remember that God has every right to punish us for our sins. To demonstrate His character, He employed this particular case of disobedience to teach the Israelites the true price for sin.

Put the Lord first (Lev. 10:3-5). Moses' response could easily be seen as insensitive. After all, Aaron's sons had just died a dramatic and sudden death, and certainly he was heartbroken. But Moses reminded him of the responsibility to God that both he and his sons had taken on. Moses brought Aaron back to God's word and reminded him to focus on God's glory.

Maybe it was Aaron's remembrance of the tragedy of the golden calf that kept him silent at this time. Maybe the deaths of many in the Israelite camp still haunted him. He had tried to make excuses, saying that the people were bent on disobedience (Ex. 32:22) and telling a story to rid himself of blame (vss. 23-24), but he learned quickly that idolatry had consequences. Aaron had a great understanding of God's holiness and was not willing to challenge it, even in his mourning. His silence was a sign of resolute repentance.

Respect the Lord's judgment (Lev. 10:6-7). Moses called Aaron and his sons to a high standard of holiness. He reminded Aaron about the Lord's faithfulness to His word and that God was completely just in His dealings with the two men. Accordingly, he expected Aaron and the rest of his sons to show respect for the Lord's judgment by not mourning visibly for Nadab and Abihu. God was making Israel a holy nation that was supposed to reveal His glory to the world (Ex. 19:6). How were the people supposed to learn to respect God's holiness if the priests could not?

We often have a hard time seeing the continuity between God in the Old Testament and God in the New Testament. But even in the New Testament, God commands that we follow Him wholeheartedly and put our love for Him even above our families (Luke 14:26). God has always demanded and will continue to demand wholehearted worship. We can praise Him for sending His own Son to pay the penalty for when we miss this mark and fall short of His glory (cf. Rom. 3:23-24).

There are times in our lives when we do not feel like praising God because we do not understand what He is doing. But at times like these, we must remember our calling as ambassadors of Christ (II Cor. 5:20), showing the world that God is good, just, wise, holy, and completely worthy of our worship.
—*Megan Hickman.*

World Missions

According to *millennialinflux.com,* America is no longer a Christian nation. "Christianity is on the decline and not just among younger generations or in certain regions of the country but across all races, genders, education and states. It is no longer the great Christian nation as we thought it was; it is falling into more secular principles such as materialism, secularism, humanism, and sexual immorality. These secular viruses infect our spiritual presence of the church in America even when we don't realize it" ("Why Does America Need Missionaries?").

The secular world, by contrast, has not haphazardly fallen, but rather pursued a purposeful agenda. Just one example is *People* magazine, which highlights Hollywood celebrity culture. Twenty years ago or so, when homosexuality was generally frowned upon, *People* would slip a photo or story that focused on homosexuals far in the back of the magazine, quite small, as if in apology for the discomfort it might cause.

Through the years, however, these photos moved up a few pages, pushing a little beyond their audience's comfort level but not blatantly enough for people to complain much. Over time, readers got used to seeing these types of photos. If the coverage bothered them, they overlooked it. As this happened in multiple venues, including with multimedia giants such as Disney, the attitude of the culture at large went from disagreement or neutrality to acceptance, and then from acceptance to celebration.

Meanwhile, the Christian community as a whole watched and drifted along with the cultural tide. Individual believers were not equipped to address the subject, and pastors hesitated to preach on it for fear of backlash. Many Christians believed churches should open their physical, mental, and emotional doors without discernment to the homosexual community to represent the unconditional love of Christ.

Now we see entire denominations not only accepting this lifestyle, but welcoming it into their pews and even into their leadership.

This cultural acclimation did not just happen. It was well-planned and pursued seriously, even religiously. Is it not ironic that the world seems more religious about its agenda than the church?

Yes, we should love the sinners. The gospel is about reaching the lost, not boarding up our church to insulate the redeemed. But there is a difference between reaching the lost and deceiving the lost into thinking they are already saved simply because God loves them. No one can be genuinely saved and still pursue a habitually sinful lifestyle. "Many Christians don't want to rock the boat or cause offense when preaching or sharing the gospel. In result, the church becomes lukewarm and the people receiving the gospel find it as an entertaining story instead of a life-changing narrative that it should be" (millenialinflux.com).

It is foolhardy to assume that America could remain moral and God-fearing simply because it once was. Reaching the world takes work.

Should the church change? Definitely. However, when we think of missionaries, we do not send out entire churches. Missionaries are individuals. If all the individual believers in our nation became the missionaries God intended, just think what could happen to America!

—*Kimberly Rae.*

The Jewish Aspect

As I mentioned last week, modern science has proved a common genetic marker for the Jewish priestly line. Studies show that over 98 percent of those who claim to be of priestly lineage based on their father's identity also carry the Y-chromosome Alu Polymorphism (YAP) marker (Rozovsky, "Raise Your Hand If You're a Kohen," chabad.org).

The director of Nephrology and Molecular Medicine in the Faculty of Medicine at Technion in Haifa states, "The simplest, most straightforward explanation is that these men have the Y-chromosome of Aaron" (Rozovsky). God appointed Aaron as the first high priest and founder of the Jewish priesthood, but why was Aaron's lineage chosen from all others?

History records that during the Exodus, eleven of the twelve tribes worshipped the golden calf. One tribe, the Levites, refrained from the abomination; as a result, God appointed them as His servants. God appointed Aaron and his four sons as the first priests, or *kohanim* (Ex. 28:1). Their sons were to propagate the priestly lineage. The rest of the line of Levi, those not descended from Aaron, identified themselves as "Levites." Although not priests, they too had roles in temple worship.

Even though there is no longer a temple, modern Jews recognize Aaron's descendants as special. They await the building of the next temple, when the representatives of Aaron's line will once again take their places as priests before God. Therefore, being a *kohen* (singular of *kohanim*) still carries obligations and requirements.

Today, kohanim get special honors in the synagogue. For example, Jews call on the kohanim first to recite the blessings when the Torah is read, and sometimes a kohen reenacts the giving of the priestly blessing (MJL, "What Are Kohanim, or Jewish 'Priests?'" myjewishlearning.com).

Jews also recognize the kohanim during the Pidyon HaBen ceremony. During this rite, Jewish parents redeem their firstborn male babies by paying the modern equivalent of five shekels to a kohen (MJL).

Although Jews consider it an honor to be a kohen, it also comes with restrictions. For example, a kohen may not marry a woman who has converted to Judaism or has been divorced. The law also forbids a kohen from having contact with a corpse of anyone other than a close family member. As a result, a kohen may not enter a funeral home or cemetery unless the deceased is a close relative (MJL).

Jewish law records many obligations that come with being a descendant of Aaron that remain in effect today. Throughout history, Jews have recognized the importance of the role. This week's lesson illuminates the seriousness of the position. God made this clear when He killed Aaron's sons Nadab and Abihu for improper worship.

Although God set the kohanim apart as special before Him, they are ordinary humans filled with imperfections and frailties. As observed in our lesson, they sin. In the Levitical priesthood, the high priests offered sacrifices for their own sins first. Only after this could they offer sacrifices for the people.

The Bible tells us that Jesus is a priest after the order of Melchizedek; He was not a descendant of Aaron. It is through Jesus, our perfect High Priest, that our sins—past, present, and future—are completely forgiven, and it is through His grace that we are saints in His kingdom.

—*Robin Fitzgerald.*

Guiding the Superintendent

As we saw in the previous lesson, the holiness of God is supreme. He is to be treated as holy, and He established very clear expectations for Israel to adhere to in how to approach Him and live under His blessing. But the recurring pattern established throughout Israel's history is a dismal one: they would start out obediently worshipping God but would soon lapse into a steady decline into wickedness and disregard for His holiness. In this lesson, we will see the consequences of neglecting God's holiness and taking His grace and mercy for granted.

DEVOTIONAL OUTLINE

1. The deaths of Nadab and Abihu (Lev. 10:1-3). Previous to this text, God had publicly consumed the sin offerings from the altar in a burst of fire. Following this, we are told that Nadab and Abihu, the sons of Aaron, presumptuously offered up their own fire to the Lord. Immediately, they themselves were consumed by fire from the Lord. We read of a similar act of presumption before God in Acts 5:1-11, in which Ananias and Sapphira met their doom.

Peter was receiving gifts from the people for the support of the church. Ananias entered and offered his gift of money from the sale of some property, but he deceptively withheld a portion of the proceeds for himself. He was immediately struck down for lying to the Holy Spirit. His wife, Sapphira, then entered and compounded her husband's sin by likewise lying about their donation, and she too was immediately struck dead.

We learn from these examples that the holiness of God is to be taken very seriously. It is to be honored and guarded at all costs. There is nothing more sacred than the Lord's holiness. We should never use God's mercy as a license to sin.

2. Nadab and Abihu taken away (Lev. 10:4-7). Relatives of the deceased were summoned to carry away the charred bodies of Nadab and Abihu. They were sternly cautioned by Moses not to outwardly grieve this loss of life; the holiness of God is to be preserved and honored above all other concerns, and in this case that meant abstaining from visible signs of mourning.

In a similar manner, an Israelite named Achan disobeyed God's clear command to stay away from the spoils of Jericho, keeping some for himself (Josh. 7:1-20). When the army of Israel then tried to attack Ai, they were severely routed due to Achan's sin—thirty-six Israelites were killed!

The spoils that were to be devoted to God alone were later found hoarded by Achan. As punishment for this sin, Achan and his entire family were executed by stoning and their bodies consumed by fire. As with Nadab and Abihu, any sympathy the people may have had for them had to be set aside in light of God's great and awesome holiness.

CHILDREN'S CORNER

This may be a disturbing text for children, since it shows how frightful God's wrath can be toward those who presume upon His requirements. Nadab and Abihu made a prominent show of worship, but their zeal was without respect for the holiness of the Lord. Specifically, they offered "strange fire." God had already specified in great detail the specific type of holy incense that was to be used for His worship (cf. Ex. 30:9, 34-38; 37:29). Any other offering was a deliberate disregard for His holiness.

—*Mike Spencer.*

SCRIPTURE LESSON TEXT

LEV. 16:1 And the LORD spake unto Moses after the death of the two sons of Aaron, when they offered before the LORD, and died;

2 And the LORD said unto Moses, Speak unto Aaron thy brother, that he come not at all times into the holy *place* within the vail before the mercy seat, which *is* upon the ark; that he die not: for I will appear in the cloud upon the mercy seat.

3 Thus shall Aaron come into the holy *place:* with a young bullock for a sin offering, and a ram for a burnt offering.

4 He shall put on the holy linen coat, and he shall have the linen breeches upon his flesh, and shall be girded with a linen girdle, and with the linen mitre shall he be attired: these *are* holy garments; therefore shall he wash his flesh in water, and *so* put them on.

5 And he shall take of the congregation of the children of Israel two kids of the goats for a sin offering, and one ram for a burnt offering.

6 And Aaron shall offer his bullock of the sin offering, which *is* for himself, and make an atonement for himself, and for his house.

7 And he shall take the two goats, and present them before the LORD *at* the door of the tabernacle of the congregation.

8 And Aaron shall cast lots upon the two goats; one lot for the LORD, and the other lot for the scapegoat.

9 And Aaron shall bring the goat upon which the LORD's lot fell, and offer him *for* a sin offering.

10 But the goat, on which the lot fell to be the scapegoat, shall be presented alive before the LORD, to make an atonement with him, *and* to let him go for a scapegoat into the wilderness.

11 And Aaron shall bring the bullock of the sin offering, which *is* for himself, and shall make an atonement for himself, and for his house, and shall kill the bullock of the sin offering which *is* for himself:

12 And he shall take a censer full of burning coals of fire from off the altar before the LORD, and his hands full of sweet incense beaten small, and bring *it* within the vail:

13 And he shall put the incense upon the fire before the LORD, that the cloud of the incense may cover the mercy seat that *is* upon the testimony, that he die not:

14 And he shall take of the blood of the bullock, and sprinkle *it* with his finger upon the mercy seat eastward; and before the mercy seat shall he sprinkle of the blood with his finger seven times.

15 Then shall he kill the goat of the sin offering, that *is* for the people, and bring his blood within the vail, and do with that blood as he did with the blood of the bullock, and sprinkle it upon the mercy seat, and before the mercy seat:

16 And he shall make an atonement for the holy *place,* because of the uncleanness of the children of Israel, and because of their transgressions in all their sins: and so shall he do for the tabernacle of the congregation, that remaineth among them in the midst of their uncleanness.

NOTES

The Day of Atonement

Lesson Text: Leviticus 16:1-16

Related Scriptures: Leviticus 23:26-32; Numbers 29:7-11;
Romans 3:21-26; Hebrews 10:4-22; Isaiah 53:4-10

TIME: 1445 B.C.   PLACE: Mount Sinai

GOLDEN TEXT—"Speak unto Aaron thy brother, that he come not at all times into the holy place . . . that he die not: for I will appear in the cloud upon the mercy seat" (Leviticus 16:2).

Introduction

One of the most important themes throughout Scripture is atonement, which refers to the reconciliation of sinners to God. In order for sinful humans to come before a holy and righteous God, our sins must be paid for.

The sacrificial system under the Mosaic covenant provided a way of reconciling the people of Israel to their God. It was only through atonement that they could be forgiven and be able to receive His blessings.

Jesus Christ came to provide the ultimate, final, and permanent atonement for our sins in a way that abolished the old sacrificial system.

This week's lesson shows how God initiated the Day of Atonement, the holiest day on the Jewish calendar. It reminded Israel of their sin and need for salvation, pointed them to the God who alone provides forgiveness and salvation, provided a means of forgiveness through faith in the Lord, and prepared them for the coming of their Messiah.

LESSON OUTLINE

I. PREPARING TO OFFER THE SACRIFICE—Lev. 16:1-10

II. OFFERING THE SACRIFICE—Lev. 16:11-16

Exposition: Verse by Verse

PREPARING TO OFFER THE SACRIFICE

LEV. 16:1 And the LORD spake unto Moses after the death of the two sons of Aaron, when they offered before the LORD, and died;

2 And the LORD said unto Moses, Speak unto Aaron thy brother, that he come not at all times into the holy place within the vail before the mercy seat, which is upon the ark; that he die not: for I will appear in the cloud upon the mercy seat.

3 Thus shall Aaron come into the holy place: with a young bullock for a sin offering, and a ram for a burnt offering.

4 He shall put on the holy linen coat, and he shall have the linen breeches upon his flesh, and shall be girded with a linen girdle, and with the linen mitre shall he be attired: these are holy garments; therefore shall he wash his flesh in water, and so put them on.

5 And he shall take of the congregation of the children of Israel two kids of the goats for a sin offering, and one ram for a burnt offering.

6 And Aaron shall offer his bullock of the sin offering, which is for himself, and make an atonement for himself, and for his house.

7 And he shall take the two goats, and present them before the LORD at the door of the tabernacle of the congregation.

8 And Aaron shall cast lots upon the two goats; one lot for the LORD, and the other lot for the scapegoat.

9 And Aaron shall bring the goat upon which the LORD's lot fell, and offer him for a sin offering.

10 But the goat, on which the lot fell to be the scapegoat, shall be presented alive before the LORD, to make an atonement with him, and to let him go for a scapegoat into the wilderness.

Aftermath of the death of Nadab and Abihu (Lev. 16:1-2). In last week's lesson, we learned that even the priests were subject to punishment if they violated the commands of God. Being anointed as priests did not mean that they were no longer guilty of sin. Nadab and Abihu went beyond what God had ordained as proper service, and it cost them their lives. Immediately following this, God instituted the Day of Atonement.

{Verse 1 establishes the timeline for the Day of Atonement, with the deaths of Nadab and Abihu being the occasion.}[Q1] God demonstrated His holiness by judging them immediately for their unwillingness to submit to His instructions. He also showed grace to the community by continually making Himself available to them. However, they had to understand that He is holy and could not be approached in a lackadaisical manner any way they pleased. God is never to be worshipped cavalierly.

God's command to Aaron not to come into the holy place inside the veil whenever he so chose has led some to suggest that Nadab and Abihu may have attempted to enter that area. This place, also known as the Holy of Holies, was not to be entered by anyone except the high priest—and then only according to very specific instructions.

In order to prevent tragedy from happening again, {God instructed Aaron to stay out of this holy place where the ark of the covenant rested with its cover known as the "mercy seat." The reason this room was so sacred was not because of the items that were in it but rather because the presence of God resided there.}[Q2] God Himself was present in a cloud above the mercy seat, or place of atonement.

No mortal sinner was able to enter into the presence of a holy God and survive. Aaron would suffer the same fate of his two sons if he entered the Holy of Holies on his own terms.

Holy garments (Lev. 16:3-4). Up to this point, all priestly activities had taken place outside the Holy of Holies. The time had come, however, for God to establish one day a year for Aaron, the high priest, to enter the Most Holy Place, and there to offer a yearly atonement for the sins of the nation (cf. Lev. 16:29-34; Heb. 9:7).

The Day of Atonement, or Yom Kippur, was important because it was what all the other sacrifices that took place continually in the outer court hinged on. The sacrifices that took place throughout the year were of no value if the sins of the people were not atoned for. The Day of Atonement took place once a year, but it was essential for the people to commune with God and to be forgiven.

Under the old covenant that was mediated by Moses, atonement provided a covering for sin. The high priest had to make atonement for his own sins, as well as the sins of the people, every year. Under the new covenant, mediated by Jesus Christ, atonement provided a removal of sin, not just a covering. The blood of Christ removed sin. His sacrifice on the cross is the full and final payment for all sin. Our sin has not merely been covered; it has been removed (cf. Heb. 9:11-26).

On this one day yearly, Aaron was to meet with the Lord in the Most Holy Place, according to God's very stringent instructions. {Aaron first had to bring with him into the tabernacle court a bull for a sin offering and a ram for a burnt offering. The sin offering was to cleanse him and his family from their sins (Lev. 16:6); the burnt offering was an act of consecration (cf. vs. 24).}[Q3]

{Aaron also had to wear specific articles of clothing on that day. It appears that contrary to the beautiful garments he wore when performing his high priestly duties among the people, he was to wear very humble garments when coming before God on this day. He wore a holy linen coat, or tunic, over a linen undergarment. He tied a linen sash around his waist and wore a linen turban on his head.}[Q4]

Before putting these garments on, Aaron had to wash himself completely. This was traditionally done by immersion. When serving in the outer court or at the altar, the high priest only had to wash his hands and feet with water that came from the holy basin (cf. Ex. 30:18-21). Entering the presence of God in the inner room, however, meant that he had to wash his entire body before putting on the holy, linen garments.

Sacrifices for atonement (Lev. 16:5-6). After washing himself and dressing in the holy garments, Aaron was to bring two male goats from the people for a sin offering as well as a ram for a burnt offering. These would be offered on behalf of the people. Before proceeding with these offerings, however, Aaron first had to offer "his bullock of the sin offering" to "make an atonement for himself, and for his house" (vs. 6; cf. vs. 3).

Here is an important distinction between the priestly ministries of Aaron and Jesus. Although serving as the high priest, Aaron still committed sin. His priestly office did not make him immune from sinning. Before he could offer sacrifices that would atone for the sin of the people, he first had to offer a sacrifice to atone for his own sin.

On the other hand, {Christ, our Great High Priest, did not offer a sacrifice for Himself but gave Himself as a sacrifice for all people. The sacrifices Aaron made had to be made repeatedly, but the sacrifice of Jesus was made only once and permanently atones for the sins of all who believe in Him. Since Jesus is without sin, He did not have to offer a sacrifice for Himself.}[Q5] Indeed, if He were guilty of sin, He would not have been able to atone for our sin. He is, however, the perfect and sinless Lamb of God who came to take away the sin of the world (John 1:29).

Aaron was a type of Christ in that he served as high priest for the people and interceded for them before God. The priesthood of Jesus superseded that of Aaron, however, since His atoning death put away sin once and for all.

Casting lots (Lev. 16:7-8). After sacrificing the bull, Aaron was then to cast lots in order to determine the purpose for each of the two goats. Casting lots was a way in which the Lord occasionally helped man to understand His will in Old Testament times. We now have the Holy Spirit and God's completed Word to guide and direct us, which is why we are not told to cast lots any longer.

The two goats were to be brought before the Lord at the entrance of the tabernacle. This shows that the goats belonged to the Lord and were to be used for His purposes. He, not Aaron, would decide what role each goat played in the atonement for sin. One of the goats would be presented before the Lord as an atoning sacrifice, while the other would be designated the scapegoat.

The purpose of the goats (Lev. 16:9-10). {The goat determined by lot to be the Lord's was to be used as a sacrifice for a sin offering on behalf of the people.}[Q6] Therefore, the sacrifices made on the Day of Atonement included a bull for the sins of the priestly family and a goat for the sins of the non-priestly community. These were supplemented by a burnt offering for each group.

{Sacrificing a goat to atone for the sins of the people was not sufficient in and of itself to deal with the nation's sin. Sin also had to be banished from the community, which is why the second goat, the scapegoat, was necessary.}[Q7]

The scapegoat was to be presented alive to the Lord and then sent away into the wilderness, symbolically taking with it the sins of the people (cf. Lev. 16:20-22). The word "scapegoat" comes from the Hebrew word *Azazel*, the precise meaning of which is uncertain. However, it carries with it the idea of a removal or dismissal of something, which in this case refers to the sins of the people. The function of the scapegoat was to symbolically carry away the sins of the people.

OFFERING THE SACRIFICE

11 And Aaron shall bring the bullock of the sin offering, which is for himself, and shall make an atone-ment for himself, and for his house, and shall kill the bullock of the sin offering which is for himself:

12 And he shall take a censer full of burning coals of fire from off the altar before the LORD, and his hands full of sweet incense beaten small, and bring it within the vail:

13 And he shall put the incense upon the fire before the LORD, that the cloud of the incense may cover the mercy seat that is upon the testimony, that he die not:

14 And he shall take of the blood of the bullock, and sprinkle it with his finger upon the mercy seat eastward; and before the mercy seat shall he sprinkle of the blood with his finger seven times.

15 Then shall he kill the goat of the sin offering, that is for the people, and bring his blood within the vail, and do with that blood as he did with the blood of the bullock, and sprinkle it upon the mercy seat, and before the mercy seat:

16 And he shall make an atone-ment for the holy place, because of the uncleanness of the children of Israel, and because of their transgressions in all their sins: and so shall he do for the tabernacle of the congregation, that remaineth among them in the midst of their uncleanness.

Sacrificing the bull (Lev. 16:11). The ritual summarized in verses 6-10 is now explained in greater detail. It began with Aaron's sacrifice of the bull for the atonement of his own sins as well as those of his family.

Aaron and the priests who descended from him continued to sin, thereby needing continual atonement. Jesus Christ, however, never sinned and is our High Priest who represents us before God at this very moment (cf. Heb. 7:25).

Burning incense before the Lord (Lev. 16:12-13). {After sacrificing the bull, Aaron then took a censer full of burning coals from the fire of the Lord, which was found at the altar of burnt offering in the tabernacle courtyard.}[Q8]

{The censer was taken before the Lord in the Most Holy Place, where it provided a cloud that covered the mercy seat on the ark.}[Q8] The resulting mist served as protection for Aaron, guarding him from directly seeing the presence of God.

The blood of the bull (Lev. 16:14). The mercy seat was the lid that rested on top of the ark of the covenant. Inside the ark were items that were reminiscent of human sin: Manna that the children of Israel complained about, the stone tablets that contained the Ten Commandments, and Aaron's staff that budded as a sign of Israel's rebellion (cf. Ex. 16:33-34; Deut. 10:2; Num. 17:10; Heb. 9:4).

Aaron was to dip his finger in the blood of the bull and sprinkle it seven times on the mercy seat. Going all the way back to Eden, God has always required blood to atone for sin. God made animal skins in order to cover Adam and Eve's shame (cf. Gen. 3:21).

Cleansing the Holy Place (Lev. 16:15-16). The next step in the atonement ritual was to sacrifice the goat that had been designated by God as the sin offering for the people. {The sacrifice of this goat, like the entire ritual, pointed toward the sacrifice of Jesus. The goat was from the people of Israel, just as Jesus was from Israel. It was chosen by God, just as Jesus was chosen by God. The goat's blood was taken into the Holy of Holies for atonement. Jesus' blood was taken to the most holy place in heaven, securing an eternal atonement for all who believe in Him (cf. Heb. 9:12).}[Q9]

The blood of the goat was to be sprinkled on and in front of the mercy seat inside the Holy of Holies, just as the blood of the bull had been (Lev. 16:15).

This was to provide atonement not only for the people but also for the Most Holy Place. In addition, the same ritual was to be followed for the entire tabernacle and all its furnishings, presumably also with the sprinkling of blood (vs. 16; cf. vss. 17-20).

{This was necessary due to the "uncleanness of the children of Israel" (vs. 16). Their sins contaminated the tabernacle each time they worshipped there. The blood from the atonement sacrifice provided a cleansing for the entire place of worship.}[Q10]

The filth that comes from human sin is corruptive by nature and has a contaminating effect. However, in His grace God has provided a permanent atonement for our sin: the blood of His Son, Jesus Christ, which removes, not just covers, our sin.

—Robert Ferguson, Jr.

QUESTIONS

1. What occasion prompted God to give instructions for the Day of Atonement?
2. Where in the tabernacle did the presence of God reside?
3. What sacrifices was Aaron to offer to the Lord for himself on the Day of Atonement?
4. What garments was Aaron to wear on this day?
5. What is a key difference between the priesthood of Jesus and the priesthood of Aaron?
6. What animal was to be presented as a sin offering for the people?
7. Why was a second goat needed?
8. What was Aaron to do after sacrificing the bull for himself?
9. How did the sacrifice of the goat in particular point to Jesus?
10. Why did the tabernacle itself have to be cleansed?

—Robert Ferguson, Jr.

Preparing to Teach the Lesson

In the previous two lessons, we have been learning much about God's holiness from the texts of Leviticus 8:1-13 and 10:1-7. There we witnessed the ordination and then the demise of Aaron's sons Nadab and Abihu because of their disregard for the standards of God's holiness.

In this week's lesson, we turn from narratives surrounding personal situations to a passage that legislates corporate holiness, the Day of Atonement. Leviticus 16:1-16 is a foundational text in the Old Testament in that it teaches Israel a perpetual rite that centers on God's holy standards. We find here amazingly relevant theological truth that we can carry into our everyday lives.

TODAY'S AIM

Facts: to illustrate the amazing grace, mercy, and forgiveness of the Lord.

Principle: to learn crucial aspects of atonement and forgiveness in order to gain a greater appreciation for God's holiness and mercy.

Application: to properly view God's forgiveness and His holiness in perfect balance, understanding both our responsibilities to God's holy standards and His merciful ways.

INTRODUCING THE LESSON

There are a number of holy days instituted in the Mosaic Law, but the Day of Atonement, or Yom Kippur, is the most solemn and important holy day on the Jewish calendar. Today, we will read a portion of the Mosaic instruction regarding this important holy day. The day was highlighted by the high priest making an atoning sacrifice for the sins of the people of Israel. This priestly act of atonement provided reconciliation between the people of Israel and God.

After the blood sacrifice was offered up, a goat (known as the "scapegoat") was released into the wilderness to symbolically carry away the sins of the people.

Thus, the Day of Atonement gives us the divine perspective, providing believers a proper balance between God's forgiveness and the holy requirements of His Word.

DEVELOPING THE LESSON

After the death of Aaron's sons Nadab and Abihu, the Lord spoke to Moses, instituting the Day of Atonement. Through the Day of Atonement, the Lord conveyed a number of very important concepts that assist us in living rightly while our faith is on trial. Other passages that refer to the Day of Atonement include Leviticus 23:26-32 and Numbers 29:7-11. Of course, these passages ultimately must be understood in light of the sacrifice of Christ (cf. Isa. 53:4-10; Rom. 3:21-26; Heb. 10:4-22).

Both God's forgiveness and His holy requirements are on full display in the Day of Atonement. God's forgiveness is seen in a number of ways. Initially, the Lord's injunction for Aaron that "he come not at all times into the holy place within the vail before the mercy seat" (Lev. 16:2) demonstrates an incredible amount of mercy. Second, the Lord's forgiveness is seen in His allowance of the scapegoat (vs. 10). The scapegoat clearly pictures Christ's atoning work on the cross. Finally, the Lord's forgiveness is seen in His atoning provision for the high priest himself. Here, the high priest is also given means to escape divine wrath despite his own sinfulness.

The Day of Atonement teaches us three important principles related to matters of holiness.

1. Attitude is important (Lev. 16:1-2). The Lord instructed that Aaron was to "come not at all times into the holy place within the vail before the mercy seat." Even the high priest must take great care when approaching the holy God. He must not take God and His blessings for granted but approach Him with the proper, humble attitude—unlike Nadab and Abihu. In Christ, we are invited to come boldly before the Lord at any time (Heb. 4:16), but this does not mean we can come to Him with proud, unrepentant hearts or a demanding attitude.

2. Preparation is important (Lev. 16:3-5). Aaron was to come into the holy place, but he was to come *with* the appropriate offerings. It was not enough for Aaron to simply report to the holy place; he was to come with the items necessary for him to fulfill his priestly duties. If we are to worship and serve the Lord in holiness, we need to give careful thought as individuals and congregations to why and how we do this. We must plan for things that are important.

3. Correct and complete execution is important (Lev. 16:6-16). In our text, Aaron is instructed on exactly what to do and when to do it. Clearly, following God's standards the right way is the emphasis. Obedience to God's Word is always of utmost importance. Indeed, obedience reveals proper preparation and proper attitude in serving the Lord.

The basic concept of the Day of Atonement finds some likeness in our courts of law. If a person has committed an offense that requires a financial payment, it is normally acceptable for anyone to make the payment to the court on behalf of the guilty party. The Day of Atonement points us, as it did the people of Israel, to the truth that God Himself has stepped forward to provide the payment for us, the guilty party. Christ, the Substitute He has provided, has paid the penalty for our sin in God's holy court through His death.

ILLUSTRATING THE LESSON

In the Day of Atonement ritual, the sacrifice of the one goat pictured the payment for sin. The release of the scapegoat pictured the removal of sin. Together, they pointed to the great truth that Jesus Christ has both paid the penalty for our sin and taken away our sin and its debt.

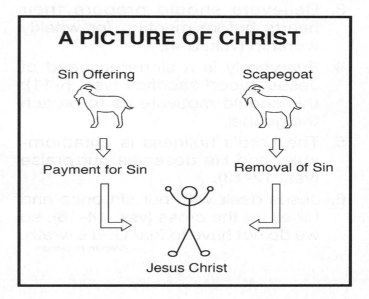

A PICTURE OF CHRIST

Sin Offering → Payment for Sin

Scapegoat → Removal of Sin

Jesus Christ

CONCLUDING THE LESSON

God's forgiveness and His holy requirements are balanced perfectly in Leviticus 16. We see His forgiveness in His specific dealings with Aaron, His allowance of the scapegoat, and His atoning provision for the high priest himself. God's holiness is also on display in the Day of Atonement as indicated by the importance of complete obedience to God.

As we seek to live out our faith, God's forgiveness and His holy standards give us much-needed guidance and assurance.

ANTICIPATING THE NEXT LESSON

In our next lesson, from Leviticus 24:10-23, we will learn more about God's holiness and the grave danger of taking it lightly.

—*Nigel C. Black.*

PRACTICAL POINTS

1. We must continue to serve and respect the Lord, even when we do not understand His ways (Lev. 16:1).
2. Coming to God in prayer is a privilege; we should treat is as such (vs. 2).
3. Believers should prepare their hearts before meeting for weekly worship (vss. 3-4).
4. Everybody is a sinner in need of Jesus' blood sacrifice (vss. 5-11); this should motivate us to preach the gospel.
5. The Lord's holiness is unfathomable, and He deserves our praise (vss. 12-13).
6. Jesus dealt with our sin once and for all on the cross (vss. 14-16), so we do not have to fear God's wrath.

—Megan Hickman.

RESEARCH AND DISCUSSION

1. How can we keep our hearts soft toward the Lord even when He brings suffering and loss into our lives (Lev. 16:1; cf. Heb. 4:16)?
2. In what ways can you prepare your heart to worship the Lord on Sunday (vs. 4)?
3. How would you counsel someone who thinks he needs to become sinless before trusting in Jesus?
4. Why do our sins need to be covered with blood? Why did they need to be covered specifically with the blood of Jesus?
5. Why do leaders and their households need to take special care in practicing righteousness (vs. 11)?

—Megan Hickman.

ILLUSTRATED HIGH POINTS

Shall he be attired (Lev. 16:4)

For most weddings, the bride wears a white dress and the groom wears a suit. The guests normally wear semi-formal or formal clothing.

Special articles of clothing are used for specific occasions. The priest's clothing symbolized righteousness. Christ clothes his true followers with His own righteousness.

Make an atonement for himself (vs. 6)

A young girl in Africa was abducted from her community and given a weapon. She was forced to attack and loot the surrounding communities.

A year and a half later, she escaped her captors and returned to her community, but what she had endured still greatly burdened her. She was filled with guilt and yearned for a way to atone for her crimes.

We cannot bear our sins on our own. Even the old-covenant priests needed atonement for their own sins. But Jesus, our great High Priest, lived a sinless life and fully atoned for the sins of those who trust Him as Lord and Saviour.

In the midst of their uncleanness (vs. 16)

I have a very energetic, playful dog. He is getting older, but he still loves to run around outside. Often to my annoyance, he loves to roll around in the dirt. Sometimes he gets so dirty that I have to put him back on his leash and clean him up a little bit before allowing him indoors.

The dirt on my dog is similar to human sin. Just as I have to clean my dog when he gets dirty, the old covenant priests had to continue cleansing the Israelites' standing before God by making sacrifices to atone for their sins.

—Chelsea Villaseñor.

Golden Text Illuminated

"Speak unto Aaron thy brother, that he come not at all times into the holy place . . . that he die not: for I will appear in the cloud upon the mercy seat" (Leviticus 16:2).

For a sinful human being, entering into the holy presence of Yahweh is a life-forfeiting prospect. Because Yahweh is supremely holy and because all humans since the Fall are sinful and therefore worthy of death, you should expect death when you enter His presence except at His sovereign discretion. This is the meaning of today's golden text.

To assuage Yahweh's righteous judgment on the Day of Atonement, much sacrificial blood had to be shed: the blood of a young bull (vss. 3, 6), a ram for a burnt offering, and two goat kids (vss. 5, 8-10, 15). Not only were Aaron's family and the rest of the people of Israel sinful before Yahweh, but even the tabernacle itself was unclean just by coming into contact with them (vs. 16).

If all this bloodshed seems extreme, then consider this: the entire ceremonial system of sacrifice under the Law was of no lasting effect in atoning for human sins. It was merely a type and shadow of the real atoning sacrifice made once and for all by Jesus Christ (cf. Heb. 10:1-4)! The sacrifices served only to impress upon the Israelites how sinful, unclean, and offensive they really were to their holy God!

Within the veil of the holiest place was the ark of the covenant, overlaid with gold. Upon the solid gold lid of the ark were the cherubim, facing each other with outstretched wings that covered the mercy seat, the earthly equivalent of the very throne of Yahweh. The presence of Yahweh was manifested in the Shekinah-glory, the glorious pillar of cloud that signaled Yahweh Himself was there.

In order for Aaron or any of his successors as high priest to survive an encounter with Yahweh's presence within the holiest place, they had to burn divinely prescribed incense on coals taken from the altar to create a cloud of smoke and incense that would obscure Aaron's vision of the Lord's mercy seat (Lev. 16:12-13).

In both the Old and the New Testaments, an encounter with Yahweh's presence meant sure death, except at His sovereign discretion.

When the Prophet Isaiah encountered a vision of the Lord in the temple, he was terrified for his very life because he realized his utter sinfulness and his unworthiness to be in the presence of Yahweh, who is holy (Isa. 6:1-5). The threefold repetition of the word meant that Yahweh's holiness is of the highest, most transcendent order, unlike anyone else in the entire universe.

When the Apostle Peter understood that he was in the presence of Yahweh in the person of Jesus Christ, he also feared for his life because, like Isaiah, he powerfully sensed his sinfulness and unworthiness (Luke 5:8). Likewise, when the Apostle John found himself in the presence of the glorified Christ, he fell to the ground as one dead, saved only by the life-bestowing touch of the Saviour (Rev. 1:13-17).

This should remind us of the supreme holiness of our God. Let no one dissuade you from this unalterable truth: the Lord is holy!

—*John Lody.*

Heart of the Lesson

The extent of God's holiness is hard for us to grasp. That is why He gave such specific requirements for how the Israelites were to worship Him. He did not intend these things to be a burden, but He did want to give them and us an illustration of the price of sin and, when the time came, what it would cost Him in the sacrifice of His Son. Knowledge of the sacrificial system gives us a greater appreciation for His mercy.

Following the death of Aaron's sons, God again emphasized His holiness among the Israelites by designating the Day of Atonement. This would be a day, occurring once each year, in which the high priest (Aaron) would atone for the sins of the people. On this day, he would enter into the holy of holies, where he would be in the Lord's presence.

Preparation for worship (Lev. 16:1-6). If Aaron tried to enter this holy space at any time other than on the Day of Atonement, he would be struck dead. This day reminded the Israelite people that though Yahweh was their God and they were His people, the Israelites certainly were not worthy of the privilege of this relationship (Deut. 7:7-9).

God gave Aaron a specific task for this day. He was to offer atonement for the sins of the people. He brought two goats with him as an offering, but before he could even perform sacrifices, he first had to cleanse himself. He had to bathe himself, put on holy garments, and offer a sacrifice for himself and his household.

Compared to the ephod described in Leviticus 10, the Atonement Day garments were relatively plain, revealing an equality between the high priest and the people (Jamieson, Fausset, Brown, *Commentary Critical and Explanatory on the Whole Bible*). Every man, even the priest, needed atonement for his sins (Rom. 3:23).

Though God gave Aaron a way to come into His presence, it was not the ultimate and permanent way that God had planned for believers through His Son, Jesus Christ. Christ serves as our perfect High Priest and eternal mediator. He is completely holy and does not need to be cleansed to atone for us because He lived a perfect life (Heb. 7:27).

The sin offering (Lev. 16:7-16). The two goats Aaron brought to sacrifice pointed forward to the reality that Jesus, the Messiah, would take care of the people's sin once and for all on the cross. One goat was sent into the wilderness, symbolically taking the people's sins far from them, and the other was offered on the altar as a blood sacrifice for them.

Christ fulfilled both of these roles for us. He not only took the wrath of the Father upon Himself by dying on the cross (Rom. 5:9), but He also cleansed us from our sins and imputed His righteousness to us. Because He lived the perfect life, we do not need to continue making sacrifices for our sins. If we have trusted in Christ as our Saviour, we no longer need to fear the Father's wrath and have the freedom to live a life of thankfulness to Him.

Though we see the extremity of God's holiness in the Old Testament, we see the extremity of His grace in the work of Christ. The Day of Atonement reminds us that we can praise God for His plan, in which "the law entered, that the offence might abound. But where sin abounded, grace did much more abound" (Rom. 5:20).

—*Megan Hickman.*

World Missions

A German man whose family was very wealthy before World War II was asked how many of the German people really were Nazis. He said, "Very few people were true Nazis, but many enjoyed the return of German pride, and many more were too busy to care. I was one of those who just thought the Nazis were a bunch of fools. So, the majority just sat back and let it all happen. Then, before we knew it, they owned us, and we had lost control, and the end of the world had come. My family lost everything. I ended up in a concentration camp and the Allies destroyed my factories" ("Why the Peaceful Majority Is Irrelevant," www.citizenwarrior.com).

Numbers matter little when it comes to influence among people. Why? Should not huge numbers of people be able to make great change? Unfortunately, the great majority are often apathetic or casual in their involvement, and their inactivity renders them effectively irrelevant.

A silent majority did not stop six million Jews from being killed in the holocaust, twenty million people in communist Russia, or seventy million in communist China. What about Rwanda, or Sudan, or Ethiopia? Were not most of its citizens non-fanatics who just wanted to live their lives?

The significant factor in political influence is not what the majority believes, but how the dedicated radicals act—the ones who have sold themselves out to an ideology or worldview.

We often hear the argument that we must accept Islam as a peaceful religion because the majority of Muslims are peaceful. But have we not seen that it is the radicals—those with the passion and commitment to carry out an agenda based on the Quran—who are the ones guiding the course of Islam?

There may indeed be nearly one billion peaceful Muslims in the world, but how much influence are they having on the direction that Islam is taking?

When our enemy, Satan, talks to his servants about Christians, does he tell them to fear the silent majority, the ones who just go along with the flow while hoping things will turn out well? Of course not! He surely considers them irrelevant to the conflict. They pose no threat to his agenda. Rather, they actually serve his purpose by their apathy and non-participation. No, Satan directs his attention to the radicals—those whose zeal for Christ is the focus of their entire existence.

Where is that minority of radical believers who are fully zealous for Christ—those who deny themselves, take up their cross daily, and follow Jesus with everything they have? Do you know of such a person? Are you such a person? Out of all the believers you know, how many would you say are truly fully committed to Christ?

The radical minority of Christians who are fully sold out to Christ are making an impact that Satan desperately needs to contest in order for his agenda to progress. But genuinely passionate believers seem few and scattered, and they are often deemed eccentric and even irrelevant by the majority of Christians, who should know better.

Do not be deceived; God's victory is assured. His sovereign plan cannot be thwarted. He even uses the evil actions of the enemy to fulfill His purposes. But He especially uses those who are fully dedicated to His service. They are His salt and His light in a world of lost sinners. Their faithfulness will be richly commended and rewarded by the Lord. Will you be counted among them?

—Kimberly Rae.

The Jewish Aspect

On September 16, Jews around the world celebrated Yom Kippur, the Day of Atonement. Jews consider Yom Kippur the holiest day of the year, when they are closest to God. For twenty-five hours, while observing Yom Kippur, Jews "afflict their souls" as they abstain from food and drink, lotions and creams, marital relations, and leather footwear. Instead, they spend the day in the synagogue praying for forgiveness.

Yom Kippur follows Rosh Hashanah, the Jewish New Year. Jews know these two holidays as "Jewish High Holidays" or "High Holy Days." During Yom Kippur, observant Jews repent of their sins and receive healing for their souls for the next year. The people participate in a twenty-five-hour fast observed from sundown to sundown as part of the holiday.

In this week's Scripture lesson, God gives Moses instructions for Aaron concerning Yom Kippur. The instructions come after the death of Aaron's two sons who died after burning unauthorized fire before the Lord, and the reiteration of these rules emphasizes the importance of following God's instructions.

This week's text is also the traditional reading for Yom Kippur morning in the Jewish synagogue. It focuses on the offerings that Aaron was to bring before God as atonement. God instructed Aaron to make expiation for himself, his household, and the entire community.

After the destruction of the second temple and the termination of the sacrificial system, the Jewish people had to figure out how to achieve atonement. Rabbis ruled that in this situation, one can perform the temple duties by reading about them since they believe that "the utterance of a person's lips is equivalent to the actual performance of the ritual" (Eisenberg, "Avodah Service," myjewishlearning.com).

Rabbis base the Avodah, which literally means "service," on the ritual that the priests performed in the ancient temple. The Avodah describes the sacrificial procedures on the Day of Atonement (Lev. 16), and it is an essential element of Yom Kippur (Eisenberg).

Jews know the period from Rosh Hashanah to Yom Kippur as the "ten days of repentance"; they see these days as an opportunity for change. Jews believe charity and prayer are important during these ten days of penitence.

Although Jews have ten days to repent and make changes, on Yom Kippur itself they believe their fate becomes sealed for the coming year. As a result, they believe Yom Kippur is the last chance to make amends and change their judgement. They hope that God will seal their names in the book of life.

During the *minhah*, or afternoon service, of Yom Kippur, Jews read from the book of Jonah. Jewish sages explain why they read this book during this service. Rabbis trust that if God accepted the repentance of the people of Nineveh, then He will forgive repenting Jews. They surmise that if He answered Jonah from the belly of the fish, God will also save them (Bernstein, "Jonah and Yom Kippur," myjewishlearning.com).

According to Scripture, nobody is saved by doing good works. Though we should be repenting of our sins daily, hoping to draw closer to God, as Christians we understand that it is when we repent and ask Christ into our lives that we pass from spiritual death unto life. All past and future sins were paid for at the Cross. When we trust in Jesus, our destiny is sealed once and for all.

—Robin Fitzgerald.

Guiding the Superintendent

We continue in our studies of the requirements for the people of Israel. They needed to scrupulously observe God's requirements for holiness in order for His presence to dwell in their midst as His chosen people. In these verses, we see the steps required of Aaron to enter the holy place in order to avoid suffering the same fiery death as his two sons.

He is instructed by Moses to don the holy garments and to prepare to bring with him a bull for his own sin offering, two rams for burnt offerings, and two goats from the people for their sin offerings. He is instructed on how to purify himself, then the Holy Place, then the tent of meeting, and finally the people of Israel. God's instructions are incredibly detailed down to the putting on and taking off of Aaron's clothes. There can be little doubt that God desires purity in His people.

DEVOTIONAL OUTLINE

1. Personal preparation (Lev. 16:1-4). Aaron was to don the holy garments in much the same way a surgeon dons his or her surgical clothing, the goal being complete cleanliness. Aaron started by bathing to ritually cleanse himself and then donned the linen undergarment and tunic. Atop this he put on the sash and turban to complete the attire. All this purified him outwardly, symbolizing the inward purity that all of us need for entering God's presence.

2. Preparation of the scapegoat (Lev. 16:5-10). The precise meaning of the Hebrew word *Azazel* is uncertain, but it has traditionally been interpreted as "scapegoat." The second goat for the offerings was to be left alive, and in verses 20 through 22 we are told that the people, represented by Aaron, placed their hands on this goat to transfer their sins from themselves onto the animal. The goat was then led away into the wilderness, taking the sins of the people with it.

3. Atonement for Aaron and his house (Lev. 16:11-14). To receive cleansing for his role as high priest, Aaron had to present a bull as a sin offering. As we learn from Hebrews 9:22, there is no forgiveness without the shedding of blood. For Aaron, the bull's blood had to be carried with him into the Most Holy Place and be sprinkled by his own hand onto the mercy seat of God. This, plus an offering of incense, allowed Aaron to survive his encounter with the Lord's holy presence.

4. Atonement for the Holy Place and Israel's sin (Lev. 16:15-16). Once purified, Aaron had to then offer a sacrifice for the purification of the people of Israel. He was instructed to do this by offering the remaining goat as a sin offering. Its blood was to be sprinkled over the mercy seat as well. He had done the same with the bull's blood, sprinkling it on the tent of meeting and on the altar. In doing this, the tabernacle was ritually purified and the people were made clean in order to begin their service to God.

CHILDREN'S CORNER

The meaning of the Day of Atonement may be difficult for children to grasp. Encourage them to focus on the fact that sin is just as much a problem for us today as it was back in Moses' time. But rather than sacrifice animals for our sins, we can receive the complete and finished atonement of Christ by placing our trust in Him as Lord and Saviour.

—*Mike Spencer.*

Scripture Lesson Text

LEV. 24:10 And the son of an Israelitish woman, whose father *was* an Egyptian, went out among the children of Israel: and this son of the Israelitish *woman* and a man of Israel strove together in the camp;

11 And the Israelitish woman's son blasphemed the name *of the* Lord, and cursed. And they brought him unto Moses: (and his mother's name *was* Shelomith, the daughter of Dibri, of the tribe of Dan:)

12 And they put him in ward, that the mind of the Lord might be shewed them.

13 And the Lord spake unto Moses, saying,

14 Bring forth him that hath cursed without the camp; and let all that heard *him* lay their hands upon his head, and let all the congregation stone him.

15 And thou shalt speak unto the children of Israel, saying, Whosoever curseth his God shall bear his sin.

16 And he that blasphemeth the name of the Lord, he shall surely be put to death, *and* all the congregation shall certainly stone him: as well the stranger, as he that is born in the land, when he blasphemeth the name *of the* Lord, shall be put to death.

17 And he that killeth any man shall surely be put to death.

18 And he that killeth a beast shall make it good; beast for beast.

19 And if a man cause a blemish in his neighbour; as he hath done, so shall it be done to him;

20 Breach for breach, eye for eye, tooth for tooth: as he hath caused a blemish in a man, so shall it be done to him *again.*

21 And he that killeth a beast, he shall restore it: and he that killeth a man, he shall be put to death.

22 Ye shall have one manner of law, as well for the stranger, as for one of your own country: for I *am* the Lord your God.

23 And Moses spake to the children of Israel, that they should bring forth him that had cursed out of the camp, and stone him with stones. And the children of Israel did as the Lord commanded Moses.

NOTES

A Blasphemer Stoned

Lesson Text: Leviticus 24:10-23

Related Scriptures: Exodus 20:1-21; Deuteronomy 13:6-18;
Matthew 12:30-32; Acts 5:1-11

TIME: 1445 B.C.   PLACE: Mount Sinai

GOLDEN TEXT—"Thou shalt not take the name of the Lord thy God in vain; for the Lord will not hold him guiltless that taketh his name in vain" (Exodus 20:7).

Introduction

As we have seen already in this unit of our study, holiness is a central and inviolable attribute of God. It cannot be compromised in any way.

This week's lesson will examine a situation in which a man cursed God and paid severely for it.

God never takes a lighthearted approach to sin, especially when someone directly confronts or challenges Him. God established the Mosaic Law with the people of Israel at the same time He was establishing them as a brand-new nation that had just spent over four hundred years in a foreign land.

In order to prevent the Israelites from following the paths of their former captors and neighbors, God gave them His law. This law was designed to regulate every aspect of life for Israel, and it was firmly grounded in the holiness of God. The people were to revere Him at all times and in all situations. Violating the holiness of God brought swift and severe judgment.

LESSON OUTLINE

I. **HOLINESS OF GOD'S NAME**—
Lev. 24:10-16

II. **SACREDNESS OF LIFE**—
Lev. 24:17-23

Exposition: Verse by Verse

HOLINESS OF GOD'S NAME

LEV. 24:10 And the son of an Israelitish woman, whose father was an Egyptian, went out among the children of Israel: and this son of the Israelitish woman and a man of Israel strove together in the camp;

11 And the Israelitish woman's son blasphemed the name of the LORD, and cursed. And they brought him unto Moses: (and his mother's name was Shelomith, the daughter of Dibri, of the tribe of Dan:)

12 And they put him in ward,

that the mind of the Lord might be shewed them.

13 And the Lord spake unto Moses, saying,

14 Bring forth him that hath cursed without the camp; and let all that heard him lay their hands upon his head, and let all the congregation stone him.

15 And thou shalt speak unto the children of Israel, saying, Whosoever curseth his God shall bear his sin.

16 And he that blasphemeth the name of the Lord, he shall surely be put to death, and all the congregation shall certainly stone him: as well the stranger, as he that is born in the land, when he blasphemeth the name of the Lord, shall be put to death.

Fight in the Israelite camp (Lev. 24:10-11). {This week's lesson begins with a narrative that tells of a man who was half Israelite and half Egyptian.}Q1 His mother, Shelomith, was from the tribe of Dan, but we know nothing about his father, except that he was Egyptian. Whether Shelomith's husband was a follower of the true God or whether he had even accompanied his wife and son when they left Egypt is unknown.

In later times, rabbinic law held that a child who had a Jewish mother and a Gentile father was considered a Jew. While the rabbinic law was much later than the time of Moses, perhaps this was the principle all along, although not yet established formally. In any case, this man was a part of the Israelite community and subject to their laws.

At the same time, being the product of a mixed marriage probably meant the man was not yet considered fully a part of the true "congregation of the Lord" (cf. Deut. 23:7-8) but was included in that group referred to as the "mixed multitude" (Ex. 12:38). These were people who had left Egypt along with the Israelites at the time of the Exodus. Some had probably joined them because they genuinely feared the Lord; others presumably saw this as an opportunity to escape their own slavery. In fact, these people might have been motivated to leave with the Israelites for any number of reasons. As we will see, they created problems during Israel's journey (cf. Num. 11:4).

The half-Israelite man became engaged in a fight with an Israelite man for an unspecified reason, and {during the scrum he uttered blasphemy against the name of the Lord in a curse. He was immediately brought to Moses, as this was a clear violation of the law (cf. Ex. 20:7).}Q2 The prohibition against cursing or blaspheming God's name had been clearly established, but the penalty for such an offense had not yet been given, so the man was brought to Moses to determine what his punishment would be.

In ancient times especially, a person's name was synonymous with the person himself and his character. {To denigrate a person's name was to make an attack on the person himself. God's name is holy just as He is holy. To curse His name is to curse God directly. It is a complete moral failure for a sinful human being to curse the name of God, who is righteous and holy.}Q3

The world is horrified when a vandal damages and desecrates a famous and treasured work of art. How much more should we be horrified at desecrating the pure holiness of the living God?

By cursing the name of God, the man reduced Him to the level of the Egyptian gods. It was not uncommon for Egyptians to curse their gods when they did not receive what they wanted from their deities. This man treated God no differently than he did the gods of his Egyptian father. God cannot be diminished to the plane of a man-made deity. The man who cursed God's name was guilty of doing this, an intolerable offense.

Waiting for God's will (Lev. 24:12). {When those who heard the man blaspheme the Lord's name brought him to Moses, the blasphemer was put in custody.}Q4 {The people did not take quick action themselves to punish the man but left the matter to God. After all, it was God whom He had offended, and without clear guidance on what to do, they were willing to wait for Him to instruct them on how to punish the man.}Q5

Waiting for the will of the Lord is not an easy thing for most of us to do. We tend to like our answers neat and tidy, and above all, quick. Yet God often requires us to wait on Him, which makes some of us uncomfortable, if not downright jittery. It is always best to wait on God for as long as necessary, as it will guard us against reacting in an irrational way and making poor decisions with disastrous results. The children of Israel often responded to God in rash fashion, but in this case they got it right. They waited for His direction in dealing with the guilty man.

The word from the Lord (Lev. 24:13-14). The people waited to hear from the Lord, and soon, presumably, God did speak to Moses. Since the life of a man was on the line in this instance, it was especially important for Moses and the people to wait for God to state what justice for this man's offense would entail. Since God had not explicitly stated previously what the punishment for blaspheming His name was, it was right and proper for Moses to wait for God to instruct him.

The first thing God told Moses was to take the man out of the camp. He was to be put to death, but to kill him inside the camp would have defiled the entire community with a corpse.

After taking him outside the camp, all those who heard the man blaspheme God were to lay their hands on his head. This was significant for at least two reasons. First, it served as testimony against the man as to his guilt and confirmed him as the guilty party. Second, the laying on of hands points back to the scapegoat, where the high priest laid his hands on the goat, signifying the transfer of the people's sin. The goat would then be sent away into the wilderness, symbolizing that the sins of the people were removed from their midst.

In this instance, the sin of the man was being returned onto his own head, outside the camp, and he would be punished for his offense. The fact that he cursed God meant that he had no reverence for the Lord. This may not seem like a big deal to many people today, but it is a serious transgression for a fallen human being to attack the character and person of God, as this man had done.

{Finally, all the people were instructed to execute the man by stoning him to death. The entire community was responsible to root out the sin among them, but only at the clear direction of the Lord.}Q6 This is not a justification for vigilante justice. It was a clear mandate from God Himself to a specific group of people for the punishment of a specific offense. In no way should this be seen as a basis for condemning someone to death based on our own whims and desire for vengeance.

Setting the precedent (Lev. 24:15-16). To show that this was not a one-time punishment simply to set an example for the people regarding the holiness of God's name, the Lord stated that any future violators would also suffer the same penalty. It was an example to be sure, but from that point forward there would be no question as to what would happen to someone who dared to blaspheme the name of the Lord.

Since the whole congregation was to participate in this man's execution, it would no doubt serve as a reminder of what would happen to those who cursed God in the future. It would also serve as a deterrent against angry speech, since an irreverent word spoken against the Lord would result in a person's execution by the community.

This statute was the same for Israelites as it was for non-Israelites who lived among them. God's name is holy and is to be regarded as such by all who acknowledge Him.

Of course, many people do not acknowledge God and curse Him continually, seemingly without any consequences. God is holy nonetheless, and such blasphemers will be held accountable. God is merciful and gives people many opportunities to repent of their hatred of God. Persistent failure to repent, however, will ultimately lead to a person's eternal destruction. Cursing God's name has never been permitted and never will be.

SACREDNESS OF LIFE

17 And he that killeth any man shall surely be put to death.

18 And he that killeth a beast shall make it good; beast for beast.

19 And if a man cause a blemish in his neighbour; as he hath done, so shall it be done to him;

20 Breach for breach, eye for eye, tooth for tooth: as he hath caused a blemish in a man, so shall it be done to him again.

21 And he that killeth a beast, he shall restore it: and he that killeth a man, he shall be put to death.

22 Ye shall have one manner of law, as well for the stranger, as for one of your own country: for I am the LORD your God.

23 And Moses spake to the children of Israel, that they should bring forth him that had cursed out of the camp, and stone him with stones. And the children of Israel did as the LORD commanded Moses.

The value of human life (Lev. 24:17). God has always placed a high value on human life. Since He is the Creator of all life, only He has the right to determine who lives and dies, along with when and under what circumstances.

{The reason human life is sacred is not only because God created us, but also because He created us in His image (Gen. 1:26-27; 5:1).}[Q7] Anyone who murders another human being is making an attack on God's sacred and unique creation, and the penalty for that is very steep (cf. 9:6).

We must always be careful, however, to distinguish between justice and a desire for vengeance. These are two very different things. Justice seeks to right that which was wrong, to bring punishment to the offender, to protect the rights of the victim, and to uphold the sacredness of human life. Vengeance, on the other hand, simply seeks to hurt the offender as much as or more than he hurt us. Vengeance must be left with God, who executes it justly (Deut. 32:35; Rom. 12:19).

As followers of Christ, our desire should be that the appropriate government authorities, would, as much as humanly possible, reflect the perfect justice of God. Given our own limitations and weaknesses as human beings ourselves, we must take every precaution to ensure that guilt is certain and the innocent are not wrongly punished.

The value of animal life (Lev. 24:18). {The difference between the value of human life and animal life is clearly seen in verse 18. Human life is protected to the point that whoever takes a life must lose his own, whereas one who takes the life of someone's animal must pay restitution.}[Q8]

This does not mean that animal life is unimportant, only that there is a great difference between animals and humans. Man is created in God's image, while animals are not. Contrary to the teachings of evolutionists and naturalists, man is not simply a highly evolved animal but rather the pinnacle of God's creation, who uniquely bears His image.

Killing an animal, in itself, was not forbidden, since animals were used for both food and sacrifice. In view here is the accidental or malicious killing of domestic animals owned by others. In ancient Israel, those who killed such an animal were to pay restitution to the owner or replace the animal.

Of course, animals not owned by people are also God's creation and are important to Him. They do not exist for humans to abuse or mistreat.

Laws of restitution (Lev. 24:19-20). {Generally, under the law anyone who brought harm to another person's being or property was to pay restitution (cf. Ex. 21:18—22:15).}[Q9] This concept is almost foreign to modern thinking and preaching. Much is said about repentance, forgiveness, reconciliation, and restoration, but very little is taught today concerning restitution.

The notion that repentance involves only an acknowledgment of guilt is not biblical. Part of repenting is, whenever possible, to make things right with those whom we have offended. Thus, God's law called for a thief not simply to apologize to the one he had stolen from, but rather to repay or replace that which was stolen—and then some.

Under the Law, restitution was an important part of community life. Ancient Israel did not have any prisons, so it was especially necessary for lawbreakers to restore what they broke or stole.

{The principle of "eye for eye, tooth for tooth" set the standard for how to punish crime (Lev. 24:20). It did not demand punishment in kind but that the punishment must fit the crime. It removed the subjectivity of punishing crime as each individual saw fit and limited how punishments could be doled out.}[Q10] Most cases that did not demand the death penalty were actually settled by restitution.

Same standard for everyone (Lev. 24:21-22). The standard of justice is summarized by stating that whoever killed an animal should make restitution, but whoever killed another human being must be put to death. The rule was not limited to just the Israelites but also applied to all those living among them, just as with the blasphemer.

Execution of the blasphemer (Lev. 24:23). The chapter closes with the people doing what God had told them to do with the blasphemer. The people took him out of the camp and stoned him to death.

The Word of God is not something simply to be agreed with or studied. It is also to be obeyed.

—*Robert Ferguson, Jr.*

QUESTIONS

1. What nationality was the man who is discussed in Leviticus 24:10?

2. Of what sin was this man guilty?

3. Why was this such a serious offense?

4. What did the people do with the man after he cursed God?

5. Why did they need to wait for God's direction?

6. Who was responsible for carrying out the final punishment God commanded?

7. Why is human life so sacred and valuable to God?

8. How is human life differentiated from animal life in God's law?

9. How were most cases involving injury to a person or his property resolved?

10. What safeguards were established by the principle of "eye for eye, tooth for tooth" (vs. 20)?

—*Robert Ferguson, Jr.*

Preparing to Teach the Lesson

The first four weeks of this quarter's series, "Faith on Trial," focus on God's holiness. We began with the consecration of Aaron and his sons (Lev. 8:1-13) and then moved to the death of Aaron's sons Nadab and Abihu (10:1-7). Last week we studied both the forgiveness and holy standards found in the institution of the Day of Atonement. Today, we will investigate the curious account of a nameless man who was executed by stoning for the crime of blasphemy. The text today will help us to truly round out our understanding of God's holiness as we look to move into Unit II of our curriculum next week.

TODAY'S AIM

Facts: to continue learning of God's holy standards and the consequences of breaking those standards.

Principle: to closely investigate the principles of divine holiness found in Leviticus 24:10-23 so that we will understand God's character and personality.

Application: to seek holiness in our lives so that we might be pleasing in God's sight and live in close relationship to Him.

INTRODUCING THE LESSON

Although the Day of Atonement served as a means of reconciling the people of Israel to their God, Israel would need to continue in obedience in order to avoid divine consequences. The stoning of a blasphemer in Leviticus 24:10-23 serves as an important reminder to every believer that God is not to be mocked (Gal. 6:7; cf. Ex. 20:1-21; Deut. 13:6-18; Matt. 12:30-32; Acts 5:1-11).

When we study the Old Testament, it is important to understand the historical and cultural context of the original readers of the Scripture. For instance, even a cursory reading of the Old Testament indicates that the people of Israel not only were aware of the surrounding pagan cultures but also struggled to avoid being profoundly influenced by their godless neighbors.

In that pagan context, personal vengeance was common and generally acceptable. And it often went beyond anything fitting the crime.

With Israel's historical context in mind, God's laws in Leviticus 24 take on a much deeper meaning. For instance, the dictate of "eye for eye, tooth for tooth" (vs. 20) was not barbaric but rather cutting edge and humane in that it institutes the idea of limited punitive damages.

DEVELOPING THE LESSON

The narrative of Leviticus 24:10-23 begins by detailing a fight between half- and full-blooded Israelites. In the midst of the struggle, the half-blooded Israelite sinned by blaspheming "the name of the Lord" (vs. 11). Ironically, the text never mentions the name of the blaspheming man (although the man's mother's name and lineage are noted). This unnamed man, his fight, and his infraction of blasphemy, are the context for the ensuing actions and teaching found in our lesson text. With the literary context in mind, verses 10-23 yield three important concepts of divine holiness for our consideration.

1. God's holy standards apply to all people equally (Lev. 24:10-12). We see here that God's holiness standards applied equally to half-blooded Israelites, full-blooded Israelites, and anyone else within the community of Israel. The reason for this is because God's laws are founded in His character, and His character never changes. He does not lower His standards for anyone.

2. Sin always has consequences (Lev. 24:13-14). The narrative indicates that both the offender and all those present were affected by the one man's sin. The offender, in this case the man who blasphemed the Lord, had to pay a blood penalty (as opposed to a monetary penalty). Being found guilty of the capital crime by the Lord Himself, the offender was not granted an appeal process or any means of making restitution; he had to pay for his crime with his own life. Yet the offender in this example was not the only one affected. The Lord required all who heard the man blaspheme to "lay their hands upon his head" (vs. 14). These witnesses had to touch the offender's head to signify that they were testifying to his guilt. The Lord then instructed that "all the congregation stone him."

So, here we see that there were multiple people affected by the man's sin: the offender, the witnesses, and the whole congregation.

3. The Lord's discipline always has a method and purpose (Lev. 24:15-23). In these verses, we observe that the crimes of blasphemy and murder were capital crimes, while the other offenses listed required either restoration or commensurate bodily injury as recompense. While God's holy standards and punishments might seem arbitrary to some, they are far from it. The standards seen in Leviticus 24 communicate clearly that not all crimes deserve equal punishment but all deserve appropriate punishment, and that the two most severe crimes are blaspheming God's name and murdering a fellow human.

God has designed His community (Israel in the Old Testament and the church in the New) so that the success as a whole is dependent on the proper functioning of each person within that community. There must be a commitment to serving the Lord in holiness, and there must be accountability.

ILLUSTRATING THE LESSON

God requires holiness of His people. His standards of holiness are spelled out in His Word, and He holds us accountable to them. Under the law, Israel was empowered to punish those who violated God's law, even to the point of execution if the law called for it.

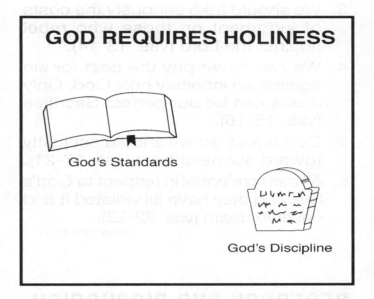

GOD REQUIRES HOLINESS

God's Standards

God's Discipline

CONCLUDING THE LESSON

God's holy standards teach us that holiness applies to all people in the community equally, sin always has consequences for both the offender and for all others who are present, and the Lord's discipline always has both a method and purpose. Thank God that He offers us examples, teaches us to pursue holiness, and holds us accountable to do so.

ANTICIPATING THE NEXT LESSON

Whereas Unit I focused on God's holiness, Unit II teaches us to see God's faithfulness even in the midst of human sin, rebellion, and ingratitude. God's response to Israel's complaints about His provision in Numbers 11 is a prime example.

—*Nigel C. Black.*

PRACTICAL POINTS

1. We must strive for unity within the church; division within God's people is an affront to God (Lev. 24:10-11).
2. We must always consult the Lord in difficult choices, especially in matters of punishment (vs. 12).
3. We should take seriously the costs of judgment on those who rebel against the Lord (vss. 13-14).
4. We can never pay the cost for sin against an infinitely holy God. Only Jesus can be our perfect Sacrifice (vss. 15-16).
5. God is just, so we should act justly toward our neighbors (vss. 17-21).
6. All men are equal in respect to God's law, and they have all violated it and deserve death (vss. 22-23).

—Megan Hickman.

RESEARCH AND DISCUSSION

1. Why is it important to be intentional about raising children in the ways of the Lord (Lev. 24:10-11)?
2. What steps can you take to ensure that you are using godly wisdom to make decisions? What are some resources God has given us to do so?
3. We obviously do not put people to death for blasphemy today. Why was it just for Moses to do this?
4. Why is it important for us to respect our church leaders when they have to make difficult decisions?
5. Should God's judgment bring comfort or fear to a believer?
6. In what way should you appeal to God's holiness while practicing evangelism?

—Megan Hickman.

ILLUSTRATED HIGH POINTS

They put him in ward (Lev. 24:12)

People who break the law can be arrested for their crimes. If they are formally charged, they may be kept in custody until trial. If later they are found guilty of their crimes in court, depending on their severity, they may be fined, sentenced to serve a prison term, or even sentenced to execution.

When the man who blasphemed the Lord's name was taken into custody, the people did not execute judgment on him immediately. But once God spoke to Moses, divine judgment was carried out by the people. This demonstration of God's judgment should make us thankful for God's abundant mercy in sending His Son to atone for our sins.

He shall restore it (vs. 21)

I myself am among the many who enjoy the convenience of online shopping; but there are some risks to shopping online. For example, a package that does not require a signature and is left on the doorstep could be stolen, it could be delivered to the wrong house, it could be lost in transit, or it could be found damaged upon delivery.

I recently had to send a part of my computer back to the supplier to be replaced because it was not working properly. The company I purchased the part from was willing to work with me to make sure the product was replaced quickly and efficiently. They allowed me to send the damaged product back, and they sent a replacement to me at no additional cost.

The company wanted to ensure its product met their standards. By maintaining their standards, they are also able to maintain their reputation. God has always proved Himself faithful to His people.

—Chelsea Villaseñor.

Golden Text Illuminated

"Thou shalt not take the name of the Lord thy God in vain; for the Lord will not hold him guiltless that taketh his name in vain" (Exodus 20:7).

The context of our golden text for this week is, of course, the giving of the Ten Commandments. Our verse is the third among the commandments and is echoed in the Lord's prayer, "Hallowed be thy name" (Matt. 6:9).

Although our verse is not taken from this week's lesson text, Leviticus 24:10 through 23, it definitely relates to it directly. In our lesson text, a man was heard to curse the name of Yahweh in the course of fighting with another man. This man was taken into custody until Moses had a chance to seek the judgment of Yahweh concerning the man's punishment. The verdict handed down from the very mouth of Yahweh was that the man must be taken outside the camp of the Israelites and stoned to death.

There was no room for mercy in the case of blasphemy against Yahweh's name. Verses 15 and 16 unequivocally state, "Whosoever curseth his God shall bear his sin. And he that blasphemeth the name of the Lord, he shall surely be put to death, and all the congregation shall certainly stone him: as well the stranger, as he that is born in the land, when he blasphemeth the name of the Lord, shall be put to death."

Now think about the way God's name is used and abused throughout our contemporary society; is blasphemy against the name of God considered a serious offense? There are certainly no criminal statutes against it in America (or if there are, they are considered antiquated and no longer enforced). In the various media, the abuse of God's holy name is commonplace, looked upon as merely a colorful form of verbal punctuation. In everyday speech among the unsaved, God's name is treated the same, or sometimes even worse. As cultural values shift away from Christianity, Christians are standing out more clearly than ever before.

Most of the many conventional phrases we consider blasphemous originated in Christian communities as well-meaning but misguided oaths, sincerely calling upon God the Father or the Lord Jesus Christ for help in various life situations.

Presumably, they were an attempt to apply the Apostle Paul's admonition, "Let your speech be alway with grace, seasoned with salt, that ye may know how ye ought to answer every man" (Col. 4:6). The problem is that this practice ignores the warnings of Jesus against all oaths (cf. Matt. 5:34-37).

An old saying warns, "The road to hell is paved with good intentions." These oaths soon fell to the use of unbelievers and quickly became vain speech that now brazenly dishonors the holy name of God and our Lord and Saviour.

One hallmark of the Reformation was the forbidding of such oaths on biblical grounds. The 1689 Baptist Confession of Faith warns, "To swear vainly or rashly by that glorious and [awesome] name . . . is sinful, and to be abhorred" (Art. 23:2).

The name of the Lord is still holy and must never be used vainly. Let us make sure that our own speech hallows that name at all times!

—John Lody.

Heart of the Lesson

Today it is very common for people to take the Lord's name in vain, most of the time thoughtlessly. But those of us who have been exposed to God's holiness and power as outlined in His Word wince when we hear His name profaned.

Taking God's name in vain demonstrates abysmal ignorance and total disregard for His authority and holiness. The name of the Lord represents His character, and it is a serious thing to defame God's character. In today's lesson, the Lord chose to give us a sense of how egregious a sin it is to dishonor His name.

The Lord's name (Lev. 24:10-11). The troublemaker in the camp was the son of an Egyptian and an Israelite. Throughout the Bible, the people of God were warned against mixed marriages, not on the basis of race but on the basis of faith (II Cor. 6:14). The man in this week's lesson text was part of the mixed multitude that followed the Israelites out of Egypt, but from what we can see, he did not consider himself one of God's people. He not only fought with an Israelite, which created tension within the camp, but he ultimately "blasphemed the name of the Lord, and cursed."

Luke 6:45 tells us that wicked words are the result of a wicked heart. Any time we sin, we rebel against the Lord. Yet the details about this man's lineage and his brawl with an Israelite suggest that his curse was not an isolated sin, but the climax of a hard heart toward God.

The word "blasphemed" itself shows us that he was not a servant of the Lord. When Jesus was accused of blasphemy, the Pharisees thought He was claiming to be God. In a sense, this word is used the same way here. This man had rejected God and His ways, putting himself in His place.

The Lord's word (Lev. 24:12-16). The man had violated the third commandment, so the Israelites put him in custody and waited on the Lord to discern his punishment. The Lord commanded that the man should be stoned by the people. Again, this is a case where the people of Israel had to trust God's wisdom. There were many times He instructed the Israelites to kill others for the sake of protecting His people from godless influence. The Lord knows the hearts of men (Prov. 21:2); because of this, He is able to be perfectly just.

This was not only punishment of a sinner, but a test of faith for God's people to see if they would obey Him.

The Lord's justice (Lev. 24:17-23). After pronouncing His verdict on the offender, the Lord went on to list examples of His impartiality (cf. Rom. 2:11). This is where the famous saying "eye for eye, tooth for tooth" makes its appearance. Notice, however, that the Lord is not talking about personal vengeance. He is giving the Israelites guidelines for a formal application of justice. Even the stoning is carried out by the whole community, not by the offended individual. The Lord gives a means of justice to the people so they do not get carried away by taking it into their own hands.

God expects us to recognize His attributes and act accordingly. He is perfectly holy and just, and those who reject Him and His ways will ultimately suffer eternal punishment. But for those of us who repent and turn to Him, He has provided abounding grace through His Son.

—*Megan Hickman.*

World Missions

How would you feel if you had to watch as someone you love was beheaded for Christ? Further, how would you feel knowing that elsewhere Christian friends were busying themselves with going to parties and spending their wealth on fashionable clothing and amusing entertainment?

Gladys Aylward, missionary to China, saw two hundred beloved students she had led to the Lord martyred one by one as each refused to recant their faith in Jesus Christ.

Two hundred Chinese students were pressured for weeks, then given one more chance to deny Christ and choose communism. A seventeen-year-old girl was called on first: "Who do you support now?"

She said, "Sir, three months ago, I thought Jesus Christ was real, and I thought the Bible was true."

Gladys watched, praying. One hundred and ninety-nine others, about to be likewise tested, also watched.

She finished, "Now after three months of your hatred, I know Jesus Christ is real, and I know the Bible is true."

She died that day, as did every single one of the two hundred.

This moment in history, and so many others, including the rescue of hundreds of orphans during a terrifying war, were experienced by the fully committed Gladys. She returned home, desperately sick, to find herself as the star of a movie—a romance!

Though the movie (*The Inn of the Sixth Happiness*) was a positive portrayal of her life, Gladys was distressed by much of it, including the false depiction of romance with a Chinese officer. Gladys had cared deeply for the man but had rejected any romantic attachment since he was not a believer.

How could she make people used to comfort and carefree living understand such hard choices?

Have times changed much? Today, persecution is still raging against Christians throughout our world. Believers are still being beheaded. Pastors are being beaten and tortured.

Meanwhile, in our lands of freedom and comfort, it is common to see flippant statements in social media posts like, "I just need coffee and Jesus."

Do we value what is holy? Do we have a commitment to Christ, a passion for His kingdom that takes priority over our own comfort and amusement? The apathetic will shrug their shoulders, avoiding difficult or uncomfortable questions. But God will use those who commit, those who give, those who go, to slash the darkness so that His light may shine upon the lost.

It may seem too awful to think about—two hundred young Christian students being beheaded. How could Gladys not feel terrible regret? As she watched the horrible deaths, she prayed the prayer she had been taught by her mentor: "If they must die, let them not be afraid of death, but let there be a meaning, O God, in their dying."

Those students who chose Christ over their earthly lives are still alive in heaven with God and have every happiness imaginable. Those who reject God will not see heaven. From an eternal perspective, there is no dilemma. The choice is as simple and as difficult as that. But even Jesus, in Gethsemane, struggled with His impending death. Still, those who follow His choice will reign with Him!

Gladys made her choice. Every one of the two hundred students made theirs. Now, in heaven with Christ, they do not regret that choice.

—Kimberly Rae.

The Jewish Aspect

An article reported that an anti-terrorism court in Pakistan sentenced a man to death for committing blasphemy on Facebook. They charged him with insulting the prophet Muhammad.

While Jewish law states that blasphemy is a punishable offense, Jews do not enforce the rule anymore (Jacobs, "Blasphemy in Judaism," myjewishlearning.com). In the broadest sense, Jews see blasphemy as anything contrary to the will of God or His power. Using a stricter definition, they define blasphemy in the older sense of the word—speaking contemptuously of God ("blasphemy," jewishvirtuallibrary.org).

In Hebrew, Jews know blasphemy as *birkat hashem*, and they call the one guilty of the offense a *megaddef*. Two main passages in the Hebrew Bible deal with blasphemy: Leviticus 24:10-23, the Scripture reading for this week, and I Kings 21:8-13. The penalty for the offense of blasphemy was death by stoning.

However, in the Mishnah (Sanhedrin 7:5), the penalty of stoning applies only when the person uses the Tetragrammaton to curse God. The passage states, "Let the Tetragrammaton curse the Tetragrammaton," a concept which most people find difficult to understand (Jacobs).

Jews understand that the Tetragrammaton, referred to in rabbinic literature as *HaShem*, is the word used to refer to the four-letter combination *yodh-heh-vav-heh*, the name for God used in the Hebrew Bible. Unfortunately, no one knows the actual pronunciation of the Tetragrammaton; however, some people pronounce the name as "Yahweh" and others as "Jehovah." The name appears 5410 times in the Hebrew Bible ("What is the Tetragrammaton," myjewishlearning.com), yet ancient rabbis forbade verbalizing the name outside priestly service in the temple.

In this week's lesson, the Bible tells us that the Jews brought a man before Moses accused of blasphemy. In the Hebrew, the Bible states he uttered the curse against "The Name."

Jews see Leviticus 24:10-23 and I Kings 21:8-13 as the main examples of blasphemy. Christians understand that the New Testament provides additional information about blasphemy. Matthew 26:47-68 and Mark 14:43-65 record that Jesus was betrayed, arrested, and taken to the high priest's house. There they charged Him with the crime of blasphemy.

As Christians, we know that Jesus, God in the flesh, was not blaspheming, but instead He was only claiming His true nature. Because the Jews were expecting their Messiah to look different, they could not comprehend the fullness of God's plan.

In Mark 3:22, the Jewish leaders accused Jesus of being possessed by Satan because of His ability to cast out demons. Jesus responded with an illustration to disprove their allegations. Afterward, He gave them important instructions regarding blasphemy. He stated that God forgives both sin and most blasphemy; however, a person who blasphemes the Holy Spirit will not be forgiven (vs. 29). Most scholars think this means that the person ultimately rejects Christ and the Holy Spirit.

For the Christian, blasphemy is important to understand. We must have healthy fear and reverence for God and honor Him in all we do. God's greatest purpose is to glorify Himself, so we should pray that He uses us to do so.

—Robin Fitzgerald.

Guiding the Superintendent

Understanding God's holiness proved to be a hard lesson for the Israelites, one that they continually had to relearn. It is important for us to learn from their example so that we can avoid chastisement. In Leviticus 24:10-23, we find the account of a man who blasphemed the name of God. We might not consider his sin all that serious, but this account and others should make us reconsider that opinion. This passage and the Related Scriptures make it clear that blasphemy against the Lord is a grave and deadly sin.

DEVOTIONAL OUTLINE

1. The sin of blasphemy (Lev. 24:10-12). In this passage, the son of a Hebrew woman and an Egyptian man is put in custody for the sin of blaspheming the name of God. Exodus 20:7 makes it clear that the name of God is holy and inviolable. As the third command in the Ten Commandments, abstaining from blasphemy is of essential importance for a believer.

In Deuteronomy 13:6-18, commands are given that any attempt to seduce an Israelite to commit idolatry was to be met with swift execution by stoning. Blasphemy, which often comes out in cursing, is so egregious because it presumes to place man above God as a judge. It is presumption akin to what the sons of Aaron displayed. They grew overconfident in esteeming their own status and liberty in relation to the worship of the Lord.

2. All shall have the same rule (Lev. 24:13-16). Just as in lesson 3, where the Israelites laid hands on the scapegoat, so here the people laid their hands on the blasphemer before judgment was executed upon him. The people of Israel owned up to their responsibility, both for allowing this sin and for ridding themselves of it. Just as important to note is that the sentence they were to carry out was death. In Matthew 12:31-32, we read of the tremendous gravity of blaspheming against the Holy Spirit. It is an inexcusable sin, even more so than blasphemy against Christ Himself.

Christians are blessed to be forgiven of all the offenses for which the old-covenant Israelites had to offer sacrifices again and again on a daily basis. However, we still need to be vigilant to walk in holiness. It is a grievous sin to be casual about the name of God and to treat Christ's atonement for our sins carelessly.

3. An eye for an eye (Lev. 24:17-23). All the people participated in the execution of God's judgment upon the blasphemer. Included here is a sub-lesson that gives us insight into God's standard of civil justice. The penalty must always fit the offense, and by way of explaining the severity of His judgment, God reviews several other cases for which the penalty fits the crime. What other penalty than death is fitting for the wanton denigration of the most holy name in the universe? Be thankful for the blood of Christ!

CHILDREN'S CORNER

Again, the violence depicted in today's lesson may be disturbing for young children. Focus their attention on taking the holiness of God's name seriously. Although no one is in danger of being stoned to death for abusing God's name in modern times, God still holds us accountable for misusing His name. It is still a sin that Jesus died on the cross to pay for, and as Christians we still need to show respect and reverence for God's name.

—*Mike Spencer.*

SCRIPTURE LESSON TEXT

NUM. 11:4 And the mixt multitude that *was* among them fell a lusting: and the children of Israel also wept again, and said, Who shall give us flesh to eat?

5 **We remember the fish, which we did eat in Egypt freely; the cucumbers, and the melons, and the leeks, and the onions, and the garlick:**

6 But now our soul *is* dried away: *there is* nothing at all, beside this manna, *before* our eyes.

10 **Then Moses heard the people weep throughout their families, every man in the door of his tent: and the anger of the LORD was kindled greatly; Moses also was displeased.**

11 And Moses said unto the LORD, Wherefore hast thou afflicted thy servant? and wherefore have I not found favour in thy sight, that thou layest the burden of all this people upon me?

12 **Have I conceived all this people? have I begotten them, that thou shouldest say unto me, Carry them in thy bosom, as a nursing father beareth the sucking child, unto the land which thou swarest unto their fathers?**

13 Whence should I have flesh to give unto all this people? for they weep unto me, saying, Give us flesh, that we may eat.

14 **I am not able to bear all this people alone, because *it is* too heavy for me.**

15 And if thou deal thus with me, kill me, I pray thee, out of hand, if I have found favour in thy sight; and let me not see my wretchedness.

16 **And the LORD said unto Moses, Gather unto me seventy men of the elders of Israel, whom thou knowest to be the elders of the people, and officers over them; and bring them unto the tabernacle of the congregation, that they may stand there with thee.**

17 And I will come down and talk with thee there: and I will take of the spirit which *is* upon thee, and will put *it* upon them; and they shall bear the burden of the people with thee, that thou bear *it* not thyself alone.

18 **And say thou unto the people, Sanctify yourselves against to morrow, and ye shall eat flesh: for ye have wept in the ears of the LORD, saying, Who shall give us flesh to eat? for *it was* well with us in Egypt: therefore the LORD will give you flesh, and ye shall eat.**

19 Ye shall not eat one day, nor two days, nor five days, neither ten days, nor twenty days;

20 *But* **even a whole month, until it come out at your nostrils, and it be loathsome unto you: because that ye have despised the LORD which *is* among you, and have wept before him, saying, Why came we forth out of Egypt?**

21 And Moses said, The people, among whom I *am, are* six hundred thousand footmen; and thou hast said, I will give them flesh, that they may eat a whole month.

22 **Shall the flocks and the herds be slain for them, to suffice them? or shall all the fish of the sea be gathered together for them, to suffice them?**

23 And the LORD said unto Moses, Is the LORD's hand waxed short? thou shalt see now whether my word shall come to pass unto thee or not.

NOTES

Complaints About Manna

Lesson Text: Numbers 11:4-6, 10-23

Related Scriptures: Exodus 16:1-8; I Corinthians 10:1-6; Mark 8:1-9

TIME: about 1444 B.C.   PLACE: Desert of Paran

GOLDEN TEXT—"And the Lord said unto Moses, Is the Lord's hand waxed short? thou shalt see now whether my word shall come to pass unto thee or not" (Numbers 11:23).

Introduction

Perhaps one of the strangest aspects of human behavior is the tendency to complain. It is strange in the sense that while virtually no one likes it, almost everyone does it.

What makes complaining particularly strange is that it never accomplishes what we want. It does not improve anything and does not truly address what may be a valid list of wrongdoings. Grumbling against circumstances does nothing to change those circumstances.

Complaining about things is not action. It just makes you and those around you miserable. It is impossible to complain and be grateful at the same time.

Sometimes even God's family complains about or to God. We get upset or angry with how our lives turn out, and we gripe at Him because we want something different than what He has provided. This week's lesson shows that complaining against God is never the right way to approach Him.

LESSON OUTLINE

I. **COMPLAINING AGAINST GOD**—Num. 11:4-6

II. **COMPLAINING TO GOD**—Num. 11:10-15

III. **GOD IS THE SOLUTION**—Num. 11:16-23

Exposition: Verse by Verse

COMPLAINING AGAINST GOD

NUM. 11:4 And the mixt multitude that was among them fell a lusting: and the children of Israel also wept again, and said, Who shall give us flesh to eat?

5 We remember the fish, which we did eat in Egypt freely; the cucumbers, and the melons, and the leeks, and the onions, and the garlick:

6 But now our soul is dried away: there is nothing at all, beside this manna, before our eyes.

Distorting the facts (Num. 11:4-5). So far in Israel's brief history following the Exodus from Egypt, God had supernaturally delivered them from the Egyptian army at the Red Sea (Ex. 14) and provided water (15:22-27; 17:1-7) and food (chap. 16) for them. All this was done before they reached Mount Sinai. Over and over again, God showed Himself to be faithful and loving to the children of Israel. Yet time and again, they complained against Him.

We now reach a point in the wilderness narrative where Israel had left Sinai on their journey to the Promised Land (Num. 10:11-12). Soon after leaving, however, they began to complain once again.

There was nothing easy or cozy about traveling with such a multitude through the desert. Likewise, God never promised that life would be easy for His children today. Hard times have a way of bringing out the worst in us, and we can easily wind up guilty of losing faith and perspective.

{The people who comprised the mixed multitude (the same community the blaspheming man in last week's lesson was from) began to grumble against the Lord that they had no meat to eat.}Q1 Their grumbling spread like wildfire throughout the Israelite community until it infested the entire camp.

{As the people griped about how bad life was for them now, they lost all perspective and began to reflect on the lives they left behind in Egypt. Their long period of cruel bondage (Ex. 3:7; 6:9) was suddenly remembered as a time of feasting. They longed for the food in Egypt—the fish they ate, as well as the cucumbers, melons, leeks, onions, and garlic.}Q2

The people began to have a strong craving for what they had in Egypt, so much so that it seemed they would have gladly returned there.

Complaining about how bad things are is a trap, though. When we complain, we see how bad things appear to be as opposed to how great we think things used to be. There was nothing great about the Israelites' lives in Egypt. They were bound as slaves and forced to live under terrible conditions at the hands of ruthless slave masters.

The people forgot about all of that, however, and romanticized the past. This is the danger of complaining. It makes the past seem better than it was and blinds people to the blessings God is giving them at the present time.

Exaggerating the hardships (Num. 11:6). Another problem with chronic complaining is that while it glamorizes what may have been a traumatic past, it exaggerates the troubles of the present and gives no hope for the future. {It is never good to allow ourselves to settle into an attitude of constant griping because it does not allow us to see the goodness of God.}Q3

The children of Israel greatly exaggerated their condition, stating that they were so hungry that their bodies were about to waste away to nothing. They did not remember their cruel working and living conditions in Egypt. Instead, they had a memory mirage of a smorgasbord of wonderful delicacies that had been available to them seemingly at all times. Now all they saw was the manna God provided for them that they were never truly grateful for.

The complaint that manna was all they had to eat was a gross understatement of what God had provided for them. They had their own livestock with them, as well as the goods God had allowed them to bring with them out of Egypt. They were far from destitute, but their incessant whining prevented them from realizing that. Is it not ironic that we tend to want what we do not have and despise what we do have? This predicament of the human condition that we deal with today is certainly nothing new.

COMPLAINING TO GOD

10 Then Moses heard the people weep throughout their families, every man in the door of his tent: and the anger of the Lord was kindled greatly; Moses also was displeased.

11 And Moses said unto the Lord, Wherefore hast thou afflicted thy servant? and wherefore have I not found favour in thy sight, that thou layest the burden of all this people upon me?

12 Have I conceived all this people? have I begotten them, that thou shouldest say unto me, Carry them in thy bosom, as a nursing father beareth the sucking child, unto the land which thou swarest unto their fathers?

13 Whence should I have flesh to give unto all this people? for they weep unto me, saying, Give us flesh, that we may eat.

14 I am not able to bear all this people alone, because it is too heavy for me.

15 And if thou deal thus with me, kill me, I pray thee, out of hand, if I have found favour in thy sight; and let me not see my wretchedness.

Moses' displeasure (Num. 11:10-11). The negativity that resulted from the constant complaining had now permeated the entire camp, as everyone was grumbling about how bad things had become and how much they had lost when they left Egypt. The people were now weeping openly, causing the Lord to be angry with them.

It is important to understand that complaining against God will never please Him. There is absolutely nothing wrong with taking our feelings to the Lord and asking Him for help. There is nothing wrong with trying to improve our circumstances when life gets hard. We must realize, however, that we will never get anywhere if we blame God for our hardships and struggles. We will never improve our situation if we regret coming to Him in the first place and begin longing to return to our lives of sin.

God loves us and wants to help us, but grumbling against Him only pits us against Him. Complaining all the time demonstrates a lack of faith, and God requires faith in order to please Him (cf. Heb. 11:6). It is an exercise in futility to think we can help our situation by fighting against God, who has permitted the situation and is our only source of help and hope.

Moses was also very displeased with what he was witnessing. As the leader of Israel, he often interceded on behalf of the people. In this case, however, he had grown very frustrated with both the people and the Lord. Unable to control the people, He took His frustrations to God.

{Under an extreme amount of stress, Moses questioned God's motives or wisdom in giving him this assignment.}[Q4] It is a bit reminiscent of his objection to being sent to Egypt in the first place, when God originally commissioned him (cf. Ex. 3:13—4:17). Now he was out in the desert with a large group of ungrateful, whining people who never seemed to be satisfied with anything Moses or God did for them.

The emphasis here is that Moses was actually blaming God for putting him in this situation. Just like the people who were wishing they were back in Egypt, Moses seemed to be pining for the days when he was back tending sheep anonymously with his father-in-law.

Moses' confusion (Num. 11:12-13). Moses continued his complaint by pointing out that he did not give birth to these people. In effect, he was distancing himself from them and putting the blame for the whole mess on God. In his mind, Moses had done all he could do to effectively lead these people and even plead for them before God at times. No matter what he did, though, his best efforts were never good enough.

{Moses was at a point now where he threw up his hands in disgust and blamed God for his predicament. After all, it was God who gave birth to this nation of thankless rebels, not Moses. He even questioned God's right to ask him to lead this multitude.}[Q5] God was the one who had promised to bring them to their ancestors' homeland, but it was Moses who was bearing all the burden—at least in his estimation.

Moses asked God where he was supposed to get food to feed all these people. It was not to God the people complained; it was to Moses. He did not know what to do.

Stressful situations have a way of preventing us from seeing clearly and causing us to take our eyes off of God. It is in these times that we must stay devoted to prayer and remember in the darkness what we once learned in the light. Jesus promised to be with us always (cf. Matt. 28:20), and the Lord has promised that He will never leave us or forsake us (Heb. 13:5).

Moses' despair (Num. 11:14-15). As Moses continued his diatribe against God and his grievance about the assignment he had been given, he said something that was quite true, even if it came out in the form of a complaint. He stated that he was unable to carry these people by himself. The only problem with what Moses said was that it came out of a distorted view of reality. God never expected or asked him to lead the people by himself.

What Moses forgot in all of this was that God was with him and was actually leading and providing for the people. God never left him, although Moses *felt* completely abandoned by God. Perception is not always reality, however.

{Moses, desperate for relief and seeing none, finally asked God to kill him. The only way for God to be merciful to him (according to Moses, at least) was to put him out of his misery.}[Q6]

GOD IS THE SOLUTION

16 And the LORD said unto Moses, Gather unto me seventy men of the elders of Israel, whom thou knowest to be the elders of the people, and officers over them; and bring them unto the tabernacle of the congregation, that they may stand there with thee.

17 And I will come down and talk with thee there: and I will take of the spirit which is upon thee, and will put it upon them; and they shall bear the burden of the people with thee, that thou bear it not thyself alone.

18 And say thou unto the people, Sanctify yourselves against to morrow, and ye shall eat flesh: for ye have wept in the ears of the LORD, saying, Who shall give us flesh to eat? for it was well with us in Egypt: therefore the LORD will give you flesh, and ye shall eat.

19 Ye shall not eat one day, nor two days, nor five days, neither ten days, nor twenty days;

20 But even a whole month, until it come out at your nostrils, and it be loathsome unto you: because that ye have despised the LORD which is among you, and have wept before him, saying, Why came we forth out of Egypt?

21 And Moses said, The people, among whom I am, are six hundred thousand footmen; and thou hast said, I will give them flesh, that they may eat a whole month.

22 Shall the flocks and the herds be slain for them, to suffice them? or shall all the fish of the sea be gathered together for them, to suffice them?

23 And the LORD said unto Moses, Is the LORD's hand waxed short? thou shalt see now whether my word shall come to pass unto thee or not.

Calling of seventy elders (Num. 11:16-17). {After listening to Moses' complaint, God told him to gather seventy elders among the leaders of Israel and to bring them to the tabernacle.}[Q7]

{God told Moses that He would meet with these seventy elders and give them the same Spirit that was in Moses. This is a reference to the Holy Spirit, who up to this point had endowed only Moses with power. They would assist Moses in leading the people and would be empowered by the same Spirit who empowered him.}[Q8]

A call to accountability (Num. 11:18-20a). The Lord then told Moses to tell the people to "sanctify," or consecrate themselves. They were to prepare themselves spiritually to see what the Lord would do the next day.

The people had asked where they could get meat to eat, and God made it clear it would come from Him. They had longed for Egypt, where they claimed they had plenty to eat. They would soon regret their words.

Be careful what you ask for (Num. 11:20b-21). God told Moses in very vivid language that the people would be eating meat until it came out of their nostrils and they loathed it. {It is a terrible mistake to turn the goodness of God into something bad and to think that returning to wickedness will bring relief and pleasure. God would take the thing the people wanted the most and turn it into something they detested.}[Q9]

{Moses retorted that the population numbered "six hundred thousand footmen" (vs. 21), and God was saying that He would give them meat for a month? This reflected Moses' own unbelief: he was thinking that this was an incredible promise, even for God.}[Q10] The number he cited referred to men twenty years old and older who were able to go to war (cf. Ex. 12:37; Num. 1:45-46). The total number of Israelites may have been well in excess of two million.

God's hand is not too small to provide (Num. 11:22-23). Moses argued that even if they were to slaughter all their livestock, it still would not be sufficient to feed the people for a month. Even all the fish in the sea would not be enough to cover such a great task.

God responded to Moses by asking him if the Lord's arm was too short to provide what He promised.

We can rest assured that God can and will do what He has promised. The Apostle Paul understood that God would provide all his needs, which is quite a statement considering he wrote those words from prison (Phil. 4:19). The source of God's provision for us is Christ; He is our sufficiency and is everything we need.

—Robert Ferguson, Jr.

QUESTIONS

1. What was the specific complaint of the people at the start of this passage?

2. In what way was the people's memory of life in Egypt distorted?

3. Why is constant griping a dangerous thing for us?

4. What did Moses' distress cause him to question?

5. In what way did Moses blame God for his predicament?

6. Why did Moses ask the Lord to take his life?

7. How did God respond to Moses' complaint?

8. How did God assure Moses that he would have help?

9. What hard lesson would God teach in meeting the people's desire for meat?

10. What did Moses' reply to the Lord reflect?

—Robert Ferguson, Jr.

Preparing to Teach the Lesson

With this week's lesson, we begin a new unit of studies focused on God's faithfulness. The four texts we will be studying in this unit are all situations in which Israel was challenged to see God's faithfulness through the difficulties they were experiencing. Over the next weeks, we will learn much from Israel's grumbling, complaining, and doubting. Today we begin in Numbers 11:4-6 and 10-23 as Israel complained about the manna God provided for them.

TODAY'S AIM

Facts: to observe God's faithfulness to unfaithful people.

Principle: to acquire the skill of seeing that God is faithful even through the severest difficulties in life.

Application: to develop strategies that will facilitate our seeing God's faithfulness more consistently in both the good and bad days of life.

INTRODUCING THE LESSON

When the Hebrews migrated to Egypt, they were only seventy persons in number. After four centuries, the Hebrew population had grown substantially (some estimate by roughly two million). But even with their increased numbers, they remained enslaved in Egypt until the Lord brought forth a leader and deliverer for His people in the person of Moses. The early portion of the book of Exodus chronicles the Hebrews' struggle for freedom against the tyranny of the pharaoh as their treatment actually became worse with the arrival of Moses (cf. Ex. 5:1-9).

The Hebrews, however, witnessed the ten miraculous plagues the Lord brought upon Egypt as He fought on Israel's behalf and secured their release. After their departure from Egypt, the Israel-ites witnessed the Lord's mighty power, which allowed them to pass through the Red Sea. Now as they found themselves journeying through the wilderness to the land of Canaan, the Israelites encountered new challenges, and their response was not commendable.

Despite having seen the plagues on Egypt and the miraculous parting of the Red Sea, the people doubted God's love and provision. As the difficulties of the wilderness journey set in, the people were given to complaining that questioned the very nature of God.

DEVELOPING THE LESSON

The narrative of Numbers 11:4-6 and 10-23 is full of questions and doubts. Exposed to the elements, tired from their journey, unsure of their direction, and bored with the food God gave them, Israel's faith was on trial, and they were having great difficulty seeing God's faithfulness.

1. The people's complaint (Num. 11:4-6). Initially, the questioning centered around God's provision. As the people of God journeyed deeper into the wilderness, they began to focus on what they lacked rather than on God's provision. Eventually, "the children of Israel also wept again, and said, Who shall give us flesh to eat?" Their question perhaps was a challenge, suggesting that God could not provide. But it was worse than that. God had been miraculously providing food for them all along the way in the form of the daily manna. Instead of showing gratitude to God for saving them from starvation in the desert, they complained that they had no meat to eat.

2. Moses' discouragement (Num. 11:10-15). As Moses heard the complaints of the people, he began to direct questions to the Lord: "Wherefore hast thou afflicted thy servant? and wherefore have I not found favour in thy sight, that thou layest the burden of all this people upon me?"

Here we see Moses questioning God's love for him. It seemed to Moses that God would not put him in such a position if He truly loved him. Moses continued his questioning, adding, "Have I conceived all this people? have I begotten them?" (vs. 12). This rhetorical query is meant more to make a statement than to ask a question. Moses was continuing to question God's love in the sense that he was accusing God of placing him in a situation where the people were looking to him for answers and demanding what he could not provide.

3. God's provision (Num. 11:16-23). As the narrative continues, the Lord instructed Moses to gather seventy elders to assist him in leadership. God would empower them for service and relieve Moses of some of the burden he felt. Furthermore, the Lord promised to provide the meat the people longed for. God's promised action did not prevent Moses from launching more questions at the Lord. In verses 21-22, Moses asked, "The people, among whom I am, are six hundred thousand footmen. . . . Shall the flocks and the herds be slain for them, to suffice them? or shall all the fish of the sea be gathered together for them, to suffice them?" He saw the immensity of the task, and it seemed impossible to him.

Many parents, when driving somewhere, have heard their children ask from the backseat, "Are we there yet?" Parents can quickly discern the difference between a curious or perhaps excited child simply wondering when the journey will end and a child who has grown impatient and is using a question to voice displeasure or boredom.

The questions in this chapter—at least most of them—clearly were voicing complaints and dissatisfaction with the circumstances and even with the Lord's faithful provision. Perhaps the most amazing aspect of Numbers 11 is that God remained faithful to His promises even when His people were unfaithful to Him. He did not disown Israel.

ILLUSTRATING THE LESSON

This lesson reveals the amazing faithfulness of God to His chosen people. The Lord did not abandon Israel or the promises He had made to them, even though they complained and were ungrateful for His blessings.

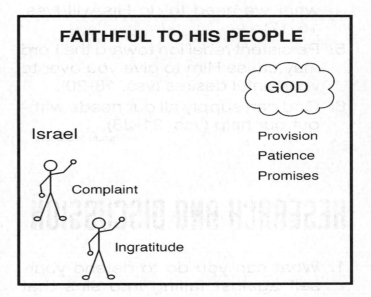

FAITHFUL TO HIS PEOPLE

CONCLUDING THE LESSON

God's faithfulness is on display in this chapter in the sense that He exhibited amazing patience and provision for His people even in the face of questions flowing from doubting hearts.

ANTICIPATING THE NEXT LESSON

Next week's lesson text immediately follows this week's text and reveals God's faithfulness to provide the meat the people longed for. Through that miraculous provision, He would also rebuke the people.

—*Nigel C. Black.*

PRACTICAL POINTS

1. We must protect our hearts against worldly influences, lest we fall into ungratefulness (Num. 11:4).
2. Satan will try to get us to look back fondly on our bondage to sin, but we must learn to love God and His righteous ways (vss. 5-6).
3. When we feel overwhelmed with responsibility, we must seek the Lord for strength (vss. 10-15).
4. The Lord has compassion on our weakness and will always provide what we need to do His will (vss. 16-17).
5. Persistent rebellion toward the Lord may cause Him to give you over to your sinful desires (vss. 18-20).
6. God can supply all our needs without our help (vss. 21-23).

—Megan Hickman.

RESEARCH AND DISCUSSION

1. What can you do to defend yourself against falling into sins that are common among unbelievers (Num. 11:4)?
2. Why do you think we sometimes look back in fondness to our lives of sin (vss. 5-6)?
3. Why is a thankful heart so essential to worship?
4. Have you ever gotten frustrated with a task that God has put before you? How should you react when this happens (vss. 11-15)?
5. How is the Lord's sovereignty at play when He gives rebellious people up to their sins (vss. 18-20)? How is His wrath different from human anger?

—Megan Hickman.

ILLUSTRATED HIGH POINTS

Who shall give us flesh to eat? (Num. 11:4)

Thanksgiving is quickly approaching. It is one of the most popular holidays of the year for people to volunteer their time to serve needy people. Many people do not have family to spend the holiday with or the resources to cook a holiday meal for themselves. Some people completely rely on social service organizations for food. Most people are grateful for these organizations, but some feel entitled, perceiving free food as a right rather than a gift.

God had completely provided for Israel, delivering them food from heaven on a daily basis, but they were ungrateful for his miraculous provision of manna. They suffered the just consequences for their ingratitude.

I am not able to bear all this people alone (vs. 14)

I worked as a counselor at a writing camp for the first time over the past summer. I was put in charge of about twenty girls. Twenty girls is not really a lot, but I had never been in that sort of position on my own before. At first, it was overwhelming for me. There were too many girls to look after, and I did not know how to handle them.

Fortunately, there was also an experienced counselor at the camp. He had only three boys to look after, so most of our writing activities were done as a mixed group, and we were able to work together to handle all of our campers properly. I do not think I would have been able to successfully lead the girl campers alone.

Although Moses was overwhelmed by the complaints of the people, the Lord gave him helpers and disciplined the contentious people.

—Chelsea Villaseñor.

Golden Text Illuminated

"And the Lord said unto Moses, Is the Lord's hand waxed short? thou shalt see now whether my word shall come to pass unto thee or not" (Numbers 11:23).

It never ceases to amaze me how quickly, after witnessing all the monumental and magnificent miracles that the Lord performed on their behalf, the Israelites of the Exodus forgot just how mightily and powerfully the Lord could work to meet their every need!

This week's golden text occurs at an extreme low point in Israel's faithfulness, since even Moses himself had by this juncture succumbed to utter hopelessness.

Influenced by the lusts of the multitude of non-Hebrews that had tagged along with them when they left Egypt, the people of Israel began to complain to the point of weeping. The reason? What they viewed as the monotony of the diet that the Lord was providing for them in the form of the miraculous manna!

The people longed for meat and vegetables such as leeks, onions, and garlic to provide the rich, delectable flavors that they longingly reminisced about having enjoyed back in Egypt. Imagine being inconsolably depressed about the taste of your food despite being led miraculously by the one true living God, who generously provides daily bread for you out of a clear blue sky! In addition, imagine that this same God had just defeated and humbled the most powerful empire on the planet and demolished their entire pantheon of false gods for the purpose of freeing your people from slavery.

Moses seems to have become completely fed up with the people at this point. Having reached the end of his rope in the face of the people's whining and weeping for such superficial cause, he asks Yahweh to just kill him outright (vs. 15). But God instead gave Moses help by spiritually anointing seventy elders to assist him in governing the people.

Yahweh also promised to give the people more than enough meat. In fact, He would give them meat for an entire month. They would become sick of it as it virtually came out of their noses (vs. 20)! This would be a calculated judgment upon them for despising the Lord's provision and throwing a pity party for themselves merely over what they felt was the blandness of their manna diet.

But Moses was still in a bad place emotionally, expressing doubt about how Yahweh could provide so much meat. Would all their livestock be slaughtered at once? Would all the fish in the ocean be suddenly dumped into their camp?

It is at this point that the Lord in effect says to Moses, "Have I suddenly become less powerful than I have shown all along? Hold your tongue, and you will see, I assure you!"

As absurd as the Israelites' self-pity was, we also often fall into feeling sorry for ourselves and lose sight of all the grace that the Lord has provided for us throughout our walk with Him.

The rightful solution for self-pity is remembering the grace that has brought us this far. We must stop and take time to erect for ourselves an Ebenezer, a personal memorial that commemorates all the times the Lord has provided for us when we saw no hope.

—*John Lody.*

Heart of the Lesson

How would it change our relationship with God if He ever went back on His promises? We would probably still worship Him, but only in the hope that we would get on His good side. That describes a lot of people today. They think they gain or lose salvation based on how God seems to feel about them at any given moment.

In the last four lessons, we have investigated God's perfect holiness, but today we turn to His amazing faithfulness. When God makes promises, He does not break them, and this is the main foundation for our hope. Considering His holiness, it should bewilder us that He is still faithful to people who fall so short of His glory (Ps. 8:4). His uncompromising faithfulness assures us that He will be true to His promises, including His promise of forgiveness and salvation through Jesus Christ. That is reason enough to worship Him!

The Israelites' discontent (Num. 11:4-6). How much time do you spend striving after things you do not yet have? Even pursuing good things with the wrong attitude can show a lack of contentment. After the Lord had already given the Israelites manna from heaven, they "fell a lusting" for some variety in their diet. They wanted meat. To make matters worse, they compared their current life unfavorably to their time in Egyptian bondage.

Though we are slow to admit it, we too sometimes fondly look back on the life that God delivered us from. We are often discontented with His plan for our lives. Sanctification can be a difficult process, and as God grows us in maturity, He often uses suffering to do it (cf. Jas. 1:2-4). We hardly ever see the fruits of suffering immediately, so we become angry with God, not believing that He is good or that His grace is sufficient (II Cor. 12:9). Even with the past evidence of God's abundant provision, we—just like the Israelites—want more.

Moses' distress (Num. 11:10-15). Moses and the Lord were both rightly furious with the people. But Moses' reaction was less than perfect: he himself began to complain to God. He rightly asked for God's help but then appeared to blame Him for his burden as a leader. His words reflect the extreme pressure he was under.

Moses acknowledged that leading the people of Israel was a burden too heavy for his own strength and followed this with a despairing request: "kill me, . . . if I have found favour in thy sight" (vs. 15). Moses believed it would be better to be killed by the Lord than to see his "wretchedness."

Sometimes the Lord exposes us to trials that reveal our sin and weakness—and we hate it. We do not like seeing our "wretchedness," but it is the very knowledge of our depravity that causes us to run to God. And before we rush to judge Moses, we should note that God did not even rebuke him but graciously provided the help he needed.

The Lord's mercy (Num. 11:16-23). Not only did the Lord grant the Israelites' request for meat at this time, He also eased Moses' burden by delegating his leadership responsibilities (vss. 17-18). He was not pleased by the people's lack of faith, but despite their doubt and complaining, He proved Himself faithful.

In our prayers, let us always remember the character of God and try to ask for His will, knowing that He will be faithful to His promises.

—*Megan Hickman.*

World Missions

They had so much: freedom, deliverance, and it was raining food! Yet they complained, "Our soul is dried away" (Num. 11:6). They longed for the old days of bondage in Egypt because that bondage had included onions, garlic, and leeks. God wanted so much for them, but they missed it because they lusted after variety in their cuisine. In complaining about God's provision, they "despised the Lord" (vs. 20).

We live in one of the richest countries in the world, but we agonize over potential recessions and our finances being tight. We have more to share than most of the people on the planet. Christians have the good news of salvation, and Americans have the resources to get that good news to the world, yet they "spent more money buying Halloween costumes for their pets" than on missions to unreached peoples. ("Missions Stats," thetravel ingteam.org). If more Americans were reached with the gospel and gave to missions, these resources could help build the church exponentially.

One missions organization lists 4.19 million full-time Christian workers on our planet. However, 95 percent of those people are working in already evangelized countries. Only 5 percent work among the unreached peoples of the world. Not everyone is called to overseas missions, but it seems that some deny this call because they do not want to leave comfortable lives ("Missions Stats").

For those who do stay, they can do much in the way of financial support. "The Church has roughly 3,000 times the financial resources and 9,000 times the manpower needed to finish the Great Commission. If every evangelical gave 10% of their income to missions we could easily support 2 million new missionaries." "Evangelical Christians could provide all of the funds needed to plant a church in each of the 6,900 unreached people groups with only 0.03% of their income" ("Missions Stats").

It seems so easy, so possible. So why is it not happening?

Apparently, of the money given to Christian causes, only 6.4% is for missions. And of that 6.4%, only .3% goes to reaching the unevangelized parts of the world. As God raises up missionaries to the unreached people of the world, we should prioritize missions in our personal giving and in our churches. Our spending shows our heart's priorities, so let us be motivated to fulfill the Great Commission.

In Bangladesh, the lost tie prayers to trees, or bow by the millions during each of the five mandatory prayer times, calling out to their gods in a language they do not even understand.

In Nepal, a temple with the great evil eye looks down upon worshippers who bang gongs or swing prayer wheels, hoping to get a god's attention.

In Iraq, a disgraced woman may strap bombs to her body and become a suicide martyr for jihad because she's been told it is the only way to assure that she will get into heaven.

There are 900 churches for every one unreached people group. Surely God has commissioned and equipped one out of 900.

Operation World (2015) reported that the world's evangelical Christians total 550 million. If there truly are 550 million followers of Christ, then each believer would only have to reach thirteen people for the entire globe to hear the gospel. We have the people; we have the money; all that is missing is our motivation.

—Kimberly Rae.

The Jewish Aspect

A story in the Jewish Talmud asks about the manna that God provided after the Jews left Egypt. The writer asks the question, "Why does the manna come every day and not once a year?"

A parable in the Talmud about a king and his son answers the question. It states that when the king gave his son what he needed once a year, the son visited only once per year. But when the father provided for his needs daily, the son called on his father every day. Because the manna was coming each day, the Israelites had to look to God every day for their sustenance (Babylonian Talmud, Yoma 76a).

Rabbis describe the manna from heaven as the perfect food—nutritionally complete and extremely delicious. Not only that, the Israelites did not have to work for the food; God gave it as a free gift. Despite these wonderful benefits, the people still murmured and complained.

As we see in this week's lesson, the Israelites—probably incited by the foreigners who traveled with them—compared God's manna unfavorably to the fish, cucumbers, melons, leeks, onions, and garlic they had eaten in Egypt. Instead of being grateful for the delicious substance of manna, they whined about having nothing else to eat.

Some commentaries explain that when the Israelite people remembered the free food of Egypt, they were remembering an era when they had no spiritual or moral responsibilities. However, when God gave them the manna, they understood the responsibilities that the gift entailed (Kamenetzky, "Fish & Chips," torah.org).

Though this view is speculative in nature, it invites us to consider an interesting question: Could it be that the Israelites were complaining less about their actual physical food and more about their new responsibilities as children of the covenant? They had just left Egypt, a place where, although they were in bondage, they had little spiritual responsibility.

Could we Christians be guilty of the same thing? Do we at times wish for our old life of sin and resent our call to righteousness? Scripture does not discuss the motivations of the Israelites at length, but we can relate to them because we all struggle with our flesh.

Many times, God asks us to do things for reasons we do not understand. Our insight is limited, and though believers have been made new in Christ, we still have a taste for sin and have to struggle against worldly attitudes and behaviors. It is possible that God will ask us to suffer for the sake of holiness. When this happens, we are called to deny ourselves to follow Christ (Matt. 16:24). In these times, we must remember to praise Him for His mercies, which, like manna, are new every morning (Lam. 3:22-23).

When we do not feel God's love for us, we must trust that He is working all things together for our good (Rom. 8:28). This can be difficult, and we may be tempted to grumble and complain (Phil. 2:14), but we must always remember where we would be without God's gift of salvation in Christ.

The Jewish Talmud states, "A truly wealthy person is one who is happy with his portion" (Avot 4:1). As Christians, we should consider God our provider. To be happy, we must be content with the set of circumstances He gives.

—Robin Fitzgerald.

Guiding the Superintendent

In this lesson, we will see God deal with the unfaithfulness of His covenant people—specifically in their lack of contentment with His miraculous provision of manna. Their complaining even had them longing to be back under the yoke of their Egyptian slave masters! In this, they were following their own selfish lusts rather than stopping to think about how amazing God's provision was and how thankful they should have been for it.

Two concurrent themes are addressed in today's lesson. The first is how God worked to foster contentment and trust in the people through the way He dealt with their complaining and rebellion. The second is how He gave Moses helpers to aid him.

DEVOTIONAL OUTLINE

1. Complaints about manna (Num. 11:4-6). The people had just suffered the chastisement of having those at the edges of their encampment consumed by fire from God for complaining (vss. 1-3). Not having learned from that judgment, the people complained again, this time about the manna God had miraculously provided. They complained loudly enough to be heard by Moses as they wept at the doors of their tents and pined for the variety of cuisine they once enjoyed as slaves. God was greatly angered by their ingratitude. Their complaining was a great offense to Him, since their ingratitude was a rejection of Him as their Protector and Provider.

2. Moses is distraught over his burden (Num. 11:10-15). Moses had reached the end of his rope with the people and their constant bickering and complaining. He confessed to God that he would rather die than go on this way. Moses was crumbling under the burden of what he perceived as an impossible situation. He launched into his own litany of complaints, climaxing with the plea that the Lord would put him out of his misery then and there.

We might think that God would be offended by his complaining too, but He responded in grace. It is evident that Moses' complaints were in actuality a desperate cry for help, which the Lord was only too pleased to supply.

3. The seventy elders (Num. 11:16-17). This is a parenthetical insertion to the main account of the people's rebellion, but it is an important one. God had Moses designate leaders among the people—seventy in number—who would help him lead and judge the people as a functioning community.

4. God promises quail (Num. 11:18-23). The people were ordered to consecrate themselves to receive a miracle from the Lord's hand. Moses was told to prepare the people to receive meat in enormous quantities, at which Moses balked, again fearing his own inability to carry out the Lord's command. God graciously comforted Moses, asking, "Is the Lord's hand waxed short?" In other words, "Do you doubt my ability to do this? Well, you'll see soon enough!"

CHILDREN'S CORNER

Parents the world over regularly have to listen to their children complain about their food. Although it would be improper to focus this week's lesson exclusively on warning about such complaints, this is undoubtedly a relevant topic for children. From a broader perspective, however, you should encourage your young students to be thankful for all the ways in which God provides for their daily needs.

—Mike Spencer.

SCRIPTURE LESSON TEXT

NUM. 11:24 And Moses went out, and told the people the words of the LORD, and gathered the seventy men of the elders of the people, and set them round about the tabernacle.

25 And the LORD came down in a cloud, and spake unto him, and took of the spirit that *was* upon him, and gave *it* unto the seventy elders: and it came to pass, *that,* when the spirit rested upon them, they prophesied, and did not cease.

26 But there remained two *of the* men in the camp, the name of the one *was* Eldad, and the name of the other Medad: and the spirit rested upon them; and they *were* of them that were written, but went not out unto the tabernacle: and they prophesied in the camp.

27 And there ran a young man, and told Moses, and said, Eldad and Medad do prophesy in the camp.

28 And Joshua the son of Nun, the servant of Moses, *one* of his young men, answered and said, My lord Moses, forbid them.

29 And Moses said unto him, Enviest thou for my sake? would God that all the LORD's people were prophets, *and* that the LORD would put his spirit upon them!

30 And Moses gat him into the camp, he and the elders of Israel.

31 And there went forth a wind from the LORD, and brought quails from the sea, and let *them* fall by the camp, as it were a day's journey on this side, and as it were a day's journey on the other side, round about the camp, and as it were two cubits *high* upon the face of the earth.

32 And the people stood up all that day, and all *that* night, and all the next day, and they gathered the quails: he that gathered least gathered ten homers: and they spread *them* all abroad for themselves round about the camp.

33 And while the flesh *was* yet between their teeth, ere it was chewed, the wrath of the LORD was kindled against the people, and the LORD smote the people with a very great plague.

34 And he called the name of that place Kibroth-hattaavah: because there they buried the people that lusted.

35 *And* the people journeyed from Kibroth-hattaavah unto Hazeroth; and abode at Hazeroth.

NOTES

God Sends Quail and Plague

Lesson Text: Numbers 11:24-35

Related Scriptures: Psalm 105:37-41; Psalm 78:18-31;
Philippians 1:15-18

TIME: about 1444 B.C.　　　　　　　　　　　　PLACE: Desert of Paran

GOLDEN TEXT—"Moses said unto him, Enviest thou for my sake? would God that all the Lord's people were prophets, and that the Lord would put his spirit upon them!" (Numbers 11:29).

Introduction

Following a craving is often a dangerous pursuit. Sadly, strong cravings are difficult to ignore and seem to never go away.

The problem I have typically experienced when I give in to a craving, or temptation, is that I am sorry I ever wanted it in the first place. At first, it feels like I cannot go without that piece of triple chocolate cake or deep-dish pizza. It feels good when it is being consumed, but I feel terrible later on. What is sad is that I know how I will feel later on, but the craving is so strong that I try not to think of that. I think it is safe to

say that I am not alone in this problem.

Last week we learned that the Israelites had a strong craving that led them to think that life in Egyptian slavery was better than the freedom God had given them. This week we will see that it is best to be careful about what we pray for because we just might get it!

LESSON OUTLINE

I. PROPHETS AMONG THE PEOPLE—Num. 11:24-30

II. PLAGUE AMONG THE PEOPLE—Num. 11:31-35

Exposition: Verse by Verse

PROPHETS AMONG THE PEOPLE

NUM. 11:24 And Moses went out, and told the people the words of the LORD, and gathered the seventy men of the elders of the people, and set them round about the tabernacle.

25 And the LORD came down in a

cloud, and spake unto him, and took of the spirit that was upon him, and gave it unto the seventy elders: and it came to pass, that, when the spirit rested upon them, they prophesied, and did not cease.

26 But there remained two of the

men in the camp, the name of the one was Eldad, and the name of the other Medad: and the spirit rested upon them; and they were of them that were written, but went not out unto the tabernacle: and they prophesied in the camp.

27 And there ran a young man, and told Moses, and said, Eldad and Medad do prophesy in the camp.

28 And Joshua the son of Nun, the servant of Moses, one of his young men, answered and said, My lord Moses, forbid them.

29 And Moses said unto him, Enviest thou for my sake? would God that all the LORD's people were prophets, and that the LORD would put his spirit upon them!

30 And Moses gat him into the camp, he and the elders of Israel.

Moses obeys the Lord (Num. 11:24). After Moses voiced his displeasure with God, as we studied in last week's lesson, God instructed him to gather seventy elders at the tabernacle. They would "bear the burden of the people" with him (vs. 17). Even after this assurance, Moses questioned God's ability to fulfill His promise to provide meat for all the multitude—a claim that seemed not quite credible.

{Although Moses was not a bastion of faith at that moment and was properly rebuked, he nonetheless did what God said and gathered seventy elders at the tabernacle.}Q1 These elders would assist Moses in providing spiritual leadership for the Israelites. They would not be able to do this in their own power, however, so they met with the Lord at the tabernacle to be equipped for the work ahead.

The seventy elders prophesy (Num. 11:25). When the seventy elders were gathered together, the Lord descended in the cloud that hovered above, speaking to Moses and imparting to the elders of Israel the Spirit who was on Moses.

The wording here does not suggest the power of the Spirit on Moses was reduced; it simply means that the same Spirit who was on Moses was now residing on the seventy elders as well. There would be no competition or disunity between Moses and the elders, because the same Spirit empowered them all.

{The result of the Spirit's coming upon the elders was that they began to prophesy.}Q2 The text does not provide specific details as to what type of prophetic activity took place, and Bible scholars are not in unison as to what actually occurred. What can be understood with clarity is that it was some type of outward behavior that was identifiable to the people as a work of the Spirit of God. Whatever it was that the elders were doing, it was clear that it was far from typical human behavior.

{This event points forward to the outpouring of the Holy Spirit on the Day of Pentecost on those believers who were gathered in Jerusalem after the ascension of Jesus (cf. Acts 2:1-4).}Q3 The fact that God was at work in the Israelite elders was obvious to those who witnessed the event and shows that God was in complete control of this situation. The prophetic activity subsided soon after it began ("did not cease" in Numbers 11:25 can be rendered "did not do it again"), but it was enough to give evidence that the Spirit who was at work in Moses was now at work in the seventy elders.

Eldad and Medad prophesy (Num. 11:26). {Although the seventy appointed elders were told to gather at the tabernacle, two of them, Eldad and Medad, were still in the camp when the Spirit of the Lord came upon all the elders.}Q4 The reason they remained in the camp is not given in the text, but no disciplinary action is recorded to have been administered for their failure to join with the others.

Instead of being disciplined or chastised, these two men received the Spirit inside the camp the same as did those who were gathered at the tabernacle. The fact that they were not at the tabernacle did not exclude them from the blessing of the empowerment of the Spirit of God. Instead, they were empowered right where they were, among the rest of the people.

{Just as the other sixty-eight elders were prophesying at the tabernacle, Eldad and Medad also prophesied in the camp.}Q4 There was no difference in the administration of the Spirit or in the administration of the prophetic gift they received. All seventy prophesied in unison.

Joshua protests against the prophesying (Num. 11:27-28). Because of the prophetic activity taking place through Eldad and Medad, it was very evident that something unusual was happening with them. Additionally, since this activity was occurring in the camp among the people, it was clearly seen by many people in the community. Since the people were not sure what was going on, confusion and unrest set in.

A young, unidentified man saw how Eldad and Medad were behaving, and his first (and perhaps natural) instinct was to report it. This young man ran and told Moses what was going on with these two elders (and now prophets). This movement of the Spirit gave evidence that God was at work in these men's lives and validated that their authority was from Him.

{Upon hearing about the activities of Eldad and Medad, however, Joshua pleaded with Moses to make them stop. To him, apparently, their absence from the tabernacle indicated they were not acting according to God's plan.}Q5 Too often we want to stop what we do not understand without trying to understand why a particular event is taking place.

Unfortunately, this happens even in the church today. Sometimes the Holy Spirit moves in a unique way in a person's life, but we are quick to dismiss it as zeal without knowledge. While we must be diligent to follow the teaching of God's Word and its proper application, we must also be careful not to discourage those who are seeking to follow the Lord. They might need instruction and correction at times, but we must not be so tied to our traditions that we reject any work or ministry that does not neatly fit with them. To do so might make us guilty of quenching the Spirit (I Thess. 5:19).

Moses' refusal (Num. 11:29-30). Moses inquired as to why Joshua demanded that Eldad and Medad be stopped from prophesying. He surmised that it was because Joshua was so devoted to him that he saw these two men as trying to compete for Moses' position of authority.

Joshua's devotion to Moses is commendable on one level, but it is also dangerous to be so committed to human leadership that we cannot see the Lord any longer. It is ultimately God whom we follow, not man. God puts human leaders over us, but they too are to follow the Lord, not displace Him.

Moses stated that he wished everyone could prophesy the way Eldad, Medad, and the other elders were prophesying. Moses did not see this as an affront to his leadership. He knew what God had called him to do and also understood that God was in control of the entire operation. He was grateful that the Spirit fell on these seventy men and longed for it to happen to everyone in the camp instead of a select few.

PLAGUE AMONG THE PEOPLE

31 And there went forth a wind from the LORD, and brought quails from the sea, and let them fall by the camp, as it were a day's journey on this side, and as it were a day's journey on the other side, round about the camp, and as it were two cubits

high upon the face of the earth.

32 And the people stood up all that day, and all that night, and all the next day, and they gathered the quails: he that gathered least gathered ten homers: and they spread them all abroad for themselves round about the camp.

33 And while the flesh was yet between their teeth, ere it was chewed, the wrath of the LORD was kindled against the people, and the LORD smote the people with a very great plague.

34 And he called the name of that place Kibroth-hattaavah: because there they buried the people that lusted.

35 And the people journeyed from Kibroth-hattaavah unto Hazeroth; and abode at Hazeroth.

God sends quail to the people (Num. 11:31). {A divinely ordered wind brought an enormous amount of quail into the Israelite camp quite suddenly.}[Q6] If anyone wondered whether or not God could provide food for such a large multitude, this definitely settled the issue.

The massive amount of quail God sent by the wind fell next to the camp, making it rather easy for the people to gather them for food. They did not have to hunt for their game. Instead, God brought the game to them. {The quail surrounded the camp on all sides up to about a day's journey away (twelve to fifteen miles). The quail were piled up two cubits (three feet) high, making this an enormous provision from the Lord.}[Q7]

God sends a plague (Num. 11:32-33). The people were delighted to see such a bountiful supply of quail all around them, going presumably as far as the eye could see. They spent the next two days gathering their unexpected delicacy to their heart's content, with each person gathering at least ten homers (about sixty bushels). The homer was the Israelites' largest unit of dry measurement.

Some of the meat would have been prepared to eat right away. It seems the rest was spread out on the ground to be dried and salted for later consumption, which was a common Egyptian method of preserving fish and fowl. This shows there was far too much to eat in one sitting. The entire camp had enough quail to feed them that day and far beyond.

{As the people began to chew the meat—even before they had swallowed and digested it—God's anger came against them. His judgment came upon them as swiftly as the quail did. Immediately, God sent a plague that struck the people down as they ate from their bounty (cf. Ps. 78:27-31).}[Q8]

This may catch the reader by surprise, but we must keep in mind that {God was still displeased by the people's incessant complaining and their often-expressed desire to return to Egypt. They had despised God's plan and provision and therefore despised God Himself.}[Q9] Some say that time heals all wounds, but time does not soften the punishment that comes from unconfessed sin. Only repentance does, and there is no record of repentance from the people.

Graves of craving (Num. 11:34-35). The place where the Israelites were encamped was renamed Kibroth-hattaavah, which means "graves of craving." The strong craving that drove them and led to their complaints against the Lord (vs. 4) resulted in a number of deaths. We are not told how many died, but it seems likely that the instigators of the complaining—those most motivated by their fleshly cravings—were the hardest hit. They got what they wanted, but they paid a heavy price.

There is no mention in the text that anyone had paused to thank the Lord for His bountiful provision. They appear to have dived right into the feast, greedily satisfying their appetites. Greed and selfishness are powerful motivators, but they always fall outside of God's will for us. They were more interested in the immediate enjoyment of the meat than in acknowledging God's goodness or being His people.

This is not to say that the people were out of line in asking God to provide for them. There would have been no problem if they had humbly prayed in faith, asking for His provision. However, the complainers followed after their craving and sought only to satisfy the flesh; they never expressed gratitude for what they had. God clearly was angry with them, not for being hungry and wanting to eat, but for allowing their cravings to dictate their behavior. It seems that whenever circumstances became difficult, the people complained.

There comes a time when God has enough of grumbling and complaining. Such an attitude reveals unbelief in the heart, which is a serious offense against the Lord. What reason do we have for not trusting in Him? He has never failed to fulfill His word. He has never lied to anyone, nor can He do so (cf. Titus 1:2; Heb. 6:18).

There is nothing wrong with having a strong craving. The problem is when the object of our craving is something other than the Lord Himself or His will for our lives. The people of Israel treated God like a hateful enemy, not a loving Father. They refused to remember the many times He had protected, delivered, and fed them in the wilderness before. They especially forgot how He brought them out of Egypt and delivered them from centuries of slavery.

{The grace of God can be seen again in Numbers 11:35 as the survivors of the plague resumed their journey, this time traveling to Hazeroth, a site of uncertain location in the wilderness. What is significant about this verse is that the journey resumed in spite of the judgment that God had just brought upon the people. God was not through with the Israelites, and He still led them.}Q10 Those who failed to believe would never be allowed to go into the Promised Land but would die along the way (cf. Heb. 3:16-19).

Be careful to avoid craving the things that are not of God. We all have a part of us that wants to go our own way and pursue our own desires. If we feed an appetite for destruction, however, we will certainly be destroyed. As followers of Jesus Christ, it is important to crave the things that will satisfy our souls and move us closer to Him. Above all, we must remember the admonition in Philippians 4:6 to make all our requests "with thanksgiving."

—Robert Ferguson, Jr.

QUESTIONS

1. How did Moses show obedience to God after first expressing distrust and anger?
2. What was the immediate result of the Spirit's coming upon the seventy elders?
3. To what future event did the Spirit's coming on the elders point?
4. Who were Eldad and Medad, and where were they prophesying?
5. Why did Joshua want Moses to stop Eldad and Medad from prophesying?
6. How did God bring quail into the Israelite camp?
7. What indicates how many quail came into the camp?
8. What happened when the people started eating?
9. Why did God send a plague on the people?
10. How was God's grace demonstrated to the people of Israel?

—Robert Ferguson, Jr.

Preparing to Teach the Lesson

Last week, we saw incredible divine patience amidst widespread questions and complaints. In this week's lesson, from Numbers 11:24-35, we find the Lord graciously fulfilling the promises He had made to Moses and to Israel (cf. vss. 16-18).

The people of Israel desired God's provision and blessing, but they were ungrateful and never seemed to be satisfied with what He gave them. They were properly rebuked and judged for their faithless attitudes, yet despite Israel's lack of faith in their powerful Saviour, we see continuing faithfulness demonstrated by the Lord. The Lord's faithfulness is truly on display in a number of ways in this week's lesson text.

TODAY'S AIM

Facts: to show that although Israel failed God time after time, the Lord always proved Himself completely faithful to His word, thus providing the ultimate example of faithfulness (cf. Ps. 78:18-31; 105:37-41).

Principle: to realize that no matter how circumstances may look or feel, God is always faithful to His people and His promises.

Application: to accept the challenge to live a life of gratefulness based upon God's unconditional love and consistently demonstrated faithfulness.

INTRODUCING THE LESSON

When times are good, we believers seem to have little trouble identifying those times with God's faithfulness. When we are the first in our family to graduate from high school or college, we acknowledge the achievement as a blessing of God. When we get that long-sought promotion or purchase our first home, we tend to identify such times with God's merciful provision for our lives.

When we fall on hard times in life, however, it is a bit more difficult for us to see God's faithfulness in those moments. When we are gripped with a serious illness or have just been laid off work or have just learned of a loved one's passing, we often need to be reminded that God is always faithful.

As the Israelites made their way through the wilderness on their way to the Promised Land, they experienced hard times and daily challenges. They found themselves in a strange and barren wilderness, traveling to an unknown place. The Lord had powerfully delivered the Israelites from enslavement in Egypt and graciously, faithfully provided food and water for them throughout their journey. Rather than gratefully acknowledge that God was providing all they needed, however, the people focused on what they wanted and what seemed to them impossible to obtain in the wilderness. God gave them manna, but they wanted meat.

DEVELOPING THE LESSON

The people had despised the divinely provided manna and demanded meat to eat (Num. 11:4-6). We might expect the Lord to just abandon these ungrateful and doubting people, but that was not at all the case. In the narrative of Numbers 11:24-35, God's faithfulness is on display in many ways.

1. A special visitation (Num. 11:24-30). God had promised to empower seventy men to help relieve Moses of the burden of leadership (vss. 16-17). Now, "the Lord came down in a cloud, and spake unto him, and took of the spirit that was upon him, and gave it unto the seventy elders: and it came to pass, that, when the spirit rested upon them, they prophesied, and did not cease" (vs. 25). Although Scripture does not closely specify the nature of this spirit of prophecy, it greatly encouraged Moses, who stated, "Would God that all the Lord's people were prophets, and that the Lord would put his spirit upon them!" (vs. 29). So, whatever this prophesying looked like, it was a very helpful, merciful outpouring of God's gracious provision for Moses and for Israel.

2. Provision of meat (Num. 11:31-32). Despite the people's ingratitude for the manna He provided, the Lord was faithful to His earlier promise (vss. 18-20) to give them the meat they longed for. Just as the Lord delivered Israel from the Egyptian army by a wind that parted the Red Sea (Ex. 14:21-22), now He sent forth a wind that brought untold numbers of quail to Israel's camp. The minimum of quail gathered by each person was "ten homers" (Num. 11:32), or some sixty bushels. Although the text does not specify how many people gathered quail, we can easily determine that the amount of quail the Lord provided was immense—far more than the people could eat.

3. A merciful judgment (Num. 11:33-35). The people got what they wanted with the miraculous provision of the quail. However, their pleasure in the quail was short-lived, for God sent them a powerful rebuke and judgment for despising the manna He gave them daily. The rebellious people were deserving of death, and the Lord unleashed a great plague upon them. However, He did not strike down all of Israel as He could have. In His judgment, He showed mercy. Although it is often difficult to see God's mercy in His acts of judgment, we must acknowledge that His judgment and discipline are always meant for our good and never approach the fullness of His wrath.

ILLUSTRATING THE LESSON

The Lord is always faithful. Indeed, Paul wrote in the New Testament, "If we believe not, yet he abideth faithful: he cannot deny himself" (II Tim. 2:13). Though Moses and the people had failed God and complained, the Lord kept His word to empower certain men to help Moses and to give the people the additional food they desired.

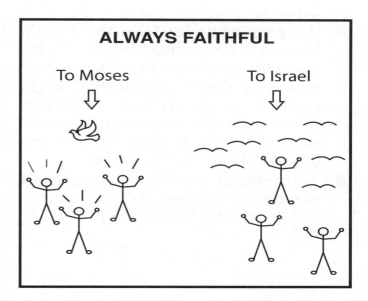

ALWAYS FAITHFUL

To Moses   To Israel

CONCLUDING THE LESSON

God's faithfulness is seen in His visitation and empowerment of Israel's leadership and in His provision of quail to all Israel. Even though we sometimes struggle with doubts and fail to live in obedience to the Lord, He remains faithful to His people.

ANTICIPATING THE NEXT LESSON

We have seen God's faithfulness to Israel against the backdrop of the people's complaints about the manna, and we have seen the Lord's faithfulness in providing the quail as He promised. As we turn next week to Numbers 12:1-16, we will see that the Lord was faithful to His servant when Moses' leadership was challenged.

—*Nigel C. Black.*

PRACTICAL POINTS

1. If we are doing the Lord's will in ministry, He will provide for our needs (Num. 11:24-25).
2. We should rejoice when God uses others to further His kingdom, not react with jealousy (vss. 26-29).
3. Even when we do not deserve it, God provides for our needs (vss. 30-31).
4. We should never take the Lord's blessings for granted; we should be good stewards of His gifts (vs. 32).
5. It is only God's mercy that holds back His wrath from us; we should never test His patience but live in keeping with true repentance (Num. 11:33; cf. Rom. 2:4).
6. Throughout our lives, we should always remember God's chastisements and blessings (Num. 11:34-35).

—Megan Hickman.

RESEARCH AND DISCUSSION

1. What does it mean to prophesy? Do people prophesy today (Matt. 7:21-23; I Cor. 14:3)? Why or why not?
2. How should we respond when someone tries to provoke us to jealousy? How can we prevent ourselves from becoming jealous of the gifts of others?
3. What does it say about our attitude toward God when we are wasteful of or ungrateful for His provision?
4. We should both fear God and understand His grace and mercy. Which of God's attributes do you tend to ignore?

—Megan Hickman.

ILLUSTRATED HIGH POINTS

The people stood up all that day (Num. 11:32)

People will sometimes do outrageous things in order to get what they want. They will stand in line for hours to be the first to get a ticket to the first showing of a new movie or to get a ticket for a concert that may sell out. They will stand outside stores waiting for them to open because the stores are having special sales promotions.

They may even stand outside stores in terrible weather all day long in order to be one of the first people to get the latest electronic device. People who are so willing to wait in line for such things show what their life priorities are. They feel they absolutely need what they wait for.

Like the people under Moses, they follow after fleeting earthly delights that neither satisfy nor provide life with any meaning.

A very great plague (vs. 33)

There are many diseases for which there still is no adequate treatment or cure. But with the advances of modern medicine, many diseases that once were life-threatening now have some form of effective treatment.

Before modern medicine, people who contracted an illness were much more likely to die than they are today. Flu shots and other such vaccinations did not exist, and the medicines that were available were not as effective in treating illnesses. In most cases, people who contracted an illness could only hope that they would regain their health without treatment.

To judge the lustful ingratitude of the Hebrew people, God sent a deadly plague. Whatever the actual nature of the plague, the people effected had no chance of surviving it.

—Chelsea Villaseñor.

Golden Text Illuminated

"Moses said unto him, Enviest thou for my sake? would God that all the Lord's people were prophets, and that the Lord would put his spirit upon them!" (Num. 11:29).

Our golden text for this week marks a continuation of last week's lesson text. God had promised to provide the Israelites with more meat than they could eat for a whole month, so much that it would come out of their noses! God also promised leadership help to Moses—seventy elders who would be anointed with the same prophetic Spirit that he had.

In this week's lesson, God makes good on this promise, but He also takes vengeance on those who followed their vain lusts into complaining about the blandness of the manna God miraculously provided to sustain His covenant people. Even as the people had just begun to eat, while the meat was still in their mouths, the Lord struck them with a plague. Although the writer of Numbers records nothing about the nature of this plague, Psalm 78 tells us that it killed the youngest and healthiest men among them (vss. 30-32).

Our golden text is Moses' response to a report that two of the seventy anointed elders were outside prophesying in the midst of the camp rather than prophesying within the tabernacle along with Moses and all the other elders. Apparently this was interpreted by some as an insult against Moses. A young man was dispatched to tell Moses of the perceived impropriety, and Joshua, upon hearing of the report, asked Moses to forbid the men from prophesying.

But Moses saw the men's prophesying in a more positive light. He rebuked those who were complaining on his behalf and attempting to rebuke the elders. For Moses, the prospect of having any sort of help in carrying the burdens of governing God's impossibly stubborn, stiffnecked people was a great blessing!

After the plague had run its course, the people buried those the plague had killed, naming that place "Kibroth-hattaavah," which translates "graves of lust." Those who had blasphemed God and brought additional misery upon Moses because of their impudent ingratitude for God's miraculous provision were to literally be a grave warning to God's people. They were to never again tempt God or trouble His anointed servants in such a manner.

If your church is blessed with a pastor who faithfully preaches God's Word and leads your congregation in prioritizing sound doctrine, outreach to the lost, and ministering to the needy of your community, I admonish you not to make his leadership more burdensome with complaining motivated by selfish or petty causes, as the people of Israel did in our lesson text. Such complaining will not go unnoticed by the Lord, who called your pastor to his commission and anointed him over you.

I exhort you rather to lighten his burdens and add to his delight in his service to God on your behalf. Be one who assists and supports his calling. As was the case with Moses, you can be sure that his desire is that all those in his spiritual charge would become fellow ministers and fellow servants of the Lord.

Rather than adding to your church's problems, become part of the solution to the glory of God!

—*John Lody.*

Heart of the Lesson

God specializes in working with sinners. Even the works that we do in His name are never perfect, but He uses them all the same. He does not need us to help Him spread the message of the gospel, but He wants us to participate in His glory. Knowing this motivates each of us to remain humble about our work for the Lord and thankful that He chose to have mercy on us.

Today we will see that Moses responded to God's mercy with humility, allowing other God-empowered followers to help him in order to further God's purposes. But we will also see the consequences of ungratefulness for God's provision as He punishes His people for their greed.

God's prophets (Num. 11:24-29). We pick up today by looking at God's fulfillment of His promise to Moses (vs. 17). Instead of keeping Moses as the only prophet for the whole camp, the Lord bestowed the prophetic gift on a group of elders as well.

Two elders prophesied within the camp under the leading of the Spirit. A young man ran to Moses to tattle on them, thinking that he would be at least a little irked and jealous of the attention they received. But Moses was not thinking about himself; he had God's purposes in mind. These men were given by God to help Moses rule the people, and this was exactly what they were doing. Moses merely responded, "Would God that all the Lord's people were prophets" (vs. 29).

Many of us have been victims of the "green monster." Jealousy is one of Satan's tools in the church. He seeks to bolster an individual's pride, even while that person is doing great work for the Lord. Have you ever been upset when someone does something better than you? How about when they cut in on your "territory"? We tend to be proud of the ways we serve, whether it is singing on the worship team or being the favorite toddler teacher. But instead of rejoicing when someone else displays giftedness in the same area, we often feel hurt.

But what is actually hurt? Our pride. Jealousy reveals idolatry in our hearts. Reacting with envy probably means that instead of aiming to please the Lord through our service, we were seeking our own glory. Selfishness and pride will keep us from rejoicing in the blessings of others for the sake of God's glory.

Moses could have hogged the power of leadership for himself; after all, he was the prophet that God chose first. But instead, he was happy to share his burden and authority with others for the sake of God's purposes.

God's allowance (Num. 11:30-35). God was similarly merciful to the Israelites. They were ungrateful for the manna He had provided, yet He still granted their request for meat. But their attitudes were revealed when they gathered at least fifty bushels each (way too much food for one person) and laid it out to eat immediately (vs. 32). There is no mention that the people acknowledged or thanked the Lord for His provision. God saw the response of their hearts—greed. So "while the flesh was yet between their teeth," He sent a plague to strike many of them dead.

Instead of being thankful for God's mercy and using it to further His work and glory, the Israelites hoarded God's gifts and were punished. Let us always be grateful for God's mercies, viewing them as a greater call to His work.

—*Megan Hickman.*

World Missions

The people of Israel, who were meant to show the world how joyful it is to be provided for by God Himself, grumbled and complained about His provision. They were meant to rejoice in having God as their Leader and King, but instead they envied God's chosen leaders. They were meant to move forward in courage and faith, but in fear they did not trust God's power to fight on their behalf and shrank back from their divinely ordained task.

God wanted to bless them. In fact, the laws and precepts He gave them were designed to promote justice and goodness. If the people followed them, God promised to richly bless them. God's intention was for all the world to see that following the one true God resulted in goodness and joy.

Yet all throughout the Old Testament, we see the same cycle: initial faithfulness, then a fall into apathy and idolatry. All this was typically followed by foreign aggression. God would do something drastic, something that was the opposite of what He desired for His people, because only hardship and suffering motivated them to seek Him again.

Is this the same legacy we will leave behind to future generations? Or do our lives show the world the joy of the goodness and faithfulness of our God? Will you be remembered for your commitment to prayer, your desire for the lost to know Christ, and your confidence in God's Word?

What if we could have a part in bringing thousands of people into Christ's kingdom? Partnering with national missionaries is one great way to reach the lost. A recent update from missionaries with Source of Light highlights changed lives:

From Togo: Recently a prisoner in Lomé's prison was saved. He had falsely accused his friend of partnering with him in a murder, and they were both in prison. After being saved, he confessed his false accusation, agreed to be punished as deemed necessary, and insisted that the judges should free his friend. The courtroom was full that day, and many people witnessed how God had changed this man's heart.

From India: Pray for an orphanage in Toranahalli that was recently started. They have seven children; four were temple prostitutes.

A report from one district in India for one month:

1. Bible studies conducted: 318
2. New fellowship groups started: 7
3. Bible lessons distributed: 2,032
4. New villages visited to share the gospel: 33

Such great work is not without opposition from the enemy. In Togo, one of the missionaries struggles with deep discouragement. His wife was nearly killed, but a miracle saved her. In another attack by the enemy, one believer who wanted to give to the church was brutally murdered.

This is war, and the devil does not want to give any ground. He seeks to kill, steal, and destroy (cf. John 10:10).

Please join this fight. Fight for God's servants through your prayers. Fight against the darkness with the light of Christ (cf. Eph. 6:12). Pray for God to protect seekers until they have a chance to believe. Pray for more laborers to allow the work to expand.

What would more greatly please God than future generations seeking to glorify Him, worship Him, and share His love through the gospel?

—*Kimberly Rae.*

The Jewish Aspect

This week's Bible lesson recounts the story of God providing quail to the Israelites in the wilderness. He did this in response to their complaints about the manna He had been giving them. The people grumbled, complained, and lusted for the meat of Egypt instead of being grateful for God's provisions (Num. 11:4-6).

Jewish rabbis write that the manna God sent was "perfect" food, so thoroughly absorbed into the body that there was no waste that needed to be excreted (Geller, "Manna from Heaven: What could be better?" reformjudaism.org). Rabbis believe the food was also delicious. They write that it tasted like "rich cream" with many satisfying tastes.

But if the manna was so perfect, why were the people so unhappy with God's food? The medieval rabbi Solomon ben Isaac, also known as Rashi, wrote that the situation was less about the actual manna and more about the people's hearts. His opinion was that the people were seeking a pretense to escape from following God (Ben-Chaim, "The Quail," mesora.org).

Just before this incident in the wilderness, God gave the Hebrew nation their new law, which was exacting and demanding. With the giving of the Law, they became bound to many rules and regulations. Rashi wrote that the Jews were rebelling not so much against the manna, but against God and His laws (Ben-Chaim).

Some people believe that the Ten Commandments are the sum of the laws given to the people at Sinai. However, the Ten Commandments are only a small portion of the 613 commandments that God gave the people. Jewish rabbis over the centuries have expounded on the 613 laws, making Judaism a comprehensive way of life, filled with rules and practices.

Jewish laws affect every aspect of a person. The laws cover every part of life—from what the Jew does when he wakes, to what he can eat, to what he can wear, to how he conducts business, to whom he can marry, to how he observes holidays and Sabbath, to how he must treat God, other people, and animals.

Jews know this set of rules and practices as *halakhah*. People often translate *halakhah* as "Jewish Law," although sometimes they translate it as "the path that one walks" ("Halakhah: Jewish Law," www.jewfaq.org).

Some rabbis believe the people recognized how drastically their lives would change with the law. Instead of rebelling against the manna in their request for meat, they actually rejected God, His law, and their new way of life.

The people wanted meat, so God granted their demands. In Numbers 11:31-33, God sends the people quail. While the people were gorging themselves on the meat, the Lord sent a plague on them.

Jesus states in John 6:48 that He is the bread of life. Following that statement, He mentions the Israelites who ate manna in the wilderness but still died. Then he declares in verse 54, "Whoso eateth my flesh, and drinketh my blood, hath eternal life."

While in the wilderness, the Israelites rebelled against God's plan for their lives and grumbled about the manna He gave them. In John 6:58, Jesus states He is the true Bread that came down from heaven. The Bible tells us that eating Jesus' flesh—depending wholly on Him for spiritual sustenance—brings eternal life.

—*Robin Fitzgerald.*

Guiding the Superintendent

This lesson deals with the fulfillment of the promise God made to Moses to provide meat for the people. Moses could not fathom where so much meat was going to come from. Even with all the miracles he had seen God perform, he still had a limited grasp of the Lord's power. Miraculously providing an abundance of meat was no problem for Him. The people would learn, yet again, the awesome power of the Lord and, even more important, the consequences of their ingratitude.

In this week's lesson, God grants their wicked desires, but only as a means to teach the people a hard but needed lesson about complaining. That lesson came in the form of a plague. It is indeed a fearsome thing to provoke the Lord.

DEVOTIONAL OUTLINE

1. The Spirit on the seventy (Num. 11:24-25). Moses got the help he so desperately needed. He was tasked with appointing seventy men who would aid him in the ministration of the duties of leading the community. Moses gathered these elders together and assembled them around the tent of meeting, where God appeared to them in His cloud of glory. God bestowed a prophetic spirit upon these elders, and they prophesied in the presence of all the people. God had shown Himself to His people; how could they now still doubt that He would provide for them?

2. Eldad and Medad (Num. 11:26-30). God is not limited by human expectations. The same power that came upon the men at the tabernacle also came upon two men who were not with the rest of the seventy, but still in the camp. When Eldad and Medad began to prophesy, bystanders sent a messenger to tell Moses of this irregularity. Even Joshua misunderstood and took offense. But Moses, understanding that this too was merely God working on his behalf, corrected him: "Enviest thou for my sake? Would God that all the Lord's people were prophets, and that the Lord would put his spirit upon them!" Moses would take all the help he could get!

3. Quail and a plague (Num. 11:31-35). Here God's promise comes to fruition. He shows the people that for Him, nothing is impossible. Even in the wilderness, God can bring forth a feast of quail to feed the multitudes of men and women who are under His care. Their complaining ended when they saw the unimaginable bounty, and they greedily ran to collect the quail and to hoard them for themselves. They had little understanding that God was using this provision to bring a much tougher lesson to His people. He would remind them that in Him alone is life and abundance.

Just as they were beginning to feast, even while the meat was still between their teeth, He sent a great plague on them, and a great many died. The people were greatly humbled.

CHILDREN'S CORNER

Although God's sending of both food and a plague upon the Israelites may be hard for children to understand, they should be encouraged to be careful about what they pray for and how they ask for it. Prayers should always be made humbly and with an understanding that not everything we might ask God for is good for us. We must trust in God's wisdom and goodness to give us only what is good for us to have.

—Mike Spencer.

SCRIPTURE LESSON TEXT

NUM. 12:1 And Miriam and Aaron spake against Moses because of the Ethiopian woman whom he had married: for he had married an Ethiopian woman.

2 And they said, Hath the LORD **indeed spoken only by Moses? hath he not spoken also by us? And the** LORD **heard** *it.*

3 (Now the man Moses *was* very meek, above all the men which *were* upon the face of the earth.)

4 And the LORD **spake suddenly unto Moses, and unto Aaron, and unto Miriam, Come out ye three unto the tabernacle of the congregation. And they three came out.**

5 And the LORD came down in the pillar of the cloud, and stood *in* the door of the tabernacle, and called Aaron and Miriam: and they both came forth.

6 And he said, Hear now my words: If there be a prophet among you, *I* **the** LORD **will make myself known unto him in a vision,** *and* **will speak unto him in a dream.**

7 My servant Moses *is* not so, who *is* faithful in all mine house.

8 With him will I speak mouth to mouth, even apparently, and not in dark speeches; and the similitude of the LORD **shall he behold: wherefore then were ye not afraid to speak against my servant Moses?**

9 And the anger of the LORD was kindled against them; and he departed.

10 And the cloud departed from off the tabernacle; and, behold, Miriam *became* **leprous,** *white* **as snow: and Aaron looked upon Miriam, and, behold,** *she was* **leprous.**

11 And Aaron said unto Moses, Alas, my lord, I beseech thee, lay not the sin upon us, wherein we have done foolishly, and wherein we have sinned.

12 Let her not be as one dead, of whom the flesh is half consumed when he cometh out of his mother's womb.

13 And Moses cried unto the LORD, saying, Heal her now, O God, I beseech thee.

14 And the LORD **said unto Moses, If her father had but spit in her face, should she not be ashamed seven days? let her be shut out from the camp seven days, and after that let her be received in** *again.*

15 And Miriam was shut out from the camp seven days: and the people journeyed not till Miriam was brought in *again.*

16 And afterward the people removed from Hazeroth, and pitched in the wilderness of Paran.

NOTES

Miriam and Aaron Oppose Moses

Lesson Text: Numbers 12:1-16

Related Scriptures: Numbers 5:1-4; II Chronicles 26:16-21;
Deuteronomy 34:5-12; Exodus 33:12-23; Hebrews 3:1-6

TIME: 1444 B.C.   PLACE: Desert of Paran

GOLDEN TEXT—"If there be a prophet among you, I the Lord will make myself known unto him in a vision, and will speak unto him in a dream" (Numbers 12:6).

Introduction

One of the greatest enemies facing the church is jealousy. Even we, the children of God, can be guilty of allowing the success or promotion of others to blind us to what God actually wants from us. If God has not given us the job or position we want, it is because He has something else for us at this time. Anything we do that is different from what God has for us should be considered a regrettable step down.

It is especially dangerous when jealousy causes us to speak against someone whom God has anointed for special service, as we see in this week's lesson. God showed that He would not tolerate anyone coming against the leader He had anointed to nurture and care for Israel as they journeyed to the Promised Land.

LESSON OUTLINE

I. AARON AND MIRIAM SPEAK AGAINST MOSES—Num. 12:1-9

II. MOSES INTERCEDES FOR MIRIAM—Num. 12:10-16

Exposition: Verse by Verse

AARON AND MIRIAM SPEAK AGAINST MOSES

NUM. 12:1 And Miriam and Aaron spake against Moses because of the Ethiopian woman whom he had married: for he had married an Ethiopian woman.

2 And they said, Hath the Lord indeed spoken only by Moses? hath he not spoken also by us? And the Lord heard it.

3 (Now the man Moses was very meek, above all the men which were upon the face of the earth.)

4 And the L𝚘𝚛𝚍 spake suddenly unto Moses, and unto Aaron, and unto Miriam, Come out ye three unto the tabernacle of the congregation. And they three came out.

5 And the L𝚘𝚛𝚍 came down in the pillar of the cloud, and stood in the door of the tabernacle, and called Aaron and Miriam: and they both came forth.

6 And he said, Hear now my words: If there be a prophet among you, I the L𝚘𝚛𝚍 will make myself known unto him in a vision, and will speak unto him in a dream.

7 My servant Moses is not so, who is faithful in all mine house.

8 With him will I speak mouth to mouth, even apparently, and not in dark speeches; and the similitude of the L𝚘𝚛𝚍 shall he behold: wherefore then were ye not afraid to speak against my servant Moses?

9 And the anger of the L𝚘𝚛𝚍 was kindled against them; and he departed.

Ethnic issues (Num. 12:1). As the Israelites traveled through the wilderness toward the Promised Land, Moses endured several challenges to his authority. There were many in the Israelite camp who at various times rebelled against his leadership. Perhaps the most significant challenge, however, came from his own brother and sister.

At some point after the plague involving the quail (11:31-35), Miriam and Aaron began to resent Moses. {Initially, the reason stated for this resentment had to do with the Ethiopian ethnicity of Moses' wife.}Q1

Ethiopia, also referred to as the land of Cush, was located to the south of Egypt. Some forty years before this time, Moses' had married Zipporah, who is identified as a Midianite (cf. Ex. 2:16-22). Some have argued that Midian and Cush were two names for the same place and Zipporah is the one referred to in Numbers 12:1. Most scholars suggest it is more likely that Zipporah had died and Moses had married an Ethiopian woman.

The fact that Miriam and Aaron opposed Moses is significant for several reasons. First, they were his sister and brother. Second, and more important, their opposition meant that both the prophetic and priestly offices were now seeking to undermine Moses' divinely held position of authority.

Miriam is mentioned as a prophetess among the women (cf. Ex. 15:20), while Aaron was appointed by God to be the high priest of Israel (cf. 28:1). Prophet and priest thus allied themselves against God's appointed mediator over Israel. Miriam's prominence and the judgment she subsequently suffered indicate that she was the instigator who influenced her brother Aaron to join her in bringing their grievance.

With the problems caused by the complaining of the mixed multitude (Num. 11:4)—which led to the quail and the plague—and the blaspheming of God's name by the son of an Egyptian man (Lev. 24:10-11), perhaps Miriam and Aaron were suggesting that Moses was hypocritical for having a wife of non-Israelite descent. Whatever particular objection they voiced concerning Moses' wife, it was, as we will see, nothing but a smokescreen for their real reason for resenting their brother.

Miriam and Aaron's jealousy (Num. 12:2-3). {Although Miriam and Aaron grumbled against Moses' Ethiopian wife, they revealed the jealousy within their own hearts by asking their real question: Did God speak only through Moses? The implication here is that God also spoke through them, prophetess and priest, just the same. Why, then, did Moses reserve such great authority for himself? They resented the closeness of the relationship Moses had with God and the authority God had given him as Israel's foremost leader.}[Q2]

They clearly did not like the fact that God spoke and ruled primarily through their younger brother. In their minds, Moses did not qualify for such a leadership role any more than they did. Perhaps they wished to imply that Moses was an authoritarian who had allowed his ego to get out of control and run wild, much to the detriment of the people.

The only thing out of control in this situation was the jealousy that fueled Miriam and Aaron's complaint. In a parenthetical note, verse 3 states that Moses was the meekest man on earth. Meekness in this instance is closely associated with humility, meaning that Moses was the exact opposite of how his sister and brother portrayed him. They saw him as an egomaniac, while the commentary within the text says nothing could have been further from the truth.

God calls Moses, Miriam, and Aaron (Num. 12:4-5). {God wasted no time in getting involved in this dispute. Very suddenly, He called Moses, Aaron, and Miriam to meet Him at the tabernacle, or tent of meeting, where His presence was manifested.}[Q3] God was not going to tolerate any more of the backbiting against Moses by his sister and brother, who were now going to be called to account for their envy and rebellion.

Previously we learned about a man who was punished for cursing the name of God, and now we see the seriousness of speaking against God's chosen servant. While not as serious as speaking directly against God Himself, it is still a dangerous thing to speak against those whom God has divinely chosen for a specific work. It is like saying that God did not know what He was doing when He chose that person.

God uses individuals and church committees to help God's servants find the place and ministry where they can best serve the Lord with their unique gifts. However, ultimately, it is the Lord who chooses people for service according to His will. Admittedly, we may not always understand His reasoning, but we must always be content to submit to His will. We must be content to serve in the capacity for which He has called and equipped us and to work humbly alongside our fellow servants.

{After Moses, Miriam, and Aaron gathered at the tabernacle, God descended in a pillar of cloud and stood at the entrance.}[Q4] There He called Miriam and Aaron to come and appear before Him. This moment reminds me of the many times my brother and I would get into a fight as boys, only to hear the thunderous voice of my dad calling our names. Those situations did not typically work out in a pleasurable way for me, and it was not likely things would go so well for Miriam and Aaron either.

The faithfulness of Moses (Num. 12:6-7). There was no mistaking who was speaking to Miriam and Aaron as God told them to hear His words. The pillar of cloud gave visible manifestation to the presence of the Lord.

Normally when God spoke, He did so through Moses. In this instance, however, He addressed the rebellious prophetess and priest directly. He did not provide Moses with words of defense to recite to his sister and brother. They likely would have been suspicious of that type of message, so God spoke to them directly and audibly in a way that left no doubt that He was the speaker and not Moses. In fact, Moses remained silent through all this.

{God did not deny that He spoke with and through prophets, but He typically did so by visions and dreams.}[Q5] Moses, on the other hand, was unique.

The commendation that Moses was "faithful in all mine house" (vs. 7) does not mean he was perfect. In fact, as we previously learned in Numbers 11, he at times voiced his own displeasure with God. However, Moses was faithful in what God called him to do. Though he stumbled and sinned occasionally, the consistent pattern of his life was to obey the Lord.

It is significant that God identified Moses as His servant. This points to a special relationship between God and Moses that is detailed more fully in the following verses. Moses was a prophet, to be sure (cf. Deut. 18:15), but he was more than that. He was also Israel's intercessor with the Lord and the mediator of the covenant between Israel and God.

God's unique relationship with Moses (Num. 12:8-9). {When God spoke to Moses, He did not do so through visions and dreams. Instead, He spoke to him directly. He did not use riddles or figurative speech but conversed clearly with him.}[Q6] God and Moses spoke to one another in a way that showed very close communion and fellowship.

God then asked Miriam and Aaron very pointedly why, knowing He spoke directly to Moses, they were not afraid to speak against him. What made them think they could speak against one so close to God without any repercussions? The anger of the Lord burned against Miriam and Aaron.

MOSES INTERCEDES FOR MIRIAM

10 And the cloud departed from off the tabernacle; and, behold, Miriam became leprous, white as snow: and Aaron looked upon Miriam, and, behold, she was lerous.

11 And Aaron said unto Moses, Alas, my lord, I beseech thee, lay not the sin upon us, wherein we have done foolishly, and wherein we have sinned.

12 Let her not be as one dead, of whom the flesh is half consumed when he cometh out of his mother's womb.

13 And Moses cried unto the Lord, saying, Heal her now, O God, I beseech thee.

14 And the Lord said unto Moses, If her father had but spit in her face, should she not be ashamed seven days? let her be shut out from the camp seven days, and after that let her be received in again.

15 And Miriam was shut out from the camp seven days: and the people journeyed not till Miriam was brought in again.

16 And afterward the people removed from Hazeroth, and pitched in the wilderness of Paran.

Miriam contracts leprosy (Num. 12:10). The setting just described above is that of a courtroom, where the plaintiffs, defendant, and judge are assembled. The Judge had already heard the plaintiffs' case against the defendant and called all parties together. Interestingly enough, the defendant never had to say a word, as the Judge actually doubled as his attorney and spoke for him.

{The case against Moses, spurious as it was to begin with, was dismissed entirely when the Judge left the courtroom, but His ruling against the plaintiffs became clear as Miriam instantly became leprous.}[Q7] This would surely have stunned both Moses and Aaron as they saw their sister turn completely white with this infectious skin disease.

Aaron pleads with Moses for Miriam (Num. 12:11-12). {Aaron immediately turned to Moses and asked him not to punish Miriam and him for their foolishness.}[Q8] He admitted that they had sinned and pleaded for mercy. Moses, of course, had nothing to do with Miriam's punishment; it was inflicted by God. However, this divine judgment effectively reinforced to Aaron that Moses was God's chosen servant, and he received the message loud and clear. That he understood this is seen by the fact that he addressed Moses as his "lord."

The horror Aaron felt as he saw his sister afflicted with such a terrible disease was expressed quite vividly as he compared her to a stillborn child who comes out of his mother's womb with his flesh half-eaten. Aaron realized that they both had sinned, but he did not want Miriam to die. The only thing he knew to do was to plead with Moses to intercede for her life.

Moses' prayer and God's answer (Num. 12:13-14). After Aaron turned to Moses in desperation and repentance, Moses immediately went to God with the same sense of desperation as Aaron.

Moses' prayer for Miriam shows that he did not allow feelings of anger or bitterness toward her to dominate his thoughts or attitude. In fact, there is no indication from the text at all that Moses ever harbored any resentment toward Miriam or Aaron. God was the one who had called Miriam and Aaron to account and defended Moses. Moses, on the other hand, never offered one word of self-defense or rebuttal.

{God responded to Moses' intercessory prayer for Miriam by stating that He would forgive and restore her, but her sin would not be without consequences. She would be healed and restored, but she would undergo a brief period of punishment.}Q9

The Lord explained that if Miriam's father had spit in her face, she would be required to leave the camp for seven days. This was not based on a specific statute from the Mosaic Law, but to be spat upon was to suffer contempt (cf. Deut. 25:9) and to be made ceremonially unclean (cf. Lev. 15:8).

{Miriam's offense called for more shame than that, yet God was willing to treat her graciously. She could have been sentenced to permanent banishment, but He limited her exile from the camp to just seven days.}Q10

Shutting her out of the camp for seven days was consistent with the Law's required purification process of restoring to the community at large those who naturally contracted such a disease

(cf. Lev. 14:1-9). At the conclusion of a seven-day period of isolation, Miriam would be readmitted to the camp.

Restoration of Miriam (Num. 12:15-16). The passage concludes by acknowledging that Miriam did indeed remain outside the camp for the next seven days. At the end of this time of waiting, she was received back among her people—fully restored, yet with an indelible reminder of the power of God and the evil of jealousy.

During those seven days while Miriam remained outside, the people did not move on. They remained until she could rejoin them.

Once Miriam returned, the people resumed their journey from Hazeroth through the wilderness of Paran.

—Robert Ferguson, Jr.

QUESTIONS

1. What reason does the text give initially for Miriam and Aaron's resentment of Moses?

2. What was the real reason behind their resentment?

3. What did God do immediately in response to Miriam and Aaron's words against Moses?

4. How did the Lord show His presence to Aaron, Miriam, and Moses?

5. How did God say He typically spoke with prophets?

6. How did God say He spoke with Moses?

7. In what way did God punish Miriam?

8. How did Aaron respond when he saw Miriam with leprosy?

9. How did God answer Moses' prayer on behalf of Miriam?

10. How was God gracious to Miriam even in her judgment?

—Robert Ferguson, Jr.

Preparing to Teach the Lesson

In previous lessons, we have looked at some very unflattering episodes in Israel's history: the death of Aaron's sons, the stoning of a blasphemer of God, and the people's despising the Lord's gracious provision of manna and insisting that He give them meat to eat.

It is truly amazing how the Bible records such unflattering moments in the history of the people of God. One might think that any religion's sacred text would bolster its adherents' self-confidence. But not this Book, not the Bible. The Bible shows an unfiltered, divine perspective, a perspective that glorifies God, not human beings.

This week, our text focuses, not on the people of Israel as a whole or even on Moses himself, but rather on two individuals, Aaron and Miriam (Num. 12:1-16). On the one hand, this narrative is a tale of pettiness and selfish ambition. On the other hand, it is another portrayal of the Lord's faithfulness and gracious character.

TODAY'S AIM

Facts: to learn to see God's faithfulness in the face of pettiness and betrayal of even close friends and family.

Principle: to affirm that each of our roles in God's plan is determined by God alone.

Application: to acquire the focus and determination to not be distracted from seeing God's faithfulness by the ungodly acts of those around us.

INTRODUCING THE LESSON

Anyone who has lived any length of time knows that betrayal can come from the most unlikely sources. Perhaps a coworker we thought was a friend shows himself to be anything but a friend. Perhaps someone we confided in betrays our confidence. Yes, we know that people have the unfortunate potential to disappoint us from time to time. But even having been let down in the past does not sufficiently prepare us for the worst type of betrayal—betrayal from close friends and family.

Numbers 12 relates a situation such as this when Moses' own sister and brother turned against him. Thankfully, the Bible is not a book about people but rather a book about God and His dealings with people. Throughout Numbers 12, we might be tempted to focus on Miriam and Aaron, but Moses gives us an amazing example of focusing on God in difficult times.

DEVELOPING THE LESSON

In the initial portions of the wilderness journey to Canaan, Israel repeatedly failed God. Moses too had his failings, and now Miriam and Aaron fell into sin as well. In light of all this, the text continues to show us that the Lord remained true to His word and His faithful servant Moses.

1. Accusation (Num. 12:1-3). Numbers 12 begins with a direct challenge to Moses' leadership and authority. "Miriam and Aaron spake against Moses because of the Ethiopian woman whom he had married: for he had married an Ethiopian woman." They went on to insinuate that they should have as much authority as Moses since the Lord spoke to them as well.

The timing of this display of rancor is especially unfortunate in that a large number of Israelites had just fallen to a great plague due to their disobedience (11:33). So with the people having just been judged and Miriam and Aaron now complaining, it seems that Moses' popularity was reaching a low point. Moses did not respond to the attack from his brother and sister, however.

This can probably be attributed to his "meek," or humble, character (12:3).

2. Rebuke (Num. 12:4-8). While Moses did not respond to the attack, the Lord did, and it seems He did so immediately. Verse 2 emphasizes what should be obvious: "the Lord heard it." Now He addressed those involved and preemptively initiated a confrontation. In all this, we get the firm feeling that the Lord was fighting on behalf of Moses and that Moses was completely safe in this situation.

The Lord met with and spoke to Miriam and Aaron in the tabernacle. He rebuked their attitude and reminded them of Moses' faithfulness and the unique place he had in God's plan.

3. Judgment (Num. 12:9-16). After God met with and rebuked the dissenters, He remained rightfully angry. He departed from their presence, but His just judgment came immediately. He could have justifiably destroyed them for their offense, but instead of striking down Miriam and Aaron, the Lord took a much more merciful path with them. In this, we see that the Lord's character and tendency is to firmly yet mercifully deal with us when we fall into sin.

The Lord apparently did not directly punish Aaron, but He did afflict Miriam with leprosy that would last for seven days. The implication is that Miriam was the instigator of the rebellion against Moses' leadership. If Miriam's affliction seems harsh, we need to keep it in context. Earlier, in Numbers 11, people were consumed in fiery judgment (vs. 1), and others were smitten by a severe plague (vs. 33).

We've all had bad days when things went wrong and we got upset. On days like that, we may have thought some things or even said or did some things that we are now ashamed to admit. Bad days like that have a way of warping our perception and making us feel entitled to sin.

Miriam and Aaron had a very bad day in Numbers 12. They allowed pettiness and selfish ambition to grip their hearts and manipulate their minds. It is easy to stand in judgment of them, but it is important to see how God dealt with their situation. He addressed their sin, of course, but He did so with a disposition of mercy, not vengeance.

ILLUSTRATING THE LESSON

To oppose those who are faithfully serving God is to bring on ourselves divine rebuke and judgment.

CONCLUDING THE LESSON

God graciously saw His faithful servant Moses through the opposition of his sister and brother. But He was also merciful toward Miriam and Aaron. His rebuke and restrained judgment were acts of loving concern for them.

ANTICIPATING THE NEXT LESSON

God proved His faithfulness to His people over and over again, despite repeated episodes of rebellion and unbelief. We will see in Numbers 13 that as Israel approached the Promised Land, the people again challenged God's patience with their faithless attitude.

—Nigel C. Black.

PRACTICAL POINTS

1. When we feel the need to rebuke someone, we should consider whether our feelings are sinful or justified according to God's Word (Num. 12:1).
2. We should always be meek in considering our roles in the family of God, not asserting authority where we have none (vss. 2-3).
3. God's justice is sure, so we can have peace when we are falsely accused or defamed (vss. 4-5).
4. In Christ, we can have intimacy with God and should seek a close relationship with Him (vss. 6-8)
5. Do not provoke the Lord; He will chastise His children (vss. 9-10).
6. Even after we repent, sin still often has consequences (vss. 11-16).

—Megan Hickman.

RESEARCH AND DISCUSSION

1. Are you critical of others (cf. Matt. 7:1-5)? How can you discern whether it is appropriate for you to rebuke another believer?
2. What does it mean to be meek? How do some people misunderstand this?
3. Do you have a hard time having faith in the timing of God's judgments?
4. Do you think people still receive immediate punishment for sins today? In what ways? Does it always happen this way?
5. How can church discipline lead to reconciliation? How could it be more damaging to ignore sin than to deal with it?

—Megan Hickman.

ILLUSTRATED HIGH POINTS

Speak unto him in a dream (Num. 12:6)

Most people dream, but people do not often remember their dreams. A dream is defined as a series of thoughts, images, and sensations occurring in a person's mind during sleep. Psychologists who have studied common dreams, such as flying, falling, and being chased, have found that these dreams often correlate with the dreamer's elevated level of waking anxiety.

When the Lord spoke to Aaron and Miriam, He explained that He used visions and dreams to show His will to others. God may not communicate to everyone through their dreams, but He did with His prophets.

We have done foolishly (vs. 11)

There is a lot I do not remember about high school. But I do remember one Spanish class where the students became particularly disruptive. It was the last period of the day on the Friday of an extended weekend.

The teacher was trying to maintain control of her class, but she was young and fairly new to teaching high schoolers. The class was uncontrollable. Pencils and notebooks were being tossed around the room.

Then, someone threw a book out the third-floor window. Our teacher suddenly became very serious. She rebuked the class for their childish behavior, and the student who had thrown the book from the window confessed. The class recognized that their behavior had been inappropriate and disrespectful.

The rebellion of Aaron and Miriam had reached a climax, and it took a stern rebuke from the Lord to knock some sense back into them.

—Chelsea Villaseñor.

Golden Text Illuminated

"If there be a prophet among you, I the Lord will make myself known unto him in a vision, and will speak unto him in a dream" (Numbers 12:6).

In our golden text for this week, Moses' woes in governing the Israelites continue. This time the trouble comes from members of his own family: his brother Aaron and his sister Miriam.

Apparently they were offended that Moses had at some point taken another wife. The Hebrew word translated "Ethiopian" actually means that she was dark-skinned, a descendant of Cush (cf. Gen. 10:6-8). She was most likely a member of the "mixed multitude" of non-Israelite slaves who had decided to accompany the Hebrews on their Exodus from Egypt (Ex. 12:38).

We can infer that Moses' first wife, Zipporah, the daughter of Jethro, returned to her father in Midian after their strange conflict over Gershom's circumcision (cf. 4:20-26). She remained with her father in Midian throughout Moses' mission to deliver the Israelites. She and her children, along with her father, made one recorded visit to the Israelite camp (cf. 18:1-27). She and Moses' sons probably returned to Midian with her father after this visit. By this point, Zipporah may have died, enabling Moses to remarry. There is no mention that Moses' second marriage was in any way displeasing to the Lord.

Aaron and Miriam's irritation about Moses' remarriage provided them an occasion to attempt to undermine his authority over the people. They took advantage of Moses' meekness to try to exalt their own standing, perhaps implying that his remarriage somehow indicated that Moses was no longer fit to lead.

But our text tells us that the Lord was having none of it! He immediately summoned the three of them to appear before Him at the tabernacle.

Our golden text is the beginning of the Lord's declaration to them of His verdict (Num. 12:6-8). He began by contrasting the way He usually communicated to His prophets with the special, intimate way he communicated with Moses. The Lord had never communicated with anyone as directly and personally as he did with Moses (cf. Deut. 34:10). Therefore, the Lord pointedly challenged them with the question, "Wherefore then were ye not afraid to speak against my servant Moses?" (Num. 12:8).

This question must have chilled Aaron and Miriam to the bone, since it indicated the Lord's extreme displeasure with their actions against Moses. The pillar of the Lord's glory suddenly departed from the tabernacle, leaving Miriam covered in white, leprous sores.

Moses interceded for his sister's healing, but the Lord insisted that she be shut out of the camp for seven days, after which she was accepted into the camp again, thoroughly reprimanded for her presumption.

In today's society, we tend to assume that it is our inalienable right to criticize people in leadership and authority. But this text should counter that blanket assumption, particularly regarding spiritual leadership. We should be wary of assuming it is always appropriate for us to criticize those who serve God in authority over us. We must be careful about this.

—*John Lody.*

Heart of the Lesson

Moses was a truly humble man. In fact, the Bible says he was humble "above all the men which were upon the face of the earth" (Num. 12:3). Just in the previous chapter, he had proved his humility by rejoicing in the leadership of others. He knew he needed help for the great task that God had set before him.

God promises that he shows favor to the humble but opposes the proud (Prov. 3:34). In this lesson, we see God's faithfulness in how He responds to rebellion against Moses.

The challenge (Num. 12:1-3). Moses' marriage to an Ethiopian woman had provoked criticism from his siblings, Aaron and Miriam. The text does not specify why this was a problem, but it mainly seems to have been an opportunity for Miriam and Aaron to express a longstanding complaint against Moses.

Their question was more an accusation. Because Miriam and Aaron were upset with Moses, they wanted to usurp his authority as the head prophet. They asked, "Hath the Lord indeed spoken only by Moses?" (vs. 2). This was a pretty direct challenge to Moses' authority.

The Bible's interjection that "the Lord heard it" establishes a dark turn in the narrative. God hears everything we say or think, and we should be careful to honor Him and His leaders in every way. It is here that God notes Moses' humility in implicit contrast to the pride of Miriam and Aaron. God is about to act on Moses' behalf.

The defense (Num. 12:4-9). Then something truly frightening happened: the Lord came down to defend Moses personally. He summoned Aaron and Miriam to the tabernacle and affirmed Moses as their faithful leader. God even elevated him above all other prophets by reminding Miriam and Aaron that He had not spoken to Moses through dreams, but to his face like a friend (Ex. 33:11).

God had been with Moses from the very beginning. He had exalted him above Pharaoh and would continue to exalt him. But Moses, despite the great honor that God had bestowed on him, did not give in to pride. He knew that he would be nothing without the Lord.

There is a cogent saying: true humility is not thinking less of yourself, but thinking of yourself less. While Miriam and Aaron looked to themselves and contested God's appointed leader, Moses looked to God, who came swiftly to his defense. We should always respect the leaders that God has put in place for us, entrusting ourselves to His sovereign hand (cf. Mark 12:17; John 19:11).

The judgment (Num. 12:9-16). Miriam and Aaron made the same mistake the Israelites made time and again: when they complained against Moses, they did not realize they were really challenging God. God was angry and struck Miriam with leprosy.

It was Aaron who then turned to Moses and admitted that they had been foolish. He asked Moses to intercede on their behalf to God. Moses did, and God ultimately agreed to heal Miriam.

We all have pride in our hearts, which, left unchecked, shows its face in our rebellion against God. When Moses interceded for Miriam, He asked the Lord to "let her not be as one dead" (Num. 12:12). God's Word tells us that we were all "dead in trespasses and sins" (Eph. 2:1), but then Jesus Christ came to intercede on our behalf to the Father (Rom. 8:34). Let us always be thankful for Jesus' sacrifice that allows us, despite our grievous sins, to be sons and daughters of God.

—*Megan Hickman.*

World Missions

A missionary in Togo tells a heart-rending story: a woman trusted in Christ, but she laments that her husband will not allow her baby to go to church because the child was dedicated to Voodoo. The missionary asks us to pray for her. He gave her some assistance so that she would not be forced to beg; she had been hopelessly fighting for her livelihood.

This is no story from centuries ago. It was part of a prayer letter from a national missionary at the time of this writing. His name is Sika Yawo. Sika's work is difficult. This is easily seen from what he goes on to write:

"People being baptized are from a village that is steeped in idol worship. We had to negotiate with the people before being allowed to baptize people in the river of the village. We tried having baptisms at two other times at two different rivers, and we were asked to leave."

Sika could move to America and use his talents and skills to make money instead of facing such opposition. But he knows that this is what God has planned for him and that his trials are momentary and light compared to the glory that awaits him (II Cor. 4:17-18). His struggles have an eternal purpose.

Contrast Sika with those the world calls successful, who have fame, fortune, success, power, and beauty. Robin Williams, beloved for his ability to make the world laugh, was so filled with hopelessness that he ended his own life. Elvis Presley, Michael Jackson, Marilyn Monroe, and many more American "idols" proved that having everything this world offers cannot give happiness or peace.

But this can happen to God's people as well. The Israelites, fearful and discontented, refused to appreciate God's amazing provision for them and continued to complain and grumble against Him. The result is summarized in Psalm 78:33: "Therefore their days did he consume in vanity, and their years in trouble."

What glories are missed when we let fear keep us from obeying! Sika is obeying, but he needs help. He gives thanks for a motorbike provided for one of the men in ministry. The difference between walking village to village and having a motorbike is huge. More motorbikes would provide for more national missionaries to reach more villages.

Sika cannot afford them. He needs money just to pay his children's school fees, not to mention to maintain an orphanage, a prison ministry, and many other outreaches. We, however, could help!

Has the Lord made Himself known to you? Has He called you to be part of His work? For more information about Sika's work for God in Togo, go to *www.sourcelight.org/donate* or call 1-706-342-0397.

In the book of Revelation, God says the greatest rewards for serving Him will come after we are in heaven (11:18). There is good reason for that. The apostle Paul, though he has been physically dead for thousands of years, is still reaching souls today through his writings.

You can do that too! You can give and serve now in ways that will continue long after you have passed into glory—through raising a godly family, discipling and training believers for kingdom service, supporting a missionary, donating resources, or even naming a missions organization in your will.

Imagine the rewards collecting in heaven for those who led a life of faithful service.

—*Kimberly Rae.*

The Jewish Aspect

Jews see Miriam as an amazing woman. According to Jewish rabbis, as a young girl in Egypt, she helped her mother, Yocheved, as a midwife. We know that she and her mother defied Pharaoh's decree that everyone must kill the Hebrew baby boys. This act showed evidence of Miriam's strength of character.

A Jewish tradition holds that when Pharaoh demanded that the baby boys be drowned, Miriam's father, Amram, separated from his wife so they would have no more children. Because he was a leader, many people followed his example.

Miriam saw the problems with this action. The Talmud records that Miriam spoke up to her father and stated, "You are worse than Pharaoh! Pharaoh's decree is against the boys; you are effectively causing that there are no Jewish girls also!" Miriam's actions demonstrated her bravery; people believe that it was through her urging that Amram returned to his wife and Moses was born (Silberberg, "Why Was Miriam Punished So Harshly?" chabad.org).

Jewish sages write that Miriam was a prophetess and that the spirit of prophecy came to her when she was but a child. Her earliest prophecy was regarding Moses—that her mother would give birth to a son who would free the Jewish people (Mindel, "Miriam," chabad.org).

Miriam's mother kept baby Moses hidden for three months; when that became no longer feasible, she placed him in a basket in the Nile River. Miriam followed to watch over him. Scripture records that she approached the Egyptian princess who found Moses and offered to bring a Hebrew mother— her mother—to nurse the baby. This act displayed her boldness in the face of problems.

After the Israelites crossed the Red Sea, Miriam sang a song of triumph in which the women joined. The book of Micah places Miriam as a leader of the people in the Exodus from Egypt (6:4).

Jews also believe that the Israelites had a ready water source in the wilderness, a well, because of Miriam's merit. The Jewish Zohar explains that historians attribute the well to Miriam because she stood by the waters of the Nile to ensure Moses' safety. The Midrash connects the well to Miriam's praise after the parting of the Red Sea (Shurpin, "Miriam's Well: Unraveling the Mystery," chabad.org).

In addition, Jews believe that because of Miriam and her mother's bravery in saving Hebrew babies, God rewarded the family with the two most distinguished dynasties. God gave Aaron the priesthood and Miriam royalty. Although she was not of the line of Judah, they believed she was an ancestor of King David (Mindel). Whether or not this can be substantiated, Jews obviously hold her in high esteem.

God chose to use Miriam in a big way in His plan of redemption. Yet in this week's Scripture lesson, we do not read about her great heroic feats, but her moment of weakness and humanity when she criticizes Moses' wife and challenges his leadership. Due to her actions, God punished her with leprosy.

Miriam's life story validates mankind's need for a Saviour. Even though Miriam was extraordinary, she still was not perfect. God chastises those He loves so they will not wander into sin (Heb. 12:6). He does this to keep His people close to Him. We must always remember that the works we do in His name are for His glory alone.

—*Robin Fitzgerald.*

Guiding the Superintendent

In this lesson we encounter God personally intervening in a conflict that arose between Moses and his two siblings, Aaron and Miriam. In past lessons, we have seen a very clear relationship between disobedience and dire consequences. Israel's sin forced them to learn and relearn the same lesson again and again. This week the lesson is no different and is summed up in God's question, "Wherefore then were ye not afraid?" (Num. 12:8).

Miriam and Aaron did not understand the strength of the bond between God and His chosen prophet, Moses. They presumed on their own importance and sought that which was not theirs to claim. Prideful presumption has plagued humanity since Adam and Eve. This lesson helps us to see it clearly for what it is: sin and rebellion against God Himself.

DEVOTIONAL OUTLINE

1. The contention (Num. 12:1-2). The matter of Moses' second wife is introduced here in the text, and Miriam and Aaron take issue with her ethnic background, which they see as justification for a power play for sharing authority with Moses. They condemn his marriage and question why they too should not be considered prophets, equal in status before God to their brother. In light of all they had witnessed before, it was an arrogant, presumptuous claim. But they appeared to have no qualms in brashly putting it forward.

2. The question (Num. 12:3-10). God made His appearance in spectacular fashion in the Shekinah-glory cloud at the entrance of the tabernacle. He commanded Moses, Miriam, and Aaron to come before Him, and He spoke to Miriam and Aaron directly. God is not to be trifled with. His plans and His choices are not to be questioned.

God made it very clear that Moses was His sovereignly chosen leader. He informed the two that He spoke with Moses face to face; clearly this distinguished him from all other prophets. When God's voice abruptly ceased, the cloud departed and Miriam was left leprous. This was her punishment for (apparently) instigating the rebellion against the Lord's anointed leader.

3. Moses' intercession (Num. 12:11-16). At this point, Aaron spoke up and begged Moses to intercede on behalf of Miriam, that she not be laid waste because of their sin. Moses responded with compassion and in turn begged God to remove the curse of leprosy from her. The Lord graciously agreed, but with an important stipulation.

God asked, "If her father had but spit in her face, should she not be ashamed seven days?" (vs. 14). Miriam had personally sinned against God by her rebellion and now bore His displeasure. How could she endure this disgrace for less time than if she had offended her earthly father and earned his displeasure? So the leprosy would last seven days, during which time she would be banished from the camp.

CHILDREN'S CORNER

The sin of Miriam and Aaron was presuming that they should have just as much authority as Moses. Your children should understand that not everyone is chosen to be a leader. Moses never sought the authority that God blessed him with, and we too should never assume that we should be more important than we are. God will lift us up if it is His plan to do so. Until then, we must be humble, content, and thankful for who we are and how God has blessed us.

—Mike Spencer.

SCRIPTURE LESSON TEXT

NUM. 13:1 And the Lord spake unto Moses, saying,

2 Send thou men, that they may search the land of Canaan, which I give unto the children of Israel: of every tribe of their fathers shall ye send a man, every one a ruler among them.

3 And Moses by the commandment of the Lord sent them from the wilderness of Paran: all those men *were* heads of the children of Israel.

17 And Moses sent them to spy out the land of Canaan, and said unto them, Get you up this *way* southward, and go up into the mountain:

18 And see the land, what it *is;* and the people that dwelleth therein, whether they *be* strong or weak, few or many;

19 And what the land *is* that they dwell in, whether it *be* good or bad; and what cities *they be* that they dwell in, whether in tents, or in strong holds;

20 And what the land *is,* whether it *be* fat or lean, whether there be wood therein, or not. And be ye of good courage, and bring of the fruit of the land. Now the time *was* the time of the firstripe grapes.

25 And they returned from searching of the land after forty days.

26 And they went and came to Moses, and to Aaron, and to all the congregation of the children of Israel, unto the wilderness of Paran, to Kadesh; and brought back word unto them, and unto all the congregation, and shewed them the fruit of the land.

27 And they told him, and said, We came unto the land whither thou sentest us, and surely it floweth with milk and honey; and this *is* the fruit of it.

28 Nevertheless the people *be* strong that dwell in the land, and the cities *are* walled, *and* very great: and moreover we saw the children of Anak there.

29 The Amalekites dwell in the land of the south: and the Hittites, and the Jebusites, and the Amorites, dwell in the mountains: and the Canaanites dwell by the sea, and by the coast of Jordan.

30 And Caleb stilled the people before Moses, and said, Let us go up at once, and possess it; for we are well able to overcome it.

31 But the men that went up with him said, We be not able to go up against the people; for they *are* stronger than we.

32 And they brought up an evil report of the land which they had searched unto the children of Israel, saying, The land, through which we have gone to search it, *is* a land that eateth up the inhabitants thereof; and all the people that we saw in it *are* men of a great stature.

33 And there we saw the giants, the sons of Anak, *which come* of the giants: and we were in our own sight as grasshoppers, and so we were in their sight.

NOTES

The Mission of Twelve Spies

Lesson Text: Numbers 13:1-3, 17-20, 25-33

Related Scriptures: Deuteronomy 1:1-28; Psalm 106:1-25;
I Corinthians 10:11-13

TIME: 1443 B.C.   PLACE: Desert of Paran

GOLDEN TEXT—"Caleb stilled the people before Moses, and said, Let us go up at once, and possess it; for we are well able to overcome it" (Numbers 13:30).

Introduction

The Bible never promises that living the Christian life will be easy. God never said that His children will be free from hard times and difficulties. He did say, however, that He will never leave us or forsake us (Heb. 13:5). There are many dark days we must endure, and God expects us to trust Him when we cannot see our own way. We walk by faith, not by sight, and are not to be dismayed by our surroundings.

A pastor once told me that hard times do not give people a strong character but rather reveal those who are of strong character. When we are faced with trying circumstances, we must remember that God will make us victorious and that the joy of the Lord is our strength (cf. Neh. 8:10). When we are staring down an enemy that is larger than we are and is threatening to steal everything God has given us, we must remember this: "Greater is he that is in you, than he that is in the world" (I John 4:4).

LESSON OUTLINE

I. **SELECTION OF THE TWELVE SPIES—Num. 13:1-3**

II. **MISSION OF THE TWELVE SPIES—Num. 13:17-20**

III. **REPORT OF THE TWELVE SPIES—Num. 13:25-33**

Exposition: Verse by Verse

SELECTION OF THE TWELVE SPIES

NUM. 13:1 And the Lord spake unto Moses, saying,

2 Send thou men, that they may search the land of Canaan, which I give unto the children of Israel: of every tribe of their fathers shall ye send a man, every one a ruler among them.

3 And Moses by the commandment of the Lord sent them from the wilderness of Paran: all those men were heads of the children of Israel.

The Lord's message to Moses (Num. 13:1). The opening verse of this passage makes it clear that the Lord spoke to Moses on the matter at hand. Once again, we see God at the forefront of Israel and speaking directly to Moses.

{But a request to send spies into the land to scout it and bring back a report had been presented to Moses by the people.}[Q1] Years later, in retelling the history of Israel's wilderness wandering, Moses explained that he had told the people that God had brought them to Canaan to possess the land. The people wanted spies sent out first to see what kind of land it was and what the situation was in terms of its inhabitants. This would help determine the battle strategy. It seemed like a wise plan to Moses, so he agreed with the idea of the people (cf. Deut. 1:19-23).

The fact that God spoke to Moses regarding this issue indicates that He was still leading Israel. God, of course, already knew what the land was like and who lived there. He had set out this region for His chosen people and had already determined to give it to them. But God met the Israelites where they were and guided the process, still speaking through Moses.

The selection process (Num. 13:2). While still encamped in the wilderness of Paran, which was located on the Sinai Peninsula south of Canaan, {God told Moses to go ahead and send out twelve men to spy out the land of Canaan.}[Q2] Moses never tried to get ahead of God's timing, nor did he try to develop a clever plan of his own. God was in control of the entire process.

{In order to make sure that each tribe was equally represented in this matter, one leader from each was to be chosen as that tribe's representative.}[Q3] He would represent his particular tribe and bring back a report, not only to his tribe but also to the nation as a whole. Each tribal chief was to be a part of what was designed to be a unified effort to rally the Israelites and prepare them to conquer the land God had promised them.

The sending of the spies (Num. 13:3). Moses did exactly as God commanded and sent the twelve spies out from the wilderness of Paran to scout the Promised Land. The names of the spies and the tribes they were from are chronicled in verses 4-16. This record makes clear that each tribe was represented, so no one could make a charge to the contrary. Each spy would be accountable for the fieldwork he did as well as the report he gave.

The fact that Moses did what God commanded is worthy of further comment. We have seen several instances where Moses endured various hardships, yet he remained faithful to the Lord. This is not to say that he was a perfect man. Indeed, he had moments when he argued with God and expressed fear, confusion, and anger. However, over the course of his ministry, he was amazingly consistent in obeying the Lord, and as we saw in last week's lesson, his faithfulness was commended by God (cf. 12:6-8).

MISSION OF THE TWELVE SPIES

17 And Moses sent them to spy out the land of Canaan, and said unto them, Get you up this way southward, and go up into the mountain:

18 And see the land, what it is; and the people that dwelleth therein, whether they be strong or weak, few or many;

19 And what the land is that they dwell in, whether it be good or bad; and what cities they be that they dwell in, whether in tents, or in strong holds;

20 And what the land is, whether it be fat or lean, whether there be wood therein, or not. And be ye of good courage, and bring of the fruit of the land. Now the time was the time of the firstripe grapes.

Directions on where to go (Num. 13:17-18). In order to successfully complete their scouting mission, the twelve spies had to be instructed as to what part of the land to inspect. The expedition was to begin in the Negev ("southward"), which was the south country of Canaan, on up north to the hill country ("mountain"), which would include the regions known as Judea, Samaria, and Galilee in New Testament times (cf. vss. 21-25). Their travels probably took them as far as the modern-day nation of Lebanon. This covered a distance of approximately 220 miles one way.

{Moses gave two purposes for this mission: to scout out the land and check out its people.}Q4 He wanted to know how the land was laid out and how productive it was. He also wanted to know about the people who lived there—how many there were and whether they were strong or weak.

Moses wanted to be as calculated as possible as he prepared to take the people into the Promised Land. No doubt the information gained from the spies would be helpful in his planning, as long as he did not allow human wisdom to question what God had revealed to him. As we learn in Deuteronomy 1:19-46, sending the spies was initially the people's idea. God allowed them to proceed, but He may have done so in part to test them. Would they take Him at His word when they saw adversity, or would they flee in fear?

Directions on what to look for (Num. 13:19-20). The main goal of the mission of the spies as ordered by Moses was to discover the quality of the land as well as the strength of its cities and citizens. Since none of the Israelites, including Moses, had ever seen the land, it seemed appropriate to them to scope it out and bring back a report.

As Moses sent the spies away, he told them to be of good courage. He fully expected the spies to bring back a good report because he was well aware of the description God had provided concerning the land He was giving to the Israelites. Yet Moses wanted a first-hand account from the leaders of Israel.

{Knowing that the time of harvest had arrived, Moses instructed the spies to bring back some of the fruit of the land.}Q5 This would give him and the nation firsthand information about the fruitfulness of the soil and what type of crops the land produced.

REPORT OF THE TWELVE SPIES

25 And they returned from searching of the land after forty days.

26 And they went and came to Moses, and to Aaron, and to all the congregation of the children of Israel, unto the wilderness of Paran, to Kadesh; and brought back word unto them, and unto all the congregation, and shewed them the fruit of the land.

27 And they told him, and said, We came unto the land whither thou sentest us, and surely it floweth with milk and honey; and this is the fruit of it.

28 Nevertheless the people be strong that dwell in the land, and the cities are walled, and very great: and moreover we saw the children of Anak there.

29 The Amalekites dwell in the land of the south: and the Hittites, and the Jebusites, and the Amorites, dwell in the mountains: and the Canaanites dwell by the sea, and by the coast of Jordan.

30 And Caleb stilled the people before Moses, and said, Let us go up at once, and possess it; for we are well able to overcome it.

31 But the men that went up with him said, We be not able to go up against the people; for they are stronger than we.

32 And they brought up an evil report of the land which they had searched unto the children of Israel, saying, The land, through which we have gone to search it, is a land that eateth up the inhabitants thereof; and all the people that we saw in it are men of a great stature.

33 And there we saw the giants, the sons of Anak, which come of the giants: and we were in our own sight as grasshoppers, and so we were in their sight.

Return of the spies (Num. 13:25-26). {After being gone a total of forty days, the twelve spies returned to the Israelite camp to an anxiously waiting community that included Moses, Aaron, and the people of Israel.}[Q6]

Altogether, the journey would have covered nearly five hundred miles. To do this in forty days would mean that they traveled at a rather quick pace, leaving no time for delays along the way. They were focused on their fact-finding mission and completed it in a very efficient manner.

Report of the spies (Num. 13:27-29). The twelve spies brought back a full report, along with some of the fruit of the land, as Moses had instructed. In this regard, the mission was successful. They covered the territory they were assigned and brought back fruit to be evaluated.

{The spies announced that they had inspected the land as they were commanded, and just as God had said, it flowed with milk and honey (cf. Ex. 3:8).}[Q7] This was an expression that described the bountifulness and prosperity of the land.

In giving their report on the richness of the land, the spies demonstrated the veracity of their opinion by bringing fruit from the land, just as Moses had ordered. Noteworthy was a single cluster of grapes that was so large it had to be carried on a pole by two men. The men also brought with them pomegranates and figs (Num. 13:23).

{While there was no doubt about the abundance of the land, the spies did not have such a good report concerning the people of the land. They reported that the land they saw was inhabited by strong people and was full of large and fortified cities, impregnable strongholds that could resist any attack.}[Q8]

This, of course, presented a huge problem for the Israelites. The inhabitants of the land were not going to roll out a welcome mat for a large assembly of foreigners to come and live among them. In order to live in the land, the Israelites had to conquer it, and the spies' report was clearly picturing this as an impossibility.

To make matters worse, the spies saw what they described as "the children of Anak" living there (vs. 28). This reference will be explained further a bit later, but in the most simplistic terms, it means that some of the inhabitants were gigantic in size.

The spies continued their rant by describing the geographic locations of specific peoples. The Amalekites lived in the south, the Hittites, Jebusites, and Amorites dwelled in the central hill country, and the Canaanites lived along the Mediterranean Sea and Jordan River, covering both the east and the west. As far as the spies were concerned, the people were invincible.

Caleb's contrary report (Num. 13:30). After hearing this extremely negative report, the people began to get restless, and a commotion stirred among them. The negative report of the spies was not unanimous, however. {Caleb, who was the representative from the tribe of Judah (vs. 6), quieted the people and encouraged them to move at once to occupy the land, declaring that they were fully able to defeat the enemy.}[Q9] We learn in the next chapter that one other spy, Joshua, stood with him in this conviction (14:6-9).

Caleb did not deny that the enemy was strong and large. However, He trusted that God would defeat them all and give Israel the land just as He had promised.

Rejection of Caleb's report (Num. 13:31). The other spies were not swayed by Caleb's words. No doubt they had debated this matter constantly as they made their way back to the camp. Now the men with differing viewpoints were making their respective cases before the people and trying to persuade them accordingly.

The representatives who gave the bad report contradicted Caleb by stating that the people of Israel were not able to defeat the enemy. Clearly, they thought the mission should be aborted at once. The people of the land were much stronger than the Israelites, they declared, strongly implying that it would be foolish to try to take on these vastly superior enemies.

Exaggeration of the grim picture (Num. 13:32-33). In order to further persuade the people to accept their opinion, the majority contingent greatly exaggerated the might of the inhabitants of the land. The mere fact that they stated that the inhabitants were stronger than the Israelites reveals a severe lack of faith.

To emphasize the supposed impossibility of taking possession of the land, the spies greatly overstated the size of the inhabitants. They reported that among the natives of Canaan were the "sons of Anak," who are also described as "giants," or *nephilim*. The Nephilim were giants who lived before the Flood and contributed to the violence that led to God's judgment on man at that time (cf. Gen. 6:4).

{While the people certainly were familiar with stories concerning the giants who lived prior to and during Noah's lifetime, it was impossible that those giants had any descendants after Noah, since the Nephilim were completely destroyed in the Flood and left no living offspring. This was nothing but an attempt to play on the fears of the people by calling to mind the giants of the past in describing the current inhabitants of the Promised Land.}[Q10]

Compared to the supposed Nephilim, the ten spies saw themselves as grasshoppers. The giants they saw could defeat them simply by stepping on them as a man would crush an insect. They did not see the greatness of their God. They saw only their own weakness before an enemy whose size and power they grossly exaggerated—an enemy that Caleb knew God could defeat for them.

—*Robert Ferguson, Jr.*

QUESTIONS

1. Whose idea was it to spy out the land originally?
2. How many men were chosen to spy out the land of Canaan?
3. Why was a spy chosen from each Israelite tribe?
4. What two important purposes did Moses give for the mission of the spies?
5. What did Moses tell the spies to bring back with them?
6. How long did it take for the spies to return from their mission?
7. What report did they give regarding the land itself?
8. What report did the majority of spies give concerning the people in the land?
9. How did Caleb's report contradict that of the majority?
10. What makes it clear that the majority were exaggerating the size of the inhabitants they saw?

—*Robert Ferguson, Jr.*

Preparing to Teach the Lesson

Whether it concerned the people's dissatisfaction with the God-given manna or Miriam and Aaron's rebellion, the people of God struggled mightily as they journeyed through the wilderness to the Promised Land. Repeatedly, Israel failed to trust God when confronted with difficulty.

With all their failures and faithlessness as a backdrop, the Lord's actions stand out all the more in contrast. Where Israel was impulsive, the Lord was patient; where Israel disobeyed, the Lord was completely righteous; where Israel doubted, the Lord was faithful.

As the people of Israel approached the Promised Land of Canaan, it was time for them to get their act together and solidify their faith. The narrative of the twelve spies in Numbers 13 gives us a clear picture of where Israel was spiritually.

TODAY'S AIM

Facts: to warn that we will always find obstacles we need to overcome as we obey the Lord.

Principle: to show that those who lack faith in the Lord are controlled by their circumstances.

Application: to mature in our faith to the point that we simply take God at His word and do not put Him to the test.

INTRODUCING THE LESSON

Anyone who has ever wanted something really badly knows what it is like to have to manage expectations and fight discouragement. In a sense, the Pentateuch is a five-book narrative. The plot moves forward toward the Promised Land, and Israel, as the main character, continues to look forward to the consummation of their inheritance of Canaan.

Through famine, slavery, and the wilderness journey, Israel finally found themselves at the precipice of the Promised Land. As the Lord's word came to Moses, "Send thou men, that they may search the land of Canaan, which I give unto the children of Israel" (Num. 13:2), the excitement in the camp of Israel must have been palpable.

The Lord was certainly showing forth His faithfulness once again. He was delivering on His promises.

DEVELOPING THE LESSON

As the wilderness journey seemed to be drawing to a close, Israel still had quite a way to go in their spiritual maturity. In fact, the biblical account of the twelve spies demonstrates that while there were some faithful followers of the Lord among them, the nation as a whole was not ready to enter the Promised Land.

1. The charge to the spies (Num. 13:1-3, 17-20). Numbers 13 begins with a divine command for Israel to send out "men, that they may search the land of Canaan." Correspondingly, Moses complied with the divine ordinance and the narrative is set in motion. At this early point in time, everything seemed to be in order, and Israel looked to be quickly headed into their Promised Land.

Verses 17-20 record the detailed instructions Moses gave the spies for the Canaan mission. In this section, Moses commanded the spies as follows: "See the land, what it is; and the people that dwelleth therein, whether they be strong or weak, few or many" (vs. 18).

It might be argued that Moses' commands to the spies exceeded what the Lord had intended, since the Lord simply told Moses to send men to search out the land. Was Moses wanting to determine the feasibility of a military campaign in Canaan? That is, was he going to base his obedience to God's command to enter and take possession of the land on the strength of the inhabitants of the land? It must be said, however, that there is nothing in the narrative of Moses to substantiate this hypothesis.

It should be noted that according to Deuteronomy 1:19-22, the people were the ones who first suggested the mission, and Moses agreed to it. It is possible that some of the people wanted to wait on the spies to report their findings before deciding whether they should enter the land, while Moses, without objection from the Lord, saw value in discovering the situation in Canaan so he could plan where and how to best enter the land to take possession of it. At any rate, the spy mission would act as a test of whether the people would trust and obey the Lord or give in to their fears. It was another test that they failed.

2. Report of the spies (Num. 13:25-33). The unfaithfulness of God's people was evident when the spies returned with their report. One of the spies, Caleb, urged the people to go up at once and take possession of the land. He was later joined by Joshua, who had also gone into Canaan, in encouraging obedience to the Lord (14:6-9). The other ten spies, however, "brought up an evil report of the land which they had searched unto the children of Israel" (13:32). They described Canaan as a good land flowing "with milk and honey" (vs. 27), but also as a land filled with great, walled cities and powerful, very intimidating people. They discouraged the Israelites, telling them, "We be not able to go up against the people; for they are stronger than we" (vs. 31).

The spies should have trusted the Lord in spite of the obstacles before them. They should have learned from their previous experiences in the Exodus and their time in the wilderness that God is faithful. The majority of the spies failed the test. The people would soon join them in their faithlessness and rebellion against God and His plan for them.

ILLUSTRATING THE LESSON

Those who do not trust God are controlled by their circumstances. They can see only the immensity of the obstacles and the power of the enemy. Those who trust the Lord do not ignore the obstacles, but they focus on the power of God to overcome them.

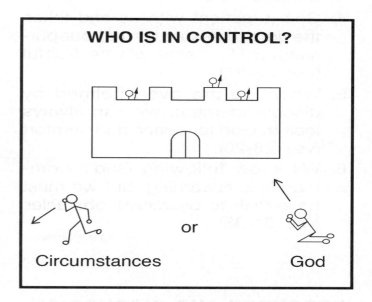

WHO IS IN CONTROL?

Circumstances   or   God

CONCLUDING THE LESSON

The unfaithfulness of God's people is on display in the report of the spies upon their return from Canaan. The fact that the Lord knew they would act this way and yet would continue with His plan for His people reveals His amazing grace and mercy.

ANTICIPATING THE NEXT LESSON

The people of God were faithless and rebellious, yet the Lord loved them and remained faithful to them. As we move into Numbers 14 and a new unit in our studies, we will see how very important it is to take God seriously.

—Nigel C. Black.

PRACTICAL POINTS

1. God sometimes calls us to search out His promises to us to demonstrate the greatness of His faithfulness (Num. 13:1-3).
2. When God calls us on a mission, we should proceed with confidence (vs. 17).
3. Even when God is with us, we must assess the situation so we can be wise in our pursuit of His will (vss. 18-20).
4. God is patient with us and takes the time to assure us that our pursuits in His name will be fruitful (vss. 25-27).
5. When we are overwhelmed by discouragement, we can always look to God for peace and comfort (vss. 28-20).
6. We know following God's commands is rewarding, but we must have faith to overcome obstacles (vss. 31-33).

—Megan Hickman.

RESEARCH AND DISCUSSION

1. Why do you think God asks us to do some things that require us to overcome great obstacles?
2. God gives us many promises in the Bible. Can you think of any? How do these encourage you?
3. Why is it dangerous (and wrong) to believe that if you are doing God's will, life will be easy?
4. The church is full of sinners, so conflict is inevitable. How should we handle conflicts when they arise (Eph. 4:1-3)?

—Megan Hickman.

ILLUSTRATED HIGH POINTS

Sent them to spy (Numbers 13:17)

An American aircraft recently carried out a reconnaissance mission. A drone was flown along the Black Sea coast of Russia. It was able to successfully complete its mission without detection.

Reconnaissance is one of the many tasks that military forces must do. Reconnaissance is the observation of an enemy or potential battleground to gain strategic information. Moses sent men to observe and garner information on both the Canaanites and the Promised Land.

Go up into the mountain (vs. 17)

My fiancé loves the outdoors. He knows a lot about various plants, animals, and birds. He also enjoys teaching me things about them. I really enjoy learning the new and interesting facts about plants and animals from him.

On one of our outings, he took me hiking. It was not much of a hike—it was one that I, as a non-hiker, could comfortably handle. We followed a path and climbed until we reached its end.

As we looked about us, we saw that the view was completely different from where we had started. We were now almost level to the tops of the trees, so we could see much more. It was beautiful! The sun was peering out from behind some clouds that sported a hint of pink. It would still have looked beautiful from a lower elevation, but now nothing obstructed our breathtaking view for miles.

Moses sent his men to climb a mountain so that they could see things they otherwise would not have been able to see of the Promised Land. They were able to survey the land, but unfortunately, they relied only on their view and not the promises of God.

—Chelsea Villaseñor.

Golden Text Illuminated

"Caleb stilled the people before Moses, and said, Let us go up at once, and possess it; for we are well able to overcome it" (Numbers 13:30).

Our golden text for this week presents us with a righteous, courageous contrast. Caleb here speaks against the majority report of the Israelite spies who were sent by Moses on a reconnaissance mission to evaluate the agricultural capacities of the land and the tactical capabilities of the Canaanite peoples they planned to attack.

Ten out of the dozen spies who were sent up to appraise the situation brought back an "evil report" (vs. 32). Only Caleb and Joshua were of the opinion that the conquest of Canaan was well within the Israelites' capabilities (cf. 14:6).

Winston Churchill once remarked that democracy is the worst form of government, except for all the other forms of government. This episode in Israelite history is a prime example of why. Sometimes the majority opinion turns out to be very wrong. Democracy is never a guarantee that a nation will be guided along the right path, only that the people as a whole are always inexcusably responsible for the consequences they incur, whether profitable or adverse.

The famous and historic stand of William Wilberforce (1759–1833) against the prevailing interests of British slavery is another example of how the minority opinion must be valued in the pursuit of a just society. Motivated by his faith in Jesus Christ as Lord and Saviour, he became a stalwart champion against the proliferation of vice and injustice.

Through many decades of overwhelming opposition, times of discour-agement, and physical infirmity, Wilberforce was a lonely voice in the halls of parliament against the immorality of vice and the injustice of slavery. Against all expectations, Wilberforce eventually led parliament to abolish the slave trade in 1807. When he retired from public life due to poor health in 1826, others took up his standard and led parliament to abolish slavery throughout the British Empire in 1833, just three days before his death.

Caleb and Joshua also maintained their faithfulness to the Lord over many years of wandering in exile along with those who were cursed for their unbelief. They also lived to see the realization of their victorious vision for God's people. Caleb and Joshua were the only survivors among the generation that was condemned to wander in the wilderness for forty years (cf. Deut. 1:35-38). Joshua, of course, became Moses' successor. He led the Israelites in their conquest of Canaan, while Caleb was granted the city of Hebron as his inheritance (cf. Josh. 14:13-14).

Being the lone faithful voice for God is never an easy role to embrace, especially in a society that is addicted to the assumption that the majority should always prevail. Standing up for God's Word will most often draw the ire and opposition of those around us. As the Apostle John wrote, "Marvel not, my brethren, if the world hate you" (I John 3:13). Jesus said, "I have chosen you out of the world, therefore the world hateth you" (John 15:19). But in these times of opposition, we can be assured of being part of the Lord's final victory.

—John Lody.

Heart of the Lesson

After a long and challenging journey through the wilderness, the Israelites had finally made it to the Promised Land. They had experienced numerous examples of God's faithfulness.

But we will see in today's text that no matter how many examples of God's faithfulness we have, we are still prone to doubt and disbelief. To fight our doubt, we must continually remind ourselves that God is good to us and has the power to fulfill all His promises.

Exploration of Canaan (Num. 13:1-3, 17-20). The Lord told the people of Israel to send the best of the best into Canaan to scout the land. These men were "heads of the children of Israel" (vs. 3), which means their opinions would be worth much more than those of laymen. They were to go and assess the strength of the people, the sophistication of their defenses, and the fruit of the land. Whatever they reported would sway the people significantly.

Sometimes there are leaders in the church who act out of fear or ambition rather than faith. Leaders have a great responsibility to make sure they are leading the people in the ways of the Lord, and the people are responsible to verify that their leaders are acting according to God's Word.

The blessings of Canaan (Num. 13:25-29). The Israelites waited in anticipation for forty days before the scouts returned. They came back with good news and bad news. The land was as plentiful and fruitful as the Lord had promised, but the residents were strong. Most of the scouts argued that the odds would be against them.

It's a good thing for us to assess challenges from all sides. This will help you be strategic about how you approach them. However, there is one thing we must always consider as Christians—the Lord is with us. Though this does not mean things will turn out exactly how we want them to, it does mean that He is sovereign and that they will turn out exactly how *He* wants them to.

We are not usually told how our challenges will be resolved, but in this case, God had already given His people the Promised Land. So despite the odds, they should have been able to walk confidently, trusting in His faithfulness.

Caleb's trust in God (Num. 13:30-33). Caleb's faith was unwavering. He insisted, "Let us go up at once, and possess it; for we are well able to overcome it" (vs. 30). But the other men feared the inhabitants of the land, picturing them as giants compared to themselves.

It is difficult to look past our own weaknesses to accomplish the Lord's work, but we focus on God's strength. If we have been commanded to do something in God's Word, we must not back down. God had specifically commanded Israel to take the Promised Land. It was the moment they had been waiting for, and they were now about to forfeit long-awaited blessings because of their fear (Deut. 1:8).

The Israelites had not conquered the Egyptians or made it through their desert wanderings in their own abilities and strength; they had been delivered by the Lord. Now was the time to overcome their fears and trust in God's faithfulness, for "God hath chosen the foolish things of the world to confound the wise" (I Cor. 1:27). As always, it would be through His power and for His glory that He would fulfill His promises.

—*Megan Hickman.*

World Missions

Some of you might be thinking, "I want to wholeheartedly serve the Lord in missions, but I can't go." Perhaps age, physical illness, or disability hinders you from what we most often see as missionary service.

But full-time service or going on a missions trip are just two ways of many to reach out in the name of Christ. You could be part of God's Great Commission by ministering through your local church, having a good testimony among the people where you live and work, or even partnering in global missions.

If you had the chance to take part in an incredible work that God is doing in Africa without having to get on a plane or leave a job, simply by sharing some resources God has already given you, would you take it?

Source of Light Ministries International (*sourcelight.org*) has national missionaries in countries all over the globe. In Uganda, in just one quarter, missionary James reports their work in 137 schools with over 8,000 students giving out Bible lessons. They have given out 29,983 lessons and have seen 4,643 decisions for Christ.

Think of it: they are already giving the gospel to over 8,000 people. They are seeing people saved. This is not a work that needs years to start up or the skill of a foreign language. It is ongoing and thriving already.

Want to be part of it?

James writes, "Please pray for those who have accepted Christ that they will stand firm in Him, and that we will have the volunteers to disciple them all. Pray also that God will continually provide for the transportation costs in caring for our vast ministry." Here are two requests that provide any believer the opportunity to be part of bringing more souls into the kingdom. Every believer can pray. Every believer can give.

His requests for the people of Uganda are profound and beautiful:

• That God will help them to overcome fear in their lives through the use of the Bible lessons (I Sam. 17:37-40).

• That the people who become Christians will truly set their affections on things above (Col. 3:2) considering our Lord's coming again (Rev. 22:20), and that they will grow in the grace and the knowledge of our Lord Jesus Christ (II Pet. 3:18). Growing in Bible knowledge is a lot easier than growing in grace. The first requires a good memory; the second requires developing a Christlike character.

• That our new believers will grow deeply in Christ, that God will give us wisdom in how to care for them, and that they will bear fruit and fellowship with other believers.

Such requests would be worthy of use in our prayers for all followers of Christ who long to see His kingdom come and His will be done on earth as it is in heaven.

James and his team in Uganda need support. You can help through your faithful prayers, through giving, or through having a representative come to your church to share more. You could raise money to buy bicycles so missionaries could travel to more villages. You could add them to your church prayer list. For more information, please visit *uganda@slmin.org* or call 706-342-0397.

No one in God's family needs to feel excluded from His service. There is much to do and an important role for anyone willing to prayerfully and humbly act!

—Kimberly Rae.

The Jewish Aspect

This week's lesson recounts the story of the twelve spies sent to scout the Promised Land. Jews know the narrative as the story of the Meraglim, the Hebrew word for spies. They state that the spies were the nobility of the Jewish people, leaders of the people (Feder, "Meraglim—The Spies," mesora.org).

In Numbers 13:3-15, Scripture lists the names of the twelve men and their tribes. There is a rabbinic tradition that the names of the various spies allude to their actions (Feder).

For example, in Numbers 13:13, Scripture states that Sethur, the son of Michael, was the representative from the tribe of Asher. Some rabbis believe his name in Hebrew alludes to the fact that he distorted the actions of God. Rashi, a medieval Jewish rabbi, stated that his hatred of God caused him to lie in his report and imply that God was weak, like "a homeowner who is unable [to] remove furniture from his house," and thus unable to drive out the inhabitants of the land (Feder).

Verse 14 states that Nahbi, son of Vophsi, was the representative from the tribe of Naphtali. Rabbis surmise that his name alludes to the fact that he concealed the words of God. Rashi expounded on the idea and stated that Nahbi concealed things and declined to report them; he observed and ignored the good things that God did (Feder).

Jewish rabbis debate the actual sin of the spies. Menachem Posner says the key to the problem was that Moses did not tell the spies to provide an assessment of whether the people could enter the land. They should have reported the facts only; they should have understood that if God willed it, he could do it ("The 12 Spies (Meraglim) in the Bible," chabad.org).

Feder concludes that the spies resented the fact that God did everything for His people. Since the spies were the nobility, the leaders of the people, their pride would not allow them to accept that they were powerless without God.

As this week's Scripture lesson shows, two spies, Joshua and Caleb, gave a report that pleased God. These two men did not take part in the sins of the other spies.

The rabbis believe Joshua's success came in part because Moses changed his name. According to Numbers 13:16, Moses added the letter *yodh* to "Oshea" (Hoshea or Hosea—"salvation" or "he saves"), which created *Yehoshua* ("Jehoshua"—"the Lord saves"), the Hebrew name for Joshua. The name change may have been a way of requesting that the young man would be steadfast in his relationship with God.

Jewish tradition holds that when Caleb started his mission, he went to the grave of the Patriarchs. There he prayed against the negative influence of his peers. He realized what he would encounter and sought help from the Lord ("Caleb," jewishencyclopedia.com).

Like the children of Israel, we all face giants in our lives. These giants often are not outside circumstances but can be our own sinful inclinations. At times, the prospect of overcoming these giants seems impossible. From the story of the twelve spies, we realize the importance of trusting in God and how He gives us the power to overcome the world. Failing to realize that God can work any miracle He desires results in negative consequences, but trust in Him always brings ultimately good results.

—*Robin Fitzgerald.*

Guiding the Superintendent

This last lesson of unit II brings us to the edge of the Promised Land of Canaan. The Israelites made it out of Egypt in miraculous fashion and survived the consequences of their many transgressions along the way. They were now poised to enter and take the land that God promised them. They were ready to begin a new life as free men and women with God as their sovereign.

But here they falter, and as we have seen over and over again in this journey, the Israelites let fear control their decisions instead of trusting in the Lord. As we will see in the next unit, this will have disastrous consequences for them.

DEVOTIONAL OUTLINE

1. The command from the Lord (Num. 13:1-3). As Sovereign over this people, God gave the command to enter the land. He directed Moses to send a man from each tribe of Israel—each one a leader among his people. These men were the best among them. They were to go into Canaan and bring back a report to help the people to go up and secure it for themselves, trusting in the Lord to fight for them as He had promised.

2. Moses' command to spy out the land (Num. 13:17-20). Moses' instructions to the men were clear: Go into the land and spy out its natural resources, the strength of its people, its cities, and its strongholds. Moses understood that the land was not free for the taking. The Israelites would have to take this land from its current occupants by force. Upon the return of the spies, God's people would use the information from their report to formulate a plan of attack for conquering the land and dispossessing the people who now dwelt there.

3. The return of the spies (Num. 13:25-33). When the men returned after forty days, they brought with them a sample of the incredible fruit of the land. They reported that the land was indeed flowing with milk and honey, just as God had said. However, ten of them described the people of the land and its fortified cities in fearful terms. They focused entirely on the size and strength of their adversaries, completely ignoring the might of the Lord to fight on their behalf. Their whole aim was to put fear and doubt into the people's hearts. Their majority report was one of cowardice and faithlessness.

Caleb and Joshua alone rebuked the naysayers, and they alone would survive the repercussions that followed this fearful report of the majority. Caleb quieted the grumbling people and attempted to encourage them to trust in God for victory, but he was overruled. The people insisted on taking the way of fear and doubt by heeding only the majority report, which intimidated them with tales of giants and monsters.

CHILDREN'S CORNER

Explain to the children that the ten spies who returned to the people with a fearful report failed to trust in what God had promised them. They saw only the might of their enemies while discounting the might of the Lord to fight for them and give them victory over those enemies. Encourage your young students to be like Caleb and Joshua, who saw the same mighty enemies but trusted that their God was far mightier and able to give them victory.

—*Mike Spencer.*

SCRIPTURE LESSON TEXT

NUM. 14:1 And all the congregation lifted up their voice, and cried; and the people wept that night.

2 And all the children of Israel murmured against Moses and against Aaron: and the whole congregation said unto them, Would God that we had died in the land of Egypt! or would God we had died in this wilderness!

3 And wherefore hath the LORD brought us unto this land, to fall by the sword, that our wives and our children should be a prey? were it not better for us to return into Egypt?

4 And they said one to another, Let us make a captain, and let us return into Egypt.

5 Then Moses and Aaron fell on their faces before all the assembly of the congregation of the children of Israel.

6 And Joshua the son of Nun, and Caleb the son of Jephunneh, which were of them that searched the land, rent their clothes:

7 And they spake unto all the company of the children of Israel, saying, The land, which we passed through to search it, is an exceeding good land.

8 If the LORD delight in us, then he will bring us into this land, and give it us; a land which floweth with milk and honey.

9 Only rebel not ye against the LORD, neither fear ye the people of the land; for they are bread for us: their defence is departed from them, and the LORD is with us: fear them not.

10 But all the congregation bade stone them with stones. And the glory of the LORD appeared in the tabernacle of the congregation before all the children of Israel.

11 And the LORD said unto Moses, How long will this people provoke me? and how long will it be ere they believe me, for all the signs which I have shewed among them?

12 I will smite them with the pestilence, and disinherit them, and will make of thee a greater nation and mightier than they.

NOTES

Rebellion of the People

Lesson Text: Numbers 14:1-12

Related Scriptures: Psalm 118:1-9; Psalm 96:1-11;
Numbers 21:4-9; Hebrews 3:8-16

TIME: about 1443 B.C.   PLACE: Kadesh

GOLDEN TEXT—"Only rebel not ye against the Lord, neither fear ye the people of the land; for they are bread for us: their defence is departed from them, and the Lord is with us: fear them not" (Numbers 14:9).

Introduction

Have you ever had to make an important decision and sought advice from multiple sources, only to get very conflicting viewpoints?

In last week's lesson, we left off with two conflicting reports brought back by a group of men who went out on a scouting mission together. They all saw the same things and had the same experiences, yet some came to one conclusion and others to a very different one.

These two opinions came from very different sources. The negative report was based on unbelief and fear, while the positive was based on faith in the Lord's promise. The people of Israel had a choice to make as to which report they were going to adopt. Their decision would determine the course of their future. Would they follow the Lord in faith, or turn away from His promise in fear and unbelief?

LESSON OUTLINE

I. THE VOICE OF FEAR—
Num. 14:1-4

II. THE VOICE OF FAITH—
Num. 14:5-10

III. THE VOICE OF JUDGMENT—
Num. 14:11-12

Exposition: Verse by Verse

THE VOICE OF FEAR

NUM. 14:1 And all the congregation lifted up their voice, and cried; and the people wept that night.

2 And all the children of Israel murmured against Moses and against Aaron: and the whole congregation said unto them, Would God that we had died in the land of Egypt! or would God we had died in this wilderness!

3 And wherefore hath the LORD brought us unto this land, to fall by

the sword, that our wives and our children should be a prey? were it not better for us to return into Egypt?

4 And they said one to another, Let us make a captain, and let us return into Egypt.

Crying and weeping all night long (Num. 14:1-2). The negative report of the majority of the spies gave the people no hope of ever securing the land God had promised them (13:27-29, 31-33). {This report reverberated throughout the community as the people wailed and wept throughout that night.}[Q1] What should have been a time of celebration and realization that God had brought Israel to the land He had promised them instead became a time of mourning because they saw only a frightening enemy instead of their omnipotent God.

Listening to the wrong voices will surely have a disastrous effect on even the most devout believers. Jesus said His sheep hear His voice and follow Him (cf. John 10:27). The children of Israel, however, were listening to the wrong voices, who were using scare tactics to prevent them from receiving what God had in store for them in the Promised Land.

God never promised us that the life of victory He has for us is free from hardships. In fact, Paul's understanding was quite the opposite: "We must through much tribulation enter into the kingdom of God" (Acts 14:22). The Lord knew the enemy was present throughout Canaan. The negative report did not catch Him off guard. Yet He promised the Israelites He would be with them. He led them out of Egypt and would also lead them into Canaan. The problem the Israelites had was that they did not believe God.

The Israelites' pattern of grumbling against Moses and Aaron whenever trouble arose continued as the people looked for someone to blame for the terrible predicament they believed they were in. This is somewhat befuddling because whenever someone grumbled against Moses, punishment and judgment soon followed. That did not seem to serve as a deterrent, though, as the people kept complaining against God's appointed leaders.

{By this time, the people were so exasperated they thought they would have been better off to have died in Egypt or in the wilderness. Anything would have been better than to have been brought to the very brink of freedom and prosperity only to have the rug pulled completely out from under them.}[Q2]

Planning to return to Egypt (Num. 14:3-4). As the Israelites bemoaned their circumstances, they shifted the blame and their anger to God. They asked each other why the Lord brought them out of Egypt to let them die in Canaan by the sword. Their wives and children would be viciously attacked by the powerful enemies throughout Canaan, and they would be powerless to defend them.

Any thinking that is rooted in unbelief will lead to bad choices every time unless it is squelched quickly. Sadly, apart from Caleb (13:30), no one in the Israelite camp had stood up to be the voice of reason when the spies' reports were initially given. Without any consideration, the people categorically rejected Caleb's exhortation and instead chose to give in to the hopeless attitude of the ten unbelieving spies.

{After lamenting their current situation, the people decided that going back to Egypt was the only thing to do.}[Q3] They knew Moses would never lead them back to Egypt, so they decided to overthrow him and choose a new leader who would help them return to where they came from. The foolishness of unbelief is staggering and will never lead to good, sound decisions.

In deciding to return to Egypt, the people were rejecting God's plan, which included His provision and protection. {It is therefore appropriate to consider what prospects they had in Egypt. Slavery, cruelty, and an angry pharaoh awaited them there.}Q4 God brought them to a place of liberty, yet they were demanding to return to a place of enslavement and hostility.

THE VOICE OF FAITH

5 Then Moses and Aaron fell on their faces before all the assembly of the congregation of the children of Israel.

6 And Joshua the son of Nun, and Caleb the son of Jephunneh, which were of them that searched the land, rent their clothes:

7 And they spake unto all the company of the children of Israel, saying, The land, which we passed through to search it, is an exceeding good land.

8 If the Lord delight in us, then he will bring us into this land, and give it us; a land which floweth with milk and honey.

9 Only rebel not ye against the Lord, neither fear ye the people of the land; for they are bread for us: their defence is departed from them, and the Lord is with us: fear them not.

10 But all the congregation bade stone them with stones. And the glory of the Lord appeared in the tabernacle of the congregation before all the children of Israel.

Falling before God (Num. 14:5-6). The nation's desire to appoint a new leader and return to Egypt was devastating to Moses and Aaron, but it was not because they felt a blow to their egos. {They fell on their faces before the people because they were witnessing full-blown unbelief.}Q5 They also knew how God always responded when His people rebelled against His word.

When we witness unbelief, it should drive us to our knees in prayer. Unbelief prevents us from receiving the blessings of God and pits us against the Lord. Moses and Aaron were not beg-

ging the people to keep them as their leaders; the people had not appointed them in the first place—God had. They were grieved by the unbelief of the people and knew that returning to Egypt was a horrible, God-dishonoring plan.

Amid all the commotion, Joshua and Caleb also stepped forward to stand in opposition to the people. These two men were the only dissenters among the twelve spies. They saw the "giants" in the land. They saw the fortified cities. They saw established civilizations throughout Canaan. They did not deny any of the details given by their comrades. What they did reject was the notion that the Israelites had no hope of taking possession of the land God had promised to them. So now they tore their clothes, a public display of grief, showing that they were appalled at the impulse to return to Egypt.

Calling for faith and courage (Num. 14:7-8). When the spies first reported on all they had seen in the land of Canaan, Caleb alone spoke in favor of taking the land and rejecting the negative recommendation to retreat. Now Caleb was joined by Joshua (who surely had given silent approval to the earlier speech) as they made one last plea to the people to go forward in faith.

The land they had seen was a good land, one filled with lush fruits and vegetables and rife with opportunity. {They had no fear of the inhabitants of the land because they knew that God was with them. God had brought them to this place not to kill them but to bless them far beyond what they could ever have imagined.}Q6 The God who had parted the Red Sea and provided food and water for them in the desert was the same God who would protect them on their journey. Joshua and Caleb knew God would do as He had promised and give them this good land.

The commonly used reference to Canaan as a "land which floweth with milk and honey" (vs. 8) points to the blessing of the land itself. God was not bringing His people to a desert wasteland. He was giving them a land that was productive; it would provide them with bountiful harvests of a variety of fruits and vegetables as well as pastureland for their livestock.

Joshua and Caleb also understood that the only way for them to succeed was for God to delight in them. Israel needed the favor of the Lord if they were going to reach their desired destination. They were not going to be able to take the land in their own strength and intellect, and they were certainly not going to enjoy God's favor and be successful if they continued in unbelief.

Warning against rebellion (Num. 14:9). {Israel's unbelief was revealed by their rebelliousness. The rebellion of which Joshua and Caleb warned their fellow Israelites points back to their insistence on returning to Egypt and rejecting God's word concerning the taking of the Promised Land.}[Q7] These actions were rebellious in nature, and the two faithful spies knew the rebellion must stop if the people were going to continue in God's blessing. To reject God's word is to invite God's wrath.

The rationale for Joshua and Caleb's faith was that the Lord was with them and had been all along. These two men trusted that God would do everything He had promised without exception. To rebel against Him was to show more faith in the wickedness of the enemy than in the goodness of God. The people had more confidence that the Canaanites would do them harm than confidence in God to protect and provide for them.

That is the problem with fear. In a sense, fear is a form of faith, but it is a perverted or distorted faith. Fear is believing that our enemy is going to prevail and do us harm, while faith is believing that God is going to accomplish that which is good for us as we follow Him.

Fear has no place in the life of a follower of Jesus Christ (cf. II Tim. 1:7). We must walk by faith, not by sight (II Cor. 5:7); the children of Israel walked by sight, not by faith. Their vision was distorted by fear, and it prevented them from seeing through the eyes of faith.

As far as Caleb and Joshua were concerned, the various inhabitants of Canaan posed no threat to the Israelites, and they saw the Canaanites as being like bread, or easy prey, for the Israelites. The Canaanites had no divine protection, for the deities they prayed to were nothing but empty idols. Israel, on the other hand, had God's presence with them, and He assured them of victory regardless of how powerful the enemy seemed.

Raging against Joshua and Caleb (Num. 14:10). {After hearing Joshua and Caleb plead for the congregation to trust the Lord and obey Him, the people responded by threatening to execute them! They wanted the most severe punishment given in ancient times: death by stoning.}[Q8]

The people were so consumed with fear and unbelief that they could no longer think clearly or even humanely. They were calling for the deaths of two leaders from their number because they gave a dissenting report that was actually based on what God had already promised. Caleb and Joshua dared to believe in the midst of a multitude of unbelievers. In addition, the desire to stone them probably also extended to Moses and Aaron, whom the rebels already wanted to replace.

Not surprisingly, the Lord was not silent when He heard this band of unbelievers rising against the leaders of Israel who spoke His word to the people. {The glory of the Lord appeared at the tent of meeting to everyone,}[Q9] leaving no doubt that He had witnessed everything that had gone on and heard everything that was said.

THE VOICE OF JUDGMENT

11 And the Lord said unto Moses, How long will this people provoke me? and how long will it be ere they believe me, for all the signs which I have shewed among them?

12 I will smite them with the pestilence, and disinherit them, and will make of thee a greater nation and mightier than they.

Although God appeared to all the people, He spoke directly to Moses. His anger against the people was not hidden at all, as He asked Moses how long the people would despise Him. How long would they continue to live so firmly entrenched in unbelief in spite of all they had seen God do?

The Lord did not pose these questions to Moses because He needed someone to talk to or because He was seeking information unknown to Him. God was angry, and He was ready to pour out His wrath on these unruly people who had rejected Him and threatened His chosen servants.

{The anger of God comes into full focus in verse 12, where He states that He would strike the people with a pestilence and destroy them. After that He would start a new nation with Moses, one that would be greater than Israel ever could become.}Q10

God is a gracious and merciful God who is slow to anger and quick to forgive, as Moses himself would acknowledge (vs. 18). However, at some point people will be held to account for continued rejection and unbelief. God said at a much earlier time that His Spirit would not always strive with man (Gen. 6:3), so it is a grave mistake to presume upon His grace and live in unbelief.

It is ironic that the Israelites were bent on destroying and replacing Moses, while God seemed intent on destroying and replacing the Israelites. We must always avoid foolish talk that rejects the will and Word of God.

It is quite stunning how quickly the tide had turned against Israel. They acted like they were now in control of their own destiny and they could go wherever they chose, even if it was back to Egypt. God, however, unmistakably made everyone understand that nothing we say or do is hidden from His sight (cf. Prov. 5:21).

How could God disown the people He had called to be His own? Would He destroy an entire nation and start over with one man as the leader? These questions will be answered in next week's lesson, as we see that God never overlooks unbelief but is merciful nonetheless. As we have learned this quarter, God's holiness cannot be compromised, but His love endures forever (cf. Ps. 52:1; Jer. 33:11).

—*Robert Ferguson, Jr.*

QUESTIONS

1. What did the Israelites do after they heard the spies' reports?
2. What did the people claim would have been better for them than entering the Promised Land?
3. Where did the people decide they should go?
4. What awaited the Israelites if they had returned there?
5. How did Moses and Aaron react to the people's rebellious plan?
6. Why were Joshua and Caleb sure they could defeat the inhabitants of Canaan?
7. What did the people's rebellion reveal? What did it consist of?
8. What did the people threaten to do to Joshua and Caleb?
9. Before whom did the glory of the Lord appear?
10. What did God say He would do to the Israelites?

—*Robert Ferguson, Jr.*

Preparing to Teach the Lesson

We learned of God's holiness in Unit I and focused on God's faithfulness in Unit II. In our final unit of lessons for this quarter, we will see how important it is to take God seriously.

Today, we will be studying Numbers 14:1-12, a narrative that graphically depicts the people's rebellion against the Lord and their fear of the inhabitants of the land of Canaan. As the people of Israel journeyed farther through the wilderness toward the Promised land, they faced temptations related to the food and the leadership God had given them. Now Israel was tempted to doubt the Lord because of the presence of the inhabitants of the land. Although Israel's temptations varied, one thing remained constant, and that was the holy character of their God. Israel needed to learn to take their God seriously if they were going to succeed in living out His good will for them.

TODAY'S AIM

Facts: to realize the negative tendency of believers to doubt God's power and plan.

Principle: to counter doubt and disbelief by reading God's Word and recalling His faithfulness.

Application: to prepare ourselves to pass the tests of faith that inevitably come throughout our lives by allowing God's Word to develop our faith and character.

INTRODUCING THE LESSON

The Lord's covenant love had been on display throughout the Exodus and journey through the wilderness. When the people were enslaved in Egypt, the Lord heard their cries and raised up a deliverer, Moses. The Lord fought for Israel, first through the ten plagues and then at the Red Sea, when He destroyed the Egyptian army. The Lord miraculously provided both manna and quail for food in a wilderness that could never sustain a people the size of the nation of Israel. The Lord mercifully dealt with failure after failure and doubt after doubt of both the people and the leadership of Israel. In all of this, the Lord certainly provided Israel many opportunities to learn to trust the One who is most trustworthy.

Israel had many opportunities to see God's faithfulness and power in action. Now, on the brink of entering the Promised Land, they must make the decision to take God's promises seriously, have faith in His word and direction, and move forward in obedience to Him. The more they learned about the inhabitants of the Land of Promise, however, the more their fear grew, feeding the doubts Israel had seemingly possessed all along about the Lord's power and plan.

Yes, the people dwelling in the land of Canaan were very powerful and lived in fortified cities. Yes, they possessed armies and would no doubt fight to the bitter end to defend themselves from being displaced. Yes, some of the indigenous Canaanites were physically imposing figures. But Israel was called to follow in faith the God who had brought them this far.

DEVELOPING THE LESSON

1. Rebellion of the people (Num. 14:1-5). Numbers 14 begins with the people's response to the evil report of the spies who had just returned from their reconnaissance work in the land: "All the congregation lifted up their voice, and cried; and the people wept that night" (vs. 1). They saw any attempt to take possession of the land God had promised them as worse than dying as slaves in Egypt or dying in the wilderness. The people of Israel bitterly complained against Moses and Aaron and even suggested that someone be appointed to replace Moses and lead them back to Egypt (vss. 2-4). Their rebellion against God and the leaders He had appointed so clouded their thinking that they thought it better to despise the Lord's miraculous deliverance and return to slavery.

2. Appeal of Joshua and Caleb (Num. 14:6-10). As if all of this were not enough, the congregation also rejected the testimony and encouragement of the faithful spies, Joshua and Caleb, who told them, "If the Lord delight in us, then he will bring us into this land, and give it us; a land which floweth with milk and honey" (vs. 8). Joshua and Caleb trusted the Lord and warned the people, "Only rebel not ye against the Lord, neither fear ye the people of the land; for they are bread for us: their defence is departed from them, and the Lord is with us: fear them not" (vs. 9). Gripped with fear and now looking for new leadership, the people would hear none of it. In fact, in their rage they probably would have stoned the two men if the glory of the Lord had not dramatically appeared in the tabernacle stopping them in their tracks.

3. Offer of God (Num. 14:11-12). The Lord spoke to Moses, condemning the people's actions and offering to destroy them and build a new nation from Moses. This was not only an expression of God's anger toward the rebellious people but also a test of Moses, as we shall see in our next lesson.

ILLUSTRATING THE LESSON

The illustration conveys the essence of human rebellion against God. As seen in the actions of the Israelites, fallen, sinful people demonstrate their disbelief and hatred of God by rejecting His promises, His leaders, and His warnings.

REBELLION AGAINST GOD

God's Promises

God's Leaders

Rejecting...

God's Warnings

CONCLUDING THE LESSON

Israel's disobedience and faithlessness seemed to be reaching a climax in Numbers 14. The text relates the people's rebellion against Moses and Aaron, as well as against Joshua and Caleb, the two spies who encouraged them to obey the Lord. Despite the impassioned, theologically sound pleas of Joshua and Caleb, Israel was determined in their refusal to enter the Promised Land. The people clearly showed that they were not taking seriously either God's promises or His warnings. They continued to reject His word, His works, and His appointed leaders. The rebellion of the people in Numbers 14 is a sad portrait of the fallen nature of man.

ANTICIPATING THE NEXT LESSON

The rebellion of the people in Numbers 14:1-12 is an unflattering instance of Israel's faithlessness and doubt. It appeared the Lord was ready to give up on His people altogether. His words to Moses in verses 11-12 opened the door for Moses to intercede on behalf of the people and seek the vindication of God's character before the world. Moses' prayer is the subject of our next lesson.

—*Nigel C. Black.*

PRACTICAL POINTS

1. Do not suffer by being rebellious against the Lord (Num 14:1-2; cf. I Pet. 3:17).
2. Even when circumstances seem to be against us, the Lord's plans are always best (Num. 14:3-4).
3. It is right to grieve over sin, but we must also do our part to correct it (vss. 5-6).
4. We should never stand down when it comes to truth, even if nobody will listen (vss. 7-9).
5. We will encounter persecution for standing up for truth, but we must persevere for Christ's glory (vs. 10).
6. Do not test the Lord's patience, for He has the power both to bless and to punish (vss. 11-12).

—Megan Hickman.

RESEARCH AND DISCUSSION

1. Have you ever cried out to God about something that you wanted but later realized that it was a sinful desire? How can we avoid this type of behavior?
2. Does it upset you when people sin? If not, why do you think this is?
3. Have you ever suffered persecution for doing the right thing? How do you know that you would be prepared to stand for Christ if you were faced with intense persecution?
4. Did God always deal immediately with sin in the Old Testament? Does He do so today?
5. Do you complain a lot? What does this say about the strength of your faith in God?

—Megan Hickman.

ILLUSTRATED HIGH POINTS

To fall by the sword (Num. 14:3)

Though army sabers are still worn by some military officers, they are normally only worn for occasions of ceremony. Swords of any kind are seldom used in combat today.

Fencing has become a popular sport around the world. It is even an event in the Olympic Games. Fencing uses a scoring system to determine the winner. Points are awarded each time a fencer touches his opponent with the weapon. A fencer may be defeated by an opponent outscoring him, but he is at no risk of falling by the sword.

The Israelites were afraid that they would "fall by the sword," that is, they feared that the Canaanites would kill them more than they trusted in the Lord's power to give them the victory.

Spake unto all the company (vs. 7)

Every President of the United States is expected to give a speech on significant occasions. Usually, his speeches are prompted by events such as a national tragedy or a national accomplishment.

Annually, he delivers a State of the Union address that summarizes the issues of the past year and his plans for the future of the nation. When the president speaks, not everyone wants to hear what he has to say, nor will everyone agree with what he says. People may even grow angry at the president's words. Still, it is vitally important for the president to communicate.

Joshua and Caleb were trying to encourage the people to trust the Lord and take possession of the Promised Land, but the Israelites were paralyzed with fear. They reacted with hostility toward Joshua and Caleb, who were faithful to the Lord.

—Chelsea Villaseñor.

Golden Text Illuminated

"Only rebel not ye against the Lord, neither fear ye the people of the land; for they are bread for us: their defence is departed from them, and the Lord is with us: fear them not" (Numbers 14:9).

The golden text for this week comes during another of Israel's worst episodes in terms of faith. Moses had sent out spies to appraise the Promised Land and its defenses. Continuing from last week's lesson text, the negative report brought back by the majority of the spies now holds sway in the minds and hearts of the people.

They have once again begun lamenting that Moses ever brought them out of Egypt. They once again accused Moses and Aaron of bringing them out of Egypt only to die, this time by the swords of the Canaanites. They even go so far as to propose that a new leader be appointed in place of Moses for the very purpose of leading them back into Egyptian slavery (vs. 4)!

What a discouraging bunch these Israelites were! It seems there was no miracle possible that could have been great enough to keep them from losing faith at every turn of adversity. When one looks back over all the wonders that God had performed on their behalf up to this point, it remains mind-boggling that these miraculous deliverances did not seem to have made any difference in their courage or confidence.

Even when Moses, Aaron, Joshua, and Caleb all rent their garments and begged the people not to rebel against the Lord and to take courage in the face of their enemies because the Lord was on their side, their response was to call for them to be stoned to death (vs. 10).

Once again, the Lord Himself had to directly intervene in the severest terms. In His wrath, Yahweh now threatened to disinherit them once and for all, to destroy them with plagues, and to start the nation over, this time beginning with Moses and his descendants.

But as it turns out, this sort of faithlessness is found throughout the course of redemptive history. From these Israelites down to the disciples of Jesus and beyond into our own personal, daily walks with God, we all tend to be too quick to lose heart in the face of adversity.

The history of Israel is one long descent from faithful beginnings down into the depths of idolatry, immorality, and injustice, at which point the Lord finally had to destroy most of them and allow the remnant to be led into captivity for seventy years. Even after that, although they had finally learned to abhor any hint of idolatry, they were still prone to faithlessness under adversity. They even descended to the point of delivering up God's own Son, their Messiah, to be crucified by their foreign oppressors, proclaiming publicly, "We have no king but Caesar" (John 19:15).

But even in this wretched condition of faltering faith, there is much encouragement. Even after this episode of rebellion, the Israelites eventually conquered Canaan under Joshua. Even after David committed adultery and murder, God established his dynasty forever. Even after Peter thrice denied Jesus, he became a leader of the early church. Our God is so gracious and powerful that He can even bring victory out of our failures. Amen!

—*John Lody.*

Heart of the Lesson

Discouragement is a powerful thing. There are generally two reactions to discouraging situations: you can either reevaluate and move forward or sink into despair. From a Christian perspective, the latter response is not a legitimate option.

God is compassionate, and our belief in His sovereign, all-powerful, loving, and faithful nature ultimately rejects the idea of despair. If He is always in control, we can trust that He is faithful to bring about His good plans for us. Our suffering is often part of this plan because trials are a huge part of our sanctification. In these times, it is important that we take God and His plan seriously, realizing that anything He puts us through is worth it for the sake of His glory.

The Israelites' despair (Num. 14:1-4). But instead of resting in the Lord's faithfulness, the Israelites gave in to despair. When they heard about the giants in the Promised Land, they basically threw a big fit and complained, once again, that they would have been better off as slaves in Egypt. Once again they rebelled against Moses, threatening to go back to Egypt (cf. Prov. 26:11).

We often compare ourselves favorably to the Israelites, thinking that we would never react so dramatically or immaturely. But the truth is, even if we do not act out in the same way, we often have the same wicked reactions within our hearts. It is easier for us to hide our blasphemous thoughts, but we must continually guard against doubt.

The leaders' exhortation (Num. 14:5-8). Today we see Moses, Aaron, Joshua, and Caleb trying to remind the Israelites of the Lord's faithfulness, which the people so often forgot. Discipling others, especially as a church leader, can be discouraging work. Moses, Aaron, Joshua, and Caleb were frustrated with the people. Even so, the leaders tried to reassure the people of the goodness of the land and the power of the Lord to deliver it to them.

But there is a foreboding backdrop to their speech as they note that God's work on their behalf depends on His delight in His people (vs. 8). It is safe to say that the Lord was not delighted. The leaders warned the people not to rebel against God, but the people's hearts were set on evil (cf. Ex. 32:22).

The Lord's wrath (Num. 14:9-12). Moses, Aaron, Joshua, and Caleb had pointed out the Israelites' sins, so the people wanted to stone them to death. When we are rebuked for sin, even if it is a gentle rebuke by someone we trust, our first instinct is to lash out. Our hearts are set on sin, but we must control our impulses and even convince ourselves to be thankful for this God-given method of sanctification.

Not only were Israel's leaders frustrated, but God Himself was grieved by the rebellion. The people rejected Him over and over again despite "all the signs" of His faithfulness (vs. 11). The Lord knows we will continue to provoke Him despite His faithfulness, and He must punish our sins. That is why He ultimately sent Christ to die for them. But just because our sins are covered by His blood does not mean we do not have to take God seriously (Rom. 6:1-2).

He reveals His wrath through the Bible by showing us His frustration with the Israelites. We are left today with an understanding of how God justly deals with unrepentant sinners, giving us a greater appreciation for His grace.

—*Megan Hickman.*

World Missions

Joshua and Caleb brought good news; the other ten brought bad news—and God's people listened to the bad news.

We still do that. Our culture has fed us the lie that the gospel is intolerant, judgmental, and unpleasant. The very word "gospel" denies this. The word means "good news!"

But the gospel is not always met with joy. Some pay a high price to share it. But though the enemies that war against it are many, and though the task is hard, victory is assured. God was with the Israelites at the edge of the Promised Land, and He is with us.

The harvest is plentiful, but the laborers are few (Matt. 9:37)! There are people who are longing and praying for the gospel, desperate for hope, waiting for good news that will bring healing and life to their souls. Why are they still waiting when there are so many of us to take it to them?

Tribal men in the jungles have asked for missionaries to come teach their tribe about Jesus, but they are still waiting because there are simply not enough missionaries available.

Children on the streets, rejected by their own society as worthless, rush by the thousands to Bible clubs where they are shown a rare and wonderful love—the love of God. So many more would come if there were room.

There are women victimized into prostitution who would leave that life if they had a safe place to go. More pregnant teenagers would choose life over abortion if there were more traveling clinics with ultrasound machines to show them their living baby's heartbeat. There are nationals who desire to be trained to reach their own people, but there is no Bible school within a hundred miles of them.

So many are waiting for the good news.

Kim Phuc Phan Thi, the famous "napalm girl" from the Vietnam War, whose photo horrified the world, was only nine when bombs fell all around her home and village. As she and her siblings and relatives ran for their lives, she was burned severely by napalm, a torturous burn that disintegrated all her clothing as she ran. It continued to burn through all her layers of skin and into her muscle tissue. She has suffered for more than forty years.

Kim, though faithful to her family's religion, felt hopeless. She knew the gods she served so faithfully did not care about her. In terrible pain and used as a propaganda tool by the communists who took over her country, Kim frequently considered ending her life. She, like all the lost, was desperately in need of the good news.

She found it in Jesus Christ. As she says of her weeks of searching the Scriptures, "How I prayed those promises were true: Peace! And joy! Abundance and true life! If it really was so, that I could possess these things, I would surrender one *thousand* hearts to this Jesus, had I that many hearts to give" (*Fire Road: The Napalm Girl's Journey Through the Horrors of War to Faith, Forgiveness, and Peace*, Tyndale).

Let us begin to see the gospel for what it truly is, the good news that the world needs. Let us never be numbered with the ten faithless spies who turned a generation away from the Promised Land. Let us stand with Caleb and Joshua and lead others to the blessed saving inheritance that God wants for them in Jesus Christ.

—*Kimberly Rae.*

The Jewish Aspect

The Bible records that Joshua from the tribe of Ephraim and Caleb from the tribe of Judah were the only two spies who tried to convince the Israelites that God would deliver the land of Canaan to His people. Knowing this, Jews ask the question, What made these two men, Joshua and Caleb, different from the other Israelites?

Jewish rabbis write that Joshua, the main student of Moses, was special; they describe him as a man of character, a hero, a devoted student, a saintly man, and a great military commander. Jews recognize that God was with Joshua, as evidenced by the miracles that occurred surrounding him, such as when the walls of Jericho fell at his command or when the sun stood still (Kesselman, "Joshua of the Bible," chabad.org).

Jewish writers describe Caleb differently than Joshua. Unlike Joshua, they portray Caleb as an average guy. In fact, they see him as an ordinary human, who, when faced with an important decision, chose the path after God's heart (Klein, "Imagining the Scroll of Caleb," reformjudaism.org).

Caleb and Joshua followed God while the rest of their peers made terrible errors because they lacked faith in Him. Because of the Israelites' sins of grumbling, murmuring, complaining, and rebellion, none of them above the age of twenty (except for Caleb and Joshua) entered the Promised Land.

In trying to explain this period of sin, a modern rabbi writes that the Israelites' problem was a problem of "remembering" (Kushner, "The Way We Were: The Need to Get Remembering Right," reformjudaism.org). In the wilderness, instead of demonstrating gratefulness, the people forgot about the many times that God provided food, water, and safety. In Kushner's words, "They have failed to learn the lessons of the past."

There's an old joke in Israel that goes like this:

"So really, how was life back in Russia?" a Sabra [a native Israeli] asks a new immigrant, just arrived in Israel from the former Soviet Union.

"I couldn't complain," he answers.

"And how were your living quarters there?"

Again, the same answer: "I couldn't complain."

"And your standard of living?"

And again, "I couldn't complain."

"Well," responds the Israeli, "if everything was so good back in Russia, why did you bother coming here?"

"Oh," replies the new [immigrant], "here I *can* complain!"

("Daddy Are We There Yet?" reformjudaism.org)

Among other things this illustration reminds us that it is human nature to grumble and complain. Yet this week's Scripture lesson teaches the importance of fighting the urge to grumble but trusting God instead.

Joshua and Caleb were different from the other ten spies; they remembered the blessings of God and looked to Him to meet their needs. As Christians, we have a choice. We can live lives full of faith like Joshua and Caleb or be faithless like the other ten men. The story of Joshua and Caleb teaches that good things come to those who remain faithful to God and are grateful for His blessings.

—*Robin Fitzgerald.*

Guiding the Superintendent

The wages of sin is certainly death, as the people of Israel were very close to discovering for themselves yet again. At the end of the last lesson, we saw the people in an uproar over the bad report brought back by ten of their spies. The people were fearful of an uncertain future and had yet to learn the peace that comes from trusting the Lord. They were to make the same mistake of ingratitude and faithlessness again and again.

The people complained and wept while Caleb and Joshua stood before them, trying to save them from themselves, to no avail. The people threatened to answer this faithful duo by stoning them to death. These two men, out of all Israel, stood alone in maintaining confident faith in God and His promise to be with them.

DEVOTIONAL OUTLINE

1. The people continue to complain (Num. 14:1-4). It is important to notice their ingratitude. The people of Israel not only complained out of fear, but they even rejected all that God had done for them till then: "Would God that we had died in the land of Egypt!" They accused Moses and Aaron of bringing them to the edge of the Promised Land only to be slaughtered. They even went so far as to seriously propose choosing a new leader for themselves to take them back to Egypt!

2. Joshua and Caleb attempt to dissuade the people (Num. 14:5-10). Moses and Aaron immediately fell on their faces to intercede for the people before God. They had seen this many times before, and they knew what sort of consequences the people's sin would provoke from the Lord. Meanwhile, Joshua and Caleb attempted to dissuade the people from their rebellious course. God always provides a witness to warn us away from our sins if we will hear it.

The two faithful men recounted the great riches and bounty that awaited in Canaan. They reminded the people of the strong arm of the Lord that was decidedly with them against the Canaanites. But as so often happened, the people did not listen to God's warnings. They relied on their own limited understanding and prepared to stone the two men who spoke for God.

3. God speaks (Num. 14:11-12). The response to the Lord is both tragic and familiar. Even after all He had done for them and all the miracles they had witnessed from Him, the people still did not trust in Him. They had seen His glory in the Shekinah cloud and pillar of fire, yet they did not believe. They had heard His voice from the tabernacle, and still they did not believe. God's anger at their disobedience provoked Him to condemn Israel, saying He would create a new, mightier nation from the descendants of Moses.

CHILDREN'S CORNER

The people of Israel had again failed to trust in the Lord. Caleb and Joshua tried to encourage the people to trust in the Lord and not rebel against His will, but they would not listen. Instead, they desired to stone Caleb and Joshua to death, just for being faithful to God! When a large group of people becomes fearful and discontented, they often resort to blaming and threatening anyone who does not agree with them. Christians must never join with such a mob. They must remain separate and faithful to the Lord.

—Mike Spencer.

SCRIPTURE LESSON TEXT

NUM. 14:13 And Moses said unto the LORD, Then the Egyptians shall hear *it,* (for thou broughtest up this people in thy might from among them;)

14 And they will tell *it* to the inhabitants of this land: *for* they have heard that thou LORD *art* among this people, that thou LORD art seen face to face, and *that* thy cloud standeth over them, and *that* thou goest before them, by day time in a pillar of a cloud, and in a pillar of fire by night.

15 Now *if* thou shalt kill *all* this people as one man, then the nations which have heard the fame of thee will speak, saying,

16 Because the LORD was not able to bring this people into the land which he sware unto them, therefore he hath slain them in the wilderness.

17 And now, I beseech thee, let the power of my LORD be great, according as thou hast spoken, saying,

18 The LORD *is* longsuffering, and of great mercy, forgiving iniquity and transgression, and by no means clearing *the guilty,* vis-iting the iniquity of the fathers upon the children unto the third and fourth *generation.*

19 Pardon, I beseech thee, the iniquity of this people according unto the greatness of thy mercy, and as thou hast forgiven this people, from Egypt even until now.

20 And the LORD said, I have pardoned according to thy word:

21 But *as* truly *as* I live, all the earth shall be filled with the glory of the LORD.

22 Because all those men which have seen my glory, and my miracles, which I did in Egypt and in the wilderness, and have tempted me now these ten times, and have not hearkened to my voice;

23 Surely they shall not see the land which I sware unto their fathers, neither shall any of them that provoked me see it:

24 But my servant Caleb, because he had another spirit with him, and hath followed me fully, him will I bring into the land whereinto he went; and his seed shall possess it.

NOTES

Moses' Prayer and God's Answer

Lesson Text: Numbers 14:13-24

Related Scriptures: Nehemiah 9:16-21; Psalms 102:1-28;
145:8-13; John 12:37-40

TIME: about 1443 B.C.   PLACE: Kadesh

GOLDEN TEXT—"The Lord is longsuffering, and of great mercy, forgiving iniquity and transgression, and by no means clearing the guilty, visiting the iniquity of the fathers upon the children unto the third and fourth generation" (Numbers 14:18).

Introduction

Interceding for people who continually try to bring harm to you is a very difficult thing to do. However, it is one of the things that makes us, as Christians, different from the rest of the world. We are to forgive, love, serve, and pray for our enemies (cf. Matt. 5:43-48; Luke 6:27-28; Rom. 12:20).

Moses was a man who walked with the Lord and learned to trust Him completely. He had loved the children of Israel since his days as a prince in Pharaoh's palace when he killed an Egyptian who was abusing an Israelite slave (cf. Ex. 2:11-12). As Moses led the Isra-

elites, there were times when he grew frustrated with them and wondered why God chose him at all, but he never wavered in his love for the people.

Loving people who do not love us in return is not easy, but God will bless us for doing so.

LESSON OUTLINE

I. MOSES' GREAT REQUEST— Num. 14:13-19

II. GOD'S GREAT JUDGMENT— Num. 14:20-24

Exposition: Verse by Verse

MOSES' GREAT REQUEST

NUM. 14:13 And Moses said unto the LORD, Then the Egyptians shall hear it, (for thou broughtest up this people in thy might from among them;)

14 And they will tell it to the inhabitants of this land: for they have heard that thou LORD art among this people, that thou LORD art seen face to face, and that thy cloud standeth over them, and that thou goest before them, by day time in a pillar of a cloud, and in a pillar of fire by night.

15 Now if thou shalt kill all this people as one man, then the nations which have heard the fame of thee will speak, saying,

16 Because the LORD was not able to bring this people into the land which he sware unto them, therefore he hath slain them in the wilderness.

17 And now, I beseech thee, let the power of my LORD be great, according as thou hast spoken, saying,

18 The LORD is longsuffering, and of great mercy, forgiving iniquity and transgression, and by no means clearing the guilty, visiting the iniquity of the fathers upon the children unto the third and fourth generation.

19 Pardon, I beseech thee, the iniquity of this people according unto the greatness of thy mercy, and as thou hast forgiven this people, from Egypt even until now.

What will the Egyptians say? (Num. 14:13-14). Because they were afraid, the children of Israel rebelled against entering the Promised Land and decided to replace Moses with another leader, one who would take them back to Egypt (vs. 4). Witnessing this was no doubt a very painful and stressful experience for Moses, {yet when God tested him by offering to destroy the people and make a new and stronger nation out of Moses, the great leader pleaded on behalf of the very people who were rejecting his leadership.}Q1

Moses began his intercession for the Israelites by reminding God that if He destroyed these people He had previously delivered, news of it would eventually reach Egypt. The Egyptians, in turn, would tell the inhabitants of Canaan. These pagan people would not only gloat over Israel's destruction but would also have reason to impugn the character and power of the God of Israel; they would not fear Him.

When the Israelites were still slaves in Egypt, Pharaoh had shown no respect for the Lord. Because of Pharaoh's hard heart, God unleashed the ten plagues on Egypt, which eventually brought about Israel's deliverance from slavery. If God brought the Israelites out of Egypt only to kill them in the wilderness, His deliverance would be incomplete. The Egyptians might still see Israel's God as powerful, but not as omnipotent or trustworthy.

There was no mistaking God's presence with Israel after they left Egypt. He had led them with a pillar of cloud by day and a pillar of fire by night. God did not hide Himself from Israel or their enemies; His presence was very visible. If the Lord now destroyed the Israelites, Moses reasoned, then the other nations would not only gloat over Israel's annihilation but also deem God to be incapable of giving them victory. His majestic presence with Israel would have been meaningless.

What would the world say? (Num. 14:15-16). Moses certainly did not deny that God was able to destroy the Israelites as He was threatening. In fact, Moses knew God was able to wipe Israel out in one fell swoop if He so chose, which is why he pleaded so earnestly for them. The false conclusion that unbelieving nations would draw from God's destruction of the people is what concerned Moses.

{If God were to destroy the Israelites because of their unbelief, then the report of the ten spies would be echoed throughout Canaan. The various peoples would rejoice and say that the Lord was unable to bring Israel into Canaan and inhabit the land, even as the spies had said.}Q2 He may have brought them out of Egypt, but He was not able to bring them into Canaan. The very thing that angered God about the spies' report would be broadcast throughout the entire land.

Moses did not doubt God's power, and he did not want anyone else to doubt it either. He wanted other nations to know that there is only one God, not only over Israel, but also over the entire world. Moses feared that if God destroyed the nation He had created, it would leave a permanent blemish on His reputation among the very people He had planned to defeat on behalf of His people.

It is important to note that Moses never said the children of Israel were undeserving of punishment. He did not disagree with God that they were rebellious and insolent. The Israelites were guilty of everything God had charged them with, and Moses knew it. So he never tried to use Israel's goodness, innocence, or ignorance as reasons why God should not punish them. {Instead, the basis for Moses' plea for Israel was the Lord's promise to give them the land, a promise that would not be kept if He destroyed the nation of Israel.}Q3

What the Lord Himself has said (Num. 14:17-18). {Moses did not want the greatness of God's power questioned; instead, he wanted it put on display for all to see. He understood that the only way for the Lord to display such greatness and maintain His integrity was through forgiving Israel's sins.}Q4 Some might expect God to annihilate those who sinned against Him. This was certainly how ancient people expected their gods to behave. What would be entirely unexpected, however, was for God to forgive them.

Forgiveness always stands out from wrath. Outbursts of anger are often displayed by people who have been wronged by someone else. It is hardly newsworthy when an offended party displays anger toward those who have offended him. What is shocking, however, is when an injured person reaches out in reconciliation instead of retaliation.

It is not natural, but entirely divine, to forgive someone. It goes against our nature to do so. Yet that is exactly what Moses was calling on God to do for Israel. Moses was appealing to His loving nature that He Himself had proclaimed (vs. 17). God is not bound by human emotions. He does not act like a petulant child; He still loves sinners in spite of their sin.

God is not subject to irrational outbursts of anger as humans are. He does not have a short fuse as some are prone to have. God does not get angry easily, and it is certainly not the first thing He demonstrates to us when we sin. If it were, none of us would even exist right now!

{God had described Himself as "longsuffering," or slow to anger (vs. 18). He is very patient with us, merciful and forgiving.}Q5

The Lord's self-description is proof that God certainly was merciful and loving in Old Testament times; these truths are not merely New Testament inventions. Some people have tried to portray God as being only wrathful and angry in the Old Testament, which is a gross misrepresentation.

God is, and always has been, gracious. However, that does not mean that He winks at sin and pretends it does not exist. What grace means is that Christ, our Substitute, bore the punishment for our sin, and this propitiated (or satisfied) God's wrath against us and brings us salvation (cf. Rom. 3:24-25). Those who do not turn to the Lord in faith and receive His forgiveness and salvation, however, remain under God's just wrath (cf. John 3:36).

Sometimes sin becomes so entrenched in us that it becomes a "family thing." Children learn certain behaviors from their parents, who learned them from their parents, and so on and on. Thus, the punishment for sin keeps going on down the family line. God does not punish a child for what the parent does, but many times children grow up and perpetuate the sins of their parents and grandparents. Those who repent, however, are forgiven of their sins.

What Moses prayed (Num. 14:19). Moses was close enough with God that he could make what on its face seems like an audacious request. He asked the Lord to pardon the people for their sin. Moses was not merely asking God to overlook Israel's sin or simply trying to help them escape punishment. He was asking God to wipe the stain from their record. They would not be destroyed but would continue to be His people under His care.

When a person is pardoned for a crime, that person's record is wiped clean. All records of the offense are eliminated, and the person can never face the punishment that is demanded by that crime. That is precisely what Moses was asking for on behalf of the Israelites.

{The basis for this plea, again, was the greatness of God's mercy, not the people's supposed goodness.}[Q6] Moses also turned to past precedent set by God, as He had already forgiven the Israelites a number of times for offenses they had committed in their journey toward Canaan. Instead of throwing up his hands in exasperation over the Israelites, Moses continued to intercede for them according to the mercy the Lord had already shown.

GOD'S GREAT JUDGMENT

20 And the Lord said, I have pardoned according to thy word:

21 But as truly as I live, all the earth shall be filled with the glory of the Lord.

22 Because all those men which have seen my glory, and my miracles, which I did in Egypt and in the wilderness, and have tempted me now these ten times, and have not hearkened to my voice;

23 Surely they shall not see the land which I sware unto their fathers, neither shall any of them that provoked me see it:

24 But my servant Caleb, because he had another spirit with him, and hath followed me fully, him will I bring into the land whereinto he went; and his seed shall possess it.

Pardon for Israel (Num. 14:20). God responded to Moses by granting his request. He affirmed that He had pardoned Israel just as Moses had asked Him to do. He would not destroy Israel as He had previously said, but He would continue to lead, guide, and protect them through the wilderness into the land He had promised to them long before, going back even to Abraham (cf. Gen. 12:1-3; 13:14-17; 15:13-16).

Punishment for the rebels (Num. 14:21-23). {The fact that God had answered Moses' prayer did not mean there would be no consequences whatsoever for Israel's rebellion.}[Q7] We should never presume that God's grace means that we are not disciplined for the sins we commit. God would not be loving if He allowed us to continue in sin completely undeterred. If He did, we would not be people who loved Him; we would end up as spoiled brats who never learned to love and serve anyone other than ourselves. The Lord disciplines those whom He loves (Heb. 12:6).

God announced to Moses that His glory would still be displayed throughout the earth. This would come both through His forgiveness and through the judgment He would bring. He would pardon the iniquity of the people, but His name would still be revered by all.

Although God would not extinguish the entire nation, He would hold the rebels accountable for their unbelief. {Those who had witnessed God's mighty hand of deliverance only to test Him over and over again would not see the Promised Land at all.}[Q8] Those who despised the Lord instead of trusting and obeying Him would never see it.

Verse 29 elaborates on this judgment, explaining that all those twenty years old and above would die in the wilderness without entering the land. It was the end of the line for a generation that refused to take God at His word and trust Him in the midst of their trials.

An exemption from the penalty (Num. 14:24). {When the ten spies were giving their negative report and discouraging the Israelites from any hope of taking possession of the land, Caleb went against popular opinion and the majority report. Although the people did not want to hear it, he spoke in accordance with God's promise and declared that they were able to take the land in spite of the presence of the giants that were there (13:30; 14:6-9).}Q9

Even though the people refused to hear Caleb's voice, the Lord heard him loud and clear. God always hears the voice of faith. The voice of faith rings loudly above the voice of unbelief in the ears of God, and He always honors faith.

{Since Caleb was willing to speak up for God, God spoke up for him and exempted him from the punishment due that generation of Israelites. Joshua would not suffer that judgment either, because he had stood with Caleb against the tide of unbelief and negativity (cf. vs. 30).}Q10 These two men were not spared from punishment because they were sinless but because they were faithful.

God identified Caleb as His servant and said that he possessed a different spirit than the other spies did. This shows that Caleb had a close walk with God, as the title "my servant" had been applied only to Moses up to this point in Numbers (12:7-8).

A true servant of God is one who follows Him no matter where He leads and is known by his faith and love for God. That is an apt description of Ca-

leb, who never wavered in his faith. At a time when the people were contemplating killing Caleb (13:10), the Lord recognized his faith and courage and commended him to Moses.

When you stand firm in your faith in the midst of trying times, you can be almost certain the world is not going to give you a prize or reward you for your faith and determination. In fact, the world is likely to despise, ridicule, and even threaten you over your stance.

God, however, rewards those who stand firm in their faith (cf. Luke 6:22-23; Jas. 1:12; I Pet. 1:6-7). Those who turn away from Him in unbelief will find themselves on the outside looking in on a land of blessing.

—*Robert Ferguson, Jr.*

QUESTIONS

1. How did Moses respond to God's offer to destroy the Israelites and start a new nation with him?
2. What did Moses argue that the pagan peoples would conclude if God destroyed Israel?
3. How would destroying the nation contradict God's own promise?
4. How did Moses want God to display His great power?
5. To what did Moses appeal in the Lord's description of Himself?
6. On what basis did Moses appeal to God to pardon the people?
7. What does being pardoned for sin not mean?
8. What judgment did the Lord pronounce on the rebels?
9. How had Caleb demonstrated his faithfulness to the Lord?
10. What two people were exempted from God's judgment?

—*Robert Ferguson, Jr.*

Preparing to Teach the Lesson

As we continue our study in the book of Numbers, we move from the people's rebellion in Numbers 14:1-12 to Moses' prayer and God's answer in verses 13-24.

In our lesson text today, we will peer through a very unique window into a prayerful conversation between Moses, the man of God, and the Lord Himself! In this dialog, we will encounter a man pleading for a rebellious people to a God who seems altogether fed up with those people. In this narrative we will also see the power of prayer on display as Moses pleads for a guilty people and the Lord turns aside from a just posture that called for their complete destruction.

It is truly a shame that Israel had gotten to this point. Their spiritual condition was not good. Their doubt and faithlessness and rebellion had been displayed over and over again. They simply were not taking God seriously.

TODAY'S AIM

Facts: to illustrate that God hears and responds to the sincere prayers of His faithful servants.

Principle: to reaffirm the power of prayer in changing circumstances, regardless of how dire the situations may seem to be.

Application: to establish a consistent prayer life that demonstrates complete trust in and dependence on the Lord.

INTRODUCING THE LESSON

The Pentateuch offers many portraits of God's character worthy of our consideration. The Bible begins in Genesis 1—2 with an extended display of God as Creator. As God dealt with humanity through Noah and then the patriarchs, we see God as Promiser. As we move into the book of Exodus, the early chapters show us God as Planner; and as the Exodus is actualized, God is seen as Protector and Saviour. Through Israel's journeys through the wilderness in Exodus and Numbers, we see God as Provider. But here in Numbers 14:13-24, we see a different side of God, a more personal side of the divine personality; we see the God of emotion.

The Lord is more than the divine Judge and more than the wise Creator. He cares about righteousness and His name. Along with being loving and merciful and holy, the Lord at times is described as becoming angry. Numbers 14:13-24 is a depiction of both the wrathful potential in God and the merciful, compassionate disposition He holds equally as firmly. This passage displays both the holiness and the love in God's character that only He can possess.

DEVELOPING THE LESSON

Numbers 14:13-24 is preceded by a number of very disappointing episodes in the history of Israel. In our study, we have seen how the people complained about God's provision of manna. Moses himself was discouraged about having to deal with these people, and Miriam and Aaron rebelled against Moses' leadership. Finally, when the spies reported that the land was impossible to conquer, the people chose to rebel against Moses and Aaron and Joshua and Caleb (vss. 1-12).

With this most recent failure of the congregation of Israel, the situation seemed to reach a tipping point from the divine perspective. The Lord said He was ready and prepared to move on from Israel completely. When added to the other discouraging instances just cited, the Lord had seemingly had enough. He said He would totally destroy Israel and build a new nation from Moses and his family.

1. Moses' intercession (Num. 14:13-19). With the Lord as angry as He was with Israel, their demise seemed all but accomplished. Yet in a strange twist, Moses, the man who had just recently complained about being burdened with these rebellious people (11:10-15), now pleaded vigorously to the Lord on behalf of them. Whether Moses saw God's offer as a test or not, that is exactly what it was. Moses saw the problem with the Lord destroying the people He had promised to take into the Promised Land, and He spoke to Him about it.

First, Moses argued that the Lord's reputation would be tarnished if He destroyed His people now (14:13-16). Egypt and the peoples of Canaan would say the Lord was unable to bring His people into the land and thus had not kept His promise. Second, he argued that the Lord's relenting and pardoning His people would be a great demonstration of His divine power and character (vss. 17-19).

2. The Lord's response (Num. 14:20-24). Moses' arguments worked! In response to Moses, the Lord vowed not to destroy all His people. In order to uphold His righteous standards, however, the Lord declared that none of the adult population who had seen His miracles and deliverance from Egypt would live to enter the Promised Land (cf. vss. 28-35). Only their descendants would possess that land.

There were exceptions to this judgment, however. The Lord said Caleb would enter the land to possess it because he had "another spirit" (vs. 24). He had urged the people to follow the Lord and take the land to possess it. Later, the Lord stated that Joshua was also an exception. He too would enter the Land of Promise (vs. 30).

ILLUSTRATING THE LESSON

Moses' prayer for His people diverted the immediate and devastating judgment of God on them and brought pardon. While Moses' situation was unique, his actions demonstrate the amazing power of prayer that faithful believers possess.

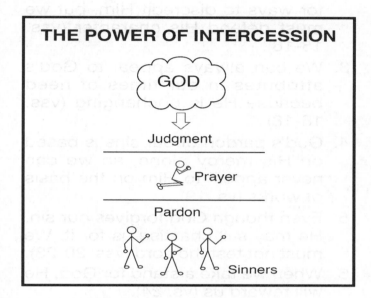

THE POWER OF INTERCESSION

GOD

Judgment

Prayer

Pardon

Sinners

CONCLUDING THE LESSON

The rebellion of the people in Numbers 14 seemed like the end of the line for God's people. But what we see is the amazing grace of God on full display. This is what Moses' prayer and God's answer was all about. The pleading of Moses was the means of moving the Lord to relent of His righteous anger. In the Lord's turning from His wrath, He showed Himself to be gracious beyond human comprehension once again (cf. Neh. 9:16-17).

ANTICIPATING THE NEXT LESSON

The rebellion of the people in Numbers 14 culminated in pressing the Lord to nearly destroy them. As we continue our studies, we will see that, unfortunately, the people's unfaithfulness persisted, as demonstrated by Korah's rebellion in Numbers 16:1-14.

—Nigel C. Black.

PRACTICAL POINTS

1. Because we declare ourselves Christians, our reputation is tied to God's; we must be careful not to defame His name (Num. 14:13-14).
2. God's enemies are always looking for ways to discredit Him, but we must defend His character (vss. 15-16).
3. We can always appeal to God's attributes in our times of need because He is unchanging (vss. 16-18).
4. God's pardon of our sins is based on His mercy alone, so we can never appeal to Him on the basis of works (vs. 19).
5. Even though God forgives our sin, He may still chastise us for it. We must not test the Lord (vss. 20-23).
6. When we take a stand for God, He will reward us (vs. 24).

—*Megan Hickman.*

RESEARCH AND DISCUSSION

1. How can a Christian's success glorify God? How can a Christian's failure glorify God?
2. How is it comforting to know that the Lord is faithful to all His promises?
3. What is the role of intercessory prayer in the Christian life?
4. Why is it so necessary to remember and rehearse God's attributes in our own prayers?
5. We often miss out on blessing when we are disobedient to God. How can this truth transform our attitudes about obedience?

—*Megan Hickman.*

ILLUSTRATED HIGH POINTS

Greatness of thy mercy (Num. 14:19)

Judges wield great power. They set bail amounts and determine a convicted person's sentence. Judges often show mercy to people who are first offenders or have endured significant hardship. They have no obligation to show such mercy, but they often choose to do so.

A short video on the internet, which has gone viral, shows a judge displaying such mercy toward a man on trial for a reckless driving charge. The man could have been imprisoned for up to three months, but the judge took into account that he had no prior traffic offenses and instead gave him a warning and a small fine. The man was so grateful that he burst into tears at the judge's decision. He was the breadwinner of his family and had a wife and two young children to care for.

The Lord constantly showed mercy toward his people, even though they did not deserve it. The Israelites were repeatedly disrespectful to God, yet He still showed them mercy.

Shall not see the land (vs. 23)

Illegal immigration is a controversial topic. Whatever views one might take on the issue, there is no denying the difficulties and hardships involved for all concerned. The opportunity to live in America is greatly desired by many.

The situation in Numbers is in many ways, of course, not analogous, but the one common denominator is the prospect of a prosperous land. An entire generation of Israelites was not allowed to enter the Promised Land, and they wandered until they died in the wilderness. Let us not shrink back from trusting the Lord's power and provision on our behalf or we might forfeit His blessings.

—*Chelsea Villaseñor.*

Golden Text Illuminated

"The Lord is longsuffering, and of great mercy, forgiving iniquity and transgression, and by no means clearing the guilty, visiting the iniquity of the fathers upon the children unto the third and fourth generation" (Numbers 14:18).

In our golden text for this week, Moses quotes the Lord's own words concerning Himself from Exodus 34:6-7. Moses is pleading for the Lord to show mercy toward the rebellious Israelites.

He calls Yahweh's attention to the fact that if He were to destroy the Israelites here and now, as He threatened to do in verse 12, the Egyptians and the Canaanites would hear of it and interpret it as a demonstration of Yahweh's powerlessness to deliver on His promises. They would say that He not only failed the Israelites, but also the patriarchs, Abraham, Isaac, and Jacob.

Moses urges the Lord instead to continue to forgive and restore the people, though they do not deserve it, just as He has done all along since bringing them up out of Egypt.

The Lord agrees to grant Moses' request, but He nevertheless punishes the current generation for their faithlessness and rebellion by denying them entrance into the Promised Land. Along with Joshua, only Caleb, who has remained faithful to the Lord, would be allowed to enter into the Promised Land. He would claim the region of Hebron for himself and his descendants.

It may seem strange to some that Moses would need to remind the Lord about His promises to the patriarchs and His reputation of forgiveness and longsuffering. Perhaps the Lord was merely testing Moses' faith, as He did when He commanded Abraham to sacrifice Isaac. Here the Lord offers Moses the honored position of becoming the patriarch of an entirely new nation of chosen people made exclusively of his own descendants.

But Moses' unfailing faithfulness will not allow him to take advantage of such a proposition. He knows that to do so would have been selfish and a blatant dishonoring of the memories of Abraham, Isaac, Jacob, and Joseph, not to mention the millions of Hebrews who toiled under oppression and bondage for four hundred years, waiting for their deliverance and the fulfillment of God's promises.

So Moses passes the test, and rather than being a replacement patriarch, he becomes so much more. Within the memory of God's people of faith, no other name is remembered with more honor than Moses except for the Lord Jesus Christ Himself.

This is because no other man of God so exemplified personal meekness and humility before God. At the same time, no other figure of faith was ever used by God to accomplish such astounding and powerful miracles on behalf of God's people. By eschewing personal promotion, Moses has become our prime example of one who, although he consistently humbled himself, became exalted by the grace and power of God. In this he foreshadowed the ultimate example of humility, our Lord Jesus Christ Himself (cf. Phil. 2:5-11).

As Paul exhorted those Philippians, so let us be encouraged today. "Let this mind be in you, which was also in Christ Jesus" (vs. 5). Humble yourself today, that God may graciously exalt you!

—*John Lody.*

Heart of the Lesson

Do you ever just rejoice in the fact that God's faithfulness is based on His own character? There are people who live in fear because they think that the security of their salvation rests on their own works. But if the fulfillment of God's promises were based on our performance, even the most righteous man would not be safe (cf. Rom. 3:23).

God's holiness is a serious matter. He cannot compromise it. It is only through His promise of salvation through faith in Jesus Christ that we are spared His wrath.

Moses appeals to God's reputation (Num. 14:13-16). Moses knew God better than anyone. So he responded with fear when the Israelites rebelled. It is interesting to note that whenever Moses approaches the Lord for the Israelites, he never defends the people's actions. Instead, he always appeals to God and His reputation.

God is totally wise and never forgets. So why did Moses feel the need to remind Him to protect His reputation? God does not need to be convinced to do what is most glorifying to Him. By appealing to Him in this way, Moses simply showed his heart for the Lord's glory and reputation. Why God challenged Moses like this is a bit of a mystery, but Moses' response honored the Lord.

Confessing God's marvelous works on your behalf is glorifying to Him. When we remind ourselves of these things, our hearts are humbled before Him. God had charged Moses to care for the people of Israel and deliver them to the Promised Land, and Moses trusted that God would fulfill this promise.

Moses' appeals to God's glory (Num. 14:17-19). Moses used the description of God's glory to beseech the Lord. He called on God's power, mercy, and forgiveness, which are all attributes that God Himself emphasized to His people. Basically, Moses immersed himself in worshipping the Lord.

The more we know about God, the better we will be able to worship Him. We can remain spiritually stagnant, satisfied with knowing God's goodness and mercy in a superficial way, or we can explore the "exceeding riches of his grace" (Eph. 2:7) and the "breadth, and length, and depth, and height" of His love (3:18). It seems like a strange concept, but the more egregious the sins of the Israelites were, the deeper Moses understood God because he was able to see that the Lord was truly faithful and merciful to an undeserving people.

God responds for His glory (Num. 14:20-24). The Lord responded to Moses' worship and pardoned the Israelites. However, the people did not go completely unpunished. God declared that the earth would be filled with His glory, but except for Caleb and Joshua, it would not be through this generation of Israelites. Those who had provoked the Lord would not see the Promised Land.

This is a stark reminder that there can be severe earthly consequences for our sins. If we refuse to carry out God's revealed will, we forfeit His blessing. The consequences may not be as obvious as they were for the Israelites, and we may never know what we miss out on, but we must trust that God's plan for our lives is better than anything we could execute ourselves.

The Lord performs everything for His own glory, but anything that He does for His glory He also does for our good. The sooner we make His glory our greatest desire, the sooner we can rejoice in Him.

—Megan Hickman.

World Missions

In a prison in the Philippines lives a man who might never be set free. He was a mafia assassin, and high-ranking people want to make sure he stays where he is.

Yet God can turn the worst things into good, for this man, Red, belongs to the Lord now. Red took a Bible lesson, and he trusted in Christ. He did Bible courses, then he taught the courses to other prisoners, and then he built a church—literally! He constructed it right inside the prison! Now he is reaching lost prisoners with the gospel and training believers for service to God.

Not long ago, Red held a Vacation Bible School at his church, and over two hundred children accepted Christ through its ministry! What kind of children come to a VBS held in a prison? One can only assume they were prisoners' children—some of the most at-risk children for future criminal activity.

Red has transformed his legacy completely. Instead of passing on his evils to others, he is now building a legacy of faith. God indeed heard this prisoner's cry and loosed him from death to life (Ps. 102:20).

Each of us is busy every day, building our own stories, whether stories of faithfulness or of disobedience. What examples will we leave behind for future generations to follow? Will our lives be testimonies to God's great justice, mercy, and love? Or will we strive for merely temporal success, show apathy toward the lost, or perhaps even model outright sinfulness? What we choose has longlasting consequences to those who are watching and will follow our examples.

There is much need for God's goodness to be manifested in our world through His servants, seen in the statistics of how many still have never heard Christ's gospel and how few are serving Him so that they can hear it.

MISSIONARIES PER RELIGION:

Tribals—714,108,000 population with 11,900 missionaries: 1 for every 60,000

Hindus—984,532,000 population with 5,500 missionaries: 1 for every 179,000

Unreligious—831,267,000 population with 11,700 missionaries: 1 for every 71,000

Muslims—1,703,146,000 population with 4,200 missionaries: 1 for every 405,500

Buddhists—520,002,000 population with 2,000 missionaries: 1 for every 260,000

According to one source, "You have a better chance of being in a plane crash than being one of the few missionaries to the unreached out of the total 2 billion Christians in the world.

"The current status quo is to do virtually nothing to reach the [Unreached People Groups] of the world. The percentages of man-power and money focused on UPGs are almost undetectable they are so small. The amount of resources that fall off the Christian table for unreached peoples is more comparable . . . with the number of skin cells you lose over a month's time: something hardly worth calling a sacrifice of the body" ("Missions Stats," thetravelingteam.org).

How God must grieve to see so many Christians, who have the true message of salvation, comfortable with just keeping it to themselves.

Let us follow the example of a former assassin who is now a missionary and create a legacy we can proudly pass on to all who will follow.

—Kimberly Rae.

The Jewish Aspect

Beginning before Rosh Hashana and continuing through Yom Kippur, Jews say *slichot*, a special set of prayers. Jews believe that after the sin with the golden calf, Moses asked God to explain His system for relating with the world. They state that His answer forms the essence of the Slichot prayers and is known as the Thirteen Attributes of Mercy (Berkovits, "Slichot and the 13 Attributes," aish.com).

In this week's Scripture lesson, Moses pleads to God for the people. The Bible tells us that following the ten spies' faithless report, the children of Israel raised their voices and murmured against Moses and Aaron.

Responding to the people's sin, God asked Moses how long the people would provoke Him. He then declared that He would punish them with pestilence and disinherit them (Num. 14:12).

Moses, as a good leader, begged that God would be merciful toward His nation. Jews believe that during this exchange, Moses invoked the Thirteen Attributes of Mercy to convince God to spare Israel (Posner, "The Twelve Spies (Meraglim) in the Bible," chabad.org).

As noted above, Jewish tradition states that God gave Moses the Thirteen Attributes of Mercy during the Israelites' episode of sin before the golden calf in the wilderness. Further, they believe the Thirteen Attributes brought salvation and forgiveness to the Jewish people for many generations.

For the Jew, the number 13 is significant. Thirteen signifies the infinite. Since there are thirteen attributes of mercy, the Jew believes that when God shows mercy, He does so without limit (Schochet, "What Are the 13 Attributes of Mercy?" chabad.org).

Although they might vary slightly, most of the lists of the thirteen attributes are very similar. Jewish mystical teaching states that the first attribute of God's mercy is that He is mighty in compassion to all creatures according to their need.

Attribute number two states that God is merciful, so that men need not be distressed. Number three declares that He is gracious with humans already in distress. Attribute four states that He is slow to anger. Jews repeat this attribute again as attribute number five, believing that the wicked might need to hear it particularly for them.

Attributes six through eight state that God is plenteous in kindness and truth. Attribute nine states that this is true "unto thousands." Attributes ten through twelve state that He forgives iniquity, transgression, and sin. The last attribute, number thirteen, states that He pardons sin (Schochet).

As mentioned earlier, Jews consider the number thirteen important to the Jewish faith. It is at the age of thirteen that a Jewish boy becomes a son of the covenant (bar mitzvah) and must begin to keep the laws of the Torah.

Many, however, consider the Thirteen Attributes of Mercy the most significant of the thirteens that appear in Judaism. It is for that reason that the Jew recites the attributes of mercy many times during the Hebrew month of Elul (August-September) and especially on the Day of Atonement.

As Christians, we understand that God is merciful. But it is important for us to consider all the different ways in which God is merciful to us. His ultimate demonstration of mercy for mankind was when He sent Jesus to the earth to die for us even though we were undeserving. Jesus perfectly embodied the Thirteen Attributes of Mercy.

—Robin Fitzgerald.

Guiding the Superintendent

In this lesson, we see the cause-and-effect nature of sin and how much we truly need a redeemer to save us from this vicious cycle.

The Lord had delivered the Israelites miraculously from the hands of the Egyptians. He had saved them by miraculously parting a large sea! The Lord had spoken to them from the Shekinah glory pillar of fire and cloud. He had traveled with them daily and had provided miraculous food from heaven to sustain them on their journey. After all this, their fear and lusts caused them to sin greatly against the Lord and turned them from trusting in Him. They rejected the Lord, and therefore they were rejected by Him.

Our studies thus far have shown us the cyclical nature not only of the sin of the Israelites but of our own sin as well. We sin, suffer consequences, beg for mercy, get reprieved, and then sin again. Thank God we have a Saviour in Jesus Christ who has redeemed us from this wicked cycle of death (cf. Rom. 7:24-25)!

DEVOTIONAL OUTLINE

1. Intercession (Num. 14:13-19). Moses sought to intercede with the Lord to turn away His wrath against the people. Even if the Lord were to start a new nation from the descendants of Moses, the destruction of the entire Israelite people would detract from His reputation among the nations. Moses' plea focused on the fact that if the Lord did such a thing, then Egypt and all the surrounding nations would conclude that He had failed in His purpose of bringing His people into the land He had promised to them.

Moses' prayer, and God's acceptance of it, raises a question about the power of prayer itself. Does prayer have the power to change God's mind? Of course not, since God does not change His mind (cf. 23:19). In what way, then, did Moses' prayer impact God's intentions? God's sovereign plans do not change because of our prayers, but He does use our prayers in bringing about His plans.

2. Pardon, but penalty (Num. 14:20-24). Moses' requested pardon for God's wicked people. God granted Moses' request; He would not simply "kill all this people as one man" (vs. 15); nevertheless, He would exact the death penalty upon them in a different way. God solemnly vowed, "As truly as I live, all the earth shall be filled with the glory of the Lord" (vs. 21). In other words, nothing that humans can do will ever detract from God's glory being magnified throughout the world.

God's alternative sentence was that none of the original generation of the Exodus would be allowed to enter the Promised Land. That generation would wander in the desert until they all died. Only those two who had remained faithful to the Lord—Caleb and Joshua—would enter the land.

CHILDREN'S CORNER

Moses is a good example of someone who always placed God's glory and the welfare of those he served above his own interests. God had offered to reinvent His chosen nation, using only Moses' family. For many people, that might have been an attractive offer. Moses too was weary from the people's constant complaining. But he was horrified by the thought that all Israel might be destroyed. He also feared what it would to do God's reputation among the nations. So he pleaded with God and put his people first.

—*Mike Spencer.*

SCRIPTURE LESSON TEXT

NUM. 16:1 Now Korah, the son of Izhar, the son of Kohath, the son of Levi, and Dathan and Abiram, the sons of Eliab, and On, the son of Peleth, sons of Reuben, took *men:*

2 And they rose up before Moses, with certain of the children of Israel, two hundred and fifty princes of the assembly, famous in the congregation, men of renown:

3 And they gathered themselves together against Moses and against Aaron, and said unto them, *Ye take* too much upon you, seeing all the congregation *are* holy, every one of them, and the LORD *is* among them: wherefore then lift ye up yourselves above the congregation of the LORD?

4 And when Moses heard *it,* he fell upon his face:

5 And he spake unto Korah and unto all his company, saying, Even to morrow the LORD will shew who *are* his, and *who is* holy; and will cause *him* to come near unto him: even *him* whom he hath chosen will he cause to come near unto him.

6 This do; Take you censers, Korah, and all his company;

7 And put fire therein, and put incense in them before the LORD to morrow: and it shall be *that* the man whom the LORD doth choose, he *shall be* holy: *ye take* too much upon you, ye sons of Levi.

8 And Moses said unto Korah, Hear, I pray you, ye sons of Levi:

9 *Seemeth it but* a small thing unto you, that the God of Israel hath separated you from the congregation of Israel, to bring you near to himself to do the service of the tabernacle of the LORD, and to stand before the congregation to minister unto them?

10 And he hath brought thee near *to him,* and all thy brethren the sons of Levi with thee: and seek ye the priesthood also?

11 For which cause *both* thou and all thy company *are* gathered together against the LORD: and what *is* Aaron, that ye murmur against him?

12 And Moses sent to call Dathan and Abiram, the sons of Eliab: which said, We will not come up:

13 *Is it* a small thing that thou hast brought us up out of a land that floweth with milk and honey, to kill us in the wilderness, except thou make thyself altogether a prince over us?

14 Moreover thou hast not brought us into a land that floweth with milk and honey, or given us inheritance of fields and vineyards: wilt thou put out the eyes of these men? we will not come up.

NOTES

Korah's Rebellion

Lesson Text: Numbers 16:1-14

Related Scriptures: Deuteronomy 11:1-7; Psalm 106:16-18

TIME: about 1443 B.C.   PLACE: Desert of Paran

GOLDEN TEXT—"Therefore thou shalt love the Lord thy God, and keep his charge, and his statutes, and his judgments, and his commandments, alway" (Deuteronomy 11:1).

Introduction

Sometimes it seems that we never learn from our mistakes—or the mistakes of others. It is bad enough to sin against God, but it is far worse to repeatedly sin against Him in the same manner. Those who do so are only inviting the wrath of God on themselves.

If we want to experience the blessings of God, we must stop any pattern of disobedience, rebellion, and unbelief that may be present in our lives.

Wise people will learn from their failures and seek God's help to not repeat them. While it is not possible to live totally sin-free lives, we can be faithfully obedient, loving, and thankful to our Lord for all He has done for us.

Apparently, the children of Israel had a hard time learning from their sins and appreciating the graciousness of God. We would be wise to learn from their mistakes so that we do not repeat them ourselves.

LESSON OUTLINE

I. KORAH REBELS AGAINST MOSES—Num. 16:1-3

II. MOSES CONFRONTS THE REBELS—Num. 16:4-11

III. THE REBELS ACCUSE MOSES—Num. 16:12-14

Exposition: Verse by Verse

KORAH REBELS AGAINST MOSES

NUM. 16:1 Now Korah, the son of Izhar, the son of Kohath, the son of Levi, and Dathan and Abiram, the sons of Eliab, and On, the son of Peleth, sons of Reuben, took men:

2 And they rose up before Moses, with certain of the children of Israel, two hundred and fifty princes of the assembly, famous in the congregation, men of renown:

3 And they gathered themselves together against Moses and against Aaron, and said unto them, Ye take too much upon you, seeing all the congregation are holy, every one of them, and the LORD is among them: wherefore then lift ye up yourselves above the congregation of the LORD?

The rebels assemble together (Num. 16:1-2). Unfounded resentment against Moses and Aaron continued, and in this week's lesson we see a new group of insurrectionists rising up against God's appointed leaders over Israel. Insubordination was a very real problem for the Israelites after they left Egypt, as the former slaves were not content or satisfied with God's direction in spite of His faithful protection and provision for them as they wandered through a foreign wilderness.

{The leader of this latest insurrection was a man named Korah, a Levite who was the grandson of Kohath.}[Q1] Kohath and his children had been chosen by God for the special service of transporting and caring for the tabernacle and its furnishings (Num. 4:1-20). Although not a priest, Korah was a noted leader among the Levites.

{Allied with Korah were Dathan, Abiram, and On, all of whom were Reubenites, descendants of Jacob's eldest son, Reuben.}[Q1] {Since the Reubenites and Kohathites both camped close together on the southside of the camp (2:10; 3:29), it is easy to see how men from these two groups would have conversed and conspired together.}[Q2]

Together, these men assembled a group of 250 others to join them in their rebellion. They were not just a random collection of men from the people; they were all respected chiefs and leaders who were well known among the people.

Charges made against Moses and Aaron (Num. 16:3). After gathering his collection of rebellious cohorts together, Korah and his fellow insurgents angrily approached Moses and Aaron to protest their leadership. The people apparently had been growing increasingly restless ever since the ten spies came back with their negative report. Although God pun-

ished the spies with a plague that cost them their lives (14:37) and pronounced judgment on the entire adult population, declaring that they would not personally enter the Promised Land (vss. 29-35), it was now clear there were still many Israelites who felt no loyalty to Moses or Aaron—or to God, for that matter.

{This large coalition led by Korah accused Moses and Aaron of going too far in exerting their authority over the people.}[Q3] At the heart of their protest was that all the people were holy, not just Moses and Aaron. As far as the rebels were concerned, they had just as much right to leadership as Moses and Aaron because they, too, were set apart to God.

Since the Lord was among all of the Israelites, Korah and his supporters asserted that Moses and Aaron were no different or better than anyone else. While it is true that God chose Israel to be a holy nation, set apart to Him (Ex. 19:6), personal holiness in their actions and attitudes was, in large measure, sadly lacking.

The rebels then charged Moses and Aaron with appointing themselves as Israel's leaders. Yet God had repeatedly affirmed Moses' leadership (cf. Ex. 4:1-5, 29-31; Num. 12). Moreover, the ordination of Aaron as high priest had taken place in the sight of all the people (Lev. 8); there should have been no question, therefore, as to the validity of his leadership.

While the Lord had a special plan for the Israelite nation as a whole, this did not negate His special calling on certain people. The Kohathites were divinely chosen specifically to transport and care for the tabernacle. That responsibility was a very prestigious calling. However, Korah was not content to do what God called him to do. He wanted a higher position, one that, undoubtedly, included the authority to tell other people what to do.

Perhaps at issue too was the people's lingering desire to choose a new leader to take them back to Egypt. Korah may have been stepping up to assume that role. In order to successfully take the people back, however, he had to replace Moses and Aaron. Together with his fellow insurrectionists, that is exactly what he set out to do.

MOSES CONFRONTS THE REBELS

6 This do; Take you censers, Korah, and all his company;

7 And put fire therein, and put incense in them before the LORD to morrow: and it shall be that the man whom the LORD doth choose, he shall be holy: ye take too much upon you, ye sons of Levi.

8 And Moses said unto Korah, Hear, I pray you, ye sons of Levi:

9 Seemeth it but a small thing unto you, that the God of Israel hath separated you from the congregation of Israel, to bring you near to himself to do the service of the tabernacle of the LORD, and to stand before the congregation to minister unto them?

10 And he hath brought thee near to him, and all thy brethren the sons of Levi with thee: and seek ye the priesthood also?

11 For which cause both thou and all thy company are gathered together against the LORD: and what is Aaron, that ye murmur against him?

Moses and Korah (Num. 16:4-5). {When Moses realized he was going to have to deal with yet another rebellion, he fell on his face in front of his accusers. This was not a position of weakness or surrender, but of grief and mourning. The people were constantly rebelling against Israel's leaders, and therefore against God Himself, and Moses knew this meant trouble for the guilty parties.}[Q4] The trouble they would bring on themselves would spill over into the entire camp if the problem was not effectively and quickly dealt with.

Staying true to his typical behavior when his authority was threatened, Moses did not defend himself but appealed to the Lord. {He did not get into a shouting match with Korah or the others; he simply stated that the Lord would make it known who His leaders were.}[Q5]

Moses had nothing to fear in this encounter because God had defended and vindicated him time and time again. There was no reason for him to get defensive against men he knew were rebelling against God's authority, not just his own. God would clear the matter up and again leave no doubt as to whom He had chosen to lead His people Israel.

Challenge to the challengers (Num. 16:6-7). Moses was a very humble man (cf. 12:3), yet he was confident that the Lord would defend him. {He instructed Korah and his entire company to take censers with fire in them and bring them before the Lord the very next morning.}[Q6]

Time was of the essence, for the insurrection could not be allowed to continue. The rebels either had to repent immediately or face God, but they would not be allowed to mount a further attack on the person or character of Moses. God would make it known once again whom He had chosen to lead Israel. There was no reason for any suspense leading up to this "showdown" because God had made it abundantly clear in the past who Israel's leaders were to be.

Moses stood firm against the challenge of Korah and his company as he returned the words they had used against him, telling them they had taken "too much" upon them—they had gone too far (vs. 7; cf. vs. 3). That is what they had accused Moses of doing, but he retorted that they in fact were the ones who had tried to grab too much for themselves. They were not satisfied with what God had for them. Korah was not content with the special role God had prepared him for. Instead, they sought the preeminent positions as Israel's political and religious leaders.

Reminder of privilege (Num. 16:8-9). Moses specifically called out the sons of Levi who had joined Korah in this rebellion. They were seeking power for themselves and the prestige that came along with it. They were not satisfied that God had already called them to a special sphere of service. Sadly, the great privilege they already enjoyed was not enough for them.

This type of attitude is also prevalent among modern-day Christians, much to the detriment of the church. Some are not content with the positions God has called them into and resent the spiritual authority that has been placed over them. Instead of simply and faithfully serving where God has placed them, they rebel against pastors, elders, and other leaders. This kind of behavior causes dissension within the body of Christ and leads to division, as it makes others feel forced to pledge allegiance to one side or the other.

Moses asked the sons of Levi if they considered it a trifling thing to have been singled out from the rest of the Israelites by God to serve the Lord in the tabernacle and to serve His people. They may not have held the most glamorous position conceivable, but it was still very significant. We should consider it an honor to do anything the Lord wants us to do. To desire only those positions that bring visibility and public acclaim is a sign of immaturity and selfishness. Some positions are obviously more visible than others, but the Lord determines who serves in what roles.

Charge of rebellion (Num. 16:10-11). Moses continued to question the Levites who were associates in the rebellion. {Now he reminded them that their appointed service had brought them near to God. They encamped near the tabernacle, and their service brought them into frequent contact with it. They were literally close to the earthly presence of God manifested in the tabernacle.}[Q7] Their privileged role should have been more than enough for them, but it was not.

Moses asked the challengers specifically why they were grumbling against Aaron. {These Levites apparently were upset that Aaron had been chosen from among all the Levites to be the high priest and that only his sons and future descendants could serve as priests.}[Q8] They were not satisfied with being servants of the Lord in the tabernacle; they had their eyes on the priesthood.

The rebels were not really grumbling against Israel's human leadership. Their complaint ultimately was against God. They did not like and did not approve of God's selection of Moses and particularly Aaron. Jealousy filled their hearts, leading them to oppose God's already clearly revealed will.

THE REBELS ACCUSE MOSES

12 And Moses sent to call Dathan and Abiram, the sons of Eliab: which said, We will not come up:

13 Is it a small thing that thou hast brought us up out of a land that floweth with milk and honey, to kill us in the wilderness, except thou make thyself altogether a prince over us?

14 Moreover thou hast not brought us into a land that floweth with milk and honey, or given us inheritance of fields and vineyards: wilt thou put out the eyes of these men? we will not come up.

Dathan and Abiram reject Moses (Num. 16:12). Dathan and his brother Abiram represented the Reubenite contingent in the rebel coalition. These two refused to come before Moses when called to do so. This shows that they were fully entrenched in their cause and had no respect for Moses' leadership or authority.

To flatly refuse the instructions of a God-ordained leader was the height of rebellion, as it showed disrespect not only to the leader but also to the One who appointed him.

Dathan and Abiram accuse Moses (Num. 16:13-14). The depravity in the hearts and minds of the two Reubenite brothers is further exemplified in their specific choice of words in describing Egypt. {They asserted that Moses had led them out of a land flowing with "milk and honey," which was exactly how God had described Canaan (cf. Ex. 3:8). Their use of this phrase to describe the place they had been delivered from was a deliberate insult and challenge to the Lord.}Q9

At no time during the long years of Hebrew slavery was Egypt ever considered a land flowing with milk and honey. For the Israelites, Egypt was a place of cruelty and bondage, not prosperity and opportunity.

{To further their case against him, Dathan and Abiram accused Moses of making himself a prince over the people of Israel. Their complaint was that Moses gloried in his authority and superior position.}Q10 They did not view him as a compassionate leader who loved them but as an opportunist who was trying to take advantage of a terrible situation and exploit them for his own benefit.

Dathan and Abiram continued their rant against Moses, next accusing him not only of bringing them out of a land flowing with milk and honey but also failing to bring them into a land that fit that description. Moses had not come through on what he had promised, and they considered that sufficient grounds on which to challenge him.

To make matters even worse, Dathan and Abiram then asserted that Moses wanted to "put out the eyes of these men" (Num. 16:14). While this may be a literal allusion to the people dying in the wilderness, it is probably a figure of speech, similar to when we speak of "pulling the wool" over someone's eyes. In this case, they clearly would have been accusing Moses of deceptive practice, blinding people to his failures and true motives.

Korah, Dathan, Abiram, On, and the other 250 men clearly had an agenda. They opposed Moses for personal reasons. They were not happy with his leadership, and they saw an opportunity for themselves to seize upon the dissatisfaction and fear of the people and wrestle leadership away from Moses and Aaron.

—Robert Ferguson, Jr.

QUESTIONS

1. Who was the leader of the rebellion against Moses, and who joined him?
2. What two tribes were involved in the rebellion against Moses and Aaron?
3. What did the rebels accuse Moses of doing?
4. Why did Moses fall on his face?
5. How did Moses respond to Korah's dispute about Israel's true leadership?
6. What did Moses tell Korah and his men to do the very next morning?
7. What privileges did Korah and the other Levites already enjoy?
8. What did the Levites have against Aaron, and what role were they seeking?
9. Why was Dathan and Abiram's description of Egypt a direct insult to the Lord?
10. Of what did Dathan and Abiram first accuse Moses?

—Robert Ferguson, Jr.

Preparing to Teach the Lesson

The events recorded in Numbers have just gotten worse and worse—from repeated complaints, to attacks on God's chosen leaders, to rebellion against God and His promises and plan. As a result, God had threatened to annihilate His people. As we come to Numbers 16, we might think things are finally going to get better. Perhaps Israel has been scared straight. Perhaps God's people will truly repent.

The narrative in Numbers 16, however, demonstrates no spiritual progress among the people. In fact, Korah's rebellion provides another new low in the history of Israel. It seems that all the discontentment and malicious motives of our earlier lessons in the book of Numbers find some level of culmination in Korah's rebellion.

TODAY'S AIM

Facts: to delve into a study of the depths of sinful propensity and examine its motives and methods.

Principle: to understand that rebellion against God's order is rebellion against the Lord Himself.

Application: to sharpen our discernment in recognizing and combating the spirit of rebellion against God and His kingdom so that our lives demonstrate a consistent desire to follow and obey God.

INTRODUCING THE LESSON

The Bible is a book that could never have been written solely by mere men; it is too condemning, too unflattering, and too unfiltered. The Bible does not speak to how good man is, and it does not go to great lengths to show man's potential for doing good. The Bible portrays man as inherently sinful and, more often than not, portrays man's negative potential.

Numbers 16 is one of many biblical passages that explores the depravity of man. Here we see men who had crossed the miraculously parted Red Sea and then watched the Egyptian army destroyed when the water collapsed upon them, but now they were committing treasonous acts as if there would be no consequences. Numbers 16 is a glimpse into sheer, unadulterated rebellion, a full dose of the negative potential found in the hearts of fallen people.

Again, the acts of Korah and his co-conspirators demonstrate that many in the camp of Israel still did not support Moses and Aaron. Indeed, there were those who supported only themselves and their own agendas, despite what God had done through Moses and Aaron in the past.

DEVELOPING THE LESSON

1. Korah's challenge (Num. 16:1-3). Korah's rebellion happened in the way that many rebellions have historically occurred—through the wicked confluence of selfish ambition and blatant disregard for proper authority. It is amazing how just a few bad people can become such a big problem. Verse 1 begins by indicating that Korah, along with Dathan, Abiram, and On, conspired together to lead some 250 other Israelite leaders in a hostile attempt to gain positions of authority for themselves and perhaps displace Moses and Aaron altogether.

While the precise motive for the rebellion is not exposed here, the passage initially indicates that Korah and his men argued that Moses and Aaron had selfishly consolidated their power for their own benefit. Korah stated, "Ye take too much upon you, seeing all the congregation are holy, every one of them, and the Lord is among them: wherefore then lift ye up yourselves above the congregation of the Lord?" (vs. 3).

2. Moses' response (Num. 16:4-14). In response, Moses promised that the next day the Lord Himself would show everyone who His true servants were. He told the rebels to appear before the Lord the next day with censers in hand.

As a Levite, Korah already held a privileged position, but he apparently sought the priesthood as well. Moses intimated that Korah and his men thirsted for power when he stated, "Seemeth it but a small thing unto you, that the God of Israel hath separated you from the congregation of Israel, to bring you near to himself to do the service of the tabernacle of the Lord, and to stand before the congregation to minister unto them?" (vs. 9).

As the dialog continues, more is gleaned. Dathan and Abiram refused to come to Moses as he had beckoned them. They reasoned, "Is it a small thing that thou hast brought us up out of a land that floweth with milk and honey, to kill us in the wilderness, except thou make thyself altogether a prince over us?" (vs. 13). Here these insurgents were claiming that Moses' leadership was inept in that he could not bring the children of Israel into the Promised Land, that Moses wished ill upon his people, and that Moses gloried in his own power over the people.

Korah and those who joined him had decided that they should take matters into their own hands. They were misled by their own desires, and they sought to mislead those around them. They failed to grasp that rebelling against Moses and Aaron was rebelling against the God who personally had appointed them to their positions of authority.

ILLUSTRATING THE LESSON

The actions of Korah and the others in Numbers 16 in rejecting God's chosen leaders for the nation illustrate the truth that those who exalt themselves find it easy to despise and denigrate those who have been exalted by God.

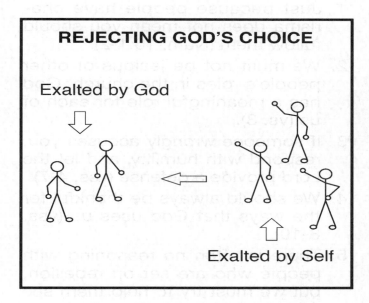

REJECTING GOD'S CHOICE

Exalted by God

Exalted by Self

CONCLUDING THE LESSON

Korah and the other rebels had convinced themselves, and now wished to convince the rest of Israel, that they deserved positions of authority equal to those of Moses and Aaron. Korah and his company thought they could do a better job than Moses and Aaron. They even believed that usurping the roles of Moses and Aaron would be an act of justice and liberation for the people of God. These men serve as a prime example of how sin can warp and manipulate one's thoughts and feelings and put them in direct opposition to God's clearly stated will.

ANTICIPATING THE NEXT LESSON

The divine judgment that resulted from Korah's rebellion is the subject of our study next week in Numbers 16:23-35. Korah and his accomplices wished to have greater influence over the people of Israel, but little did they know that the only impact they would have would be as long-remembered examples of rebellion against God.

—*Nigel C. Black.*

PRACTICAL POINTS

1. Just because people have charisma does not mean you should follow them (Num. 16:1-2).
2. We must not be jealous of other people's roles in the church. God has a meaningful role for each of us (vs. 3).
3. If someone wrongly accuses you, respond with humility, and let the Lord provide a defense (vss. 4-7).
4. We should always be thankful for the ways that God uses us (vss. 8-10).
5. There is often no reasoning with people who are set on rebellion, but we must try to help them see their error (vss. 11-12).
6. When God does not meet our expectations, we must have faith that His plans are good (vss. 13-14).

—Megan Hickman.

RESEARCH AND DISCUSSION

1. How did you deal with people using their influence for their own selfish ambitions?
2. What factors should you consider before rebuking others for misusing their power?
3. Why is it so hard to be humble in the face of accusations? Is it wrong to be upset when injustice is done to you?
4. Do you struggle with the ways in which God wants to use you in the body of Christ (cf. I Cor. 12:14-18)?
5. What should the church do if someone is not playing their proper role in the body?

—Megan Hickman.

ILLUSTRATED HIGH POINTS

They rose up (Num. 16:2)

Laws are enacted in order to protect the people of the nation. Some people, however, believe that laws do not apply to them. These people sometimes declare themselves as "Sovereign Citizens."

A "sovereign citizen" is someone who exempts himself from federal taxation, questions the legitimacy of government and its authority, and believes that he is not subject to federal laws. People who declare themselves sovereign citizens are rebelling against the constitutional authority of the federal government.

When the Israelites rebelled against Moses, they were also rebelling against the divine authority of God because it was God who chose Moses to be His representative.

Seemeth it but a small thing unto you (vs. 9)

There are many people who are dissatisfied with their appearance. Some submit themselves to undergoing plastic surgery.

Some who elect to have cosmetic surgery actually become addicted to it. They may originally plan on having just one cosmetic surgery, but continue to have further surgeries to tweak their physical appearance just a little further. Even when they reach a point where the surgeries become detrimental to both their appearance and their physical and mental health, they will not or cannot be satisfied with the way they look.

Korah, even after seeing so many blessings from the Lord and also being given a distinguished position among the Levites, still was not content with his position. He did not trust in the Lord as he should have.

—Chelsea Villaseñor.

Golden Text Illuminated

"Therefore thou shalt love the Lord thy God, and keep his charge, and his statutes, and his judgments, and his commandments, alway" (Deut. 11:1).

Our golden text today is the opposite of the subject of our lesson text. The exact problem presented by Korah's rebellion is that he and his fellow conspirators did not by any means make loving the Lord and keeping His statutes their priority. Rather, Korah and his comrades cared more about promoting their own political status.

You would think that after witnessing how the Lord dealt with those who complained against Moses in their recent past that Korah and company would have been less eager to level further complaints.

First, the complaint about the blandness and lack of variety in their divinely provided diet was swiftly punished with a plague that killed all the youngest and strongest men. Then Miriam and Aaron challenged Moses' leadership, so Miriam was made leprous and was exiled from the congregation for seven days. Finally, when those who succumbed to doubt—believing the negative report that the Canaanites were too powerful for the Israelites to defeat—called for a new leader who would return them to Egypt, the Lord condemned that entire generation to wander in the wilderness and die there without entering the Promised Land.

Now Korah, for some reason, decided that this would be an opportune time to once again challenge Moses' position as Yahweh's chosen leader of the people. Apparently the Israelites were slow learners, especially in terms of humility and submission to Yahweh's authority. After all, Yahweh's most frequent charge against them was that they were a "stiffnecked" people (Ex. 32:9; 33:3, 5; 34:9; Deut. 9:6). But, as the Lord will amply demonstrate once again in our next lesson, this challenge to Moses' leadership, like all the others, was not a good idea.

It is important to note Moses' personal reaction to Korah's challenge: "When [he] heard it, he fell upon his face" (Num. 16:4). Moses' first reaction was to humble himself before the Lord and allow God to decide who was right.

Moses told Korah and his comrades that the Lord Himself would decide this conflict. He urged them to prepare censers with fire and incense to meet with the Lord on the next day. But he also warned them that they were taking too much authority for themselves, and it would likely not go well for them. He encouraged them to appreciate the status that the Lord had already blessed them with as Levites and warned them not to become greedy for Aaron's priesthood.

But Korah and his conspirators stubbornly refused to comply with Moses' request. They repeated their accusation that Moses had cheated them out of the Promised Land and was condemning them to die in the desert; but that was the Lord's decision.

Sometimes the Lord takes us through especially hard times, either to chastise us or to purify us from sin or both. It is not easy to submit when the prospects for our future look bleak and painful. But rebellion only makes matters worse. The only way to react is with humility and submission to the Lord.

—*John Lody.*

Heart of the Lesson

Has someone ever disliked you because you refused to participate in some kind of sin? Often the hostility is masked by labeling you as self-righteous. As Christians, we know that we are not righteous in ourselves; righteousness is mercifully given to us through Christ. But God does expect us to act righteously in response to His gifts. Because of this, we should always choose to fear God over man, worshipping Him with our obedience and enduring any resulting persecution.

Today we will see how Moses endured persecution for righteously leading God's people. But even though man was against him, God upheld His humble servant and punished the proud (Prov. 29:23; Matt. 23:12).

Korah's accusation (Num. 16:1-3). Moses had to endure many power struggles during his leadership, and this was one of them. Korah, along with other "men of renown" from the tribe of Reuben, came to challenge Moses and Aaron. They accused Moses of hoarding power for himself, rather than genuinely representing God.

Notice that Korah gathered men who were "famous in the congregation" in order to sway the people to rebel against Moses. This goes to show that just because someone is popular or charismatic does not mean he is right. Even Christians can be misled, so we must always search the Scriptures for ultimate truth (Acts 17:11). And even though God had repeatedly verified Moses as His chosen leader, the Israelites rebelled.

What was Moses asking the Israelites to do that was so offensive to them? One possibility: he wanted them to repent, but Korah and his followers did not want to admit that they had sinned against the Lord or to endure any consequences. Korah did not want a judge pointing out his sin, so he claimed that all the members of the congregation were holy, therefore concluding that Moses had no right to order them around.

Moses' response (Num. 16:4-7). The text notes that Moses "fell on his face" at this accusation. This is a striking sign of humility in the face of provocation. Moses did not feel the need to show his strength. Instead, he told Korah that God would once again show them who was holy among them.

The Levites' envy (Num. 16:8-11). Moses pleaded with the Levites to be content in the position that God had given them. He pointed out that the position of honor they had been given was no "small thing." Moses also pointed out that the Levites, despite thinking they were murmuring against Aaron and Moses, were actually murmuring against the Lord.

It is extremely important for us to be content in the roles that God has put us in (cf. Phil. 4:11). Envy reveals a distrust of God's goodness and wisdom; it causes us to think that either we know better or that God does not really want to give us good gifts (cf. Matt. 7:11).

The Levites' blame (Num. 16:12-14). Moses had been speaking with Korah as a representative of the mutiny, but when he called the sons of Eliab (Dathan and Abiram), they refused to come and speak to Moses face to face.

Though the Israelites had brought their desert wandering on themselves by refusing to conquer the Promised Land, the men blamed Moses for their sin. But despite Korah's mass rebellion, Moses had the Lord on his side, and God would deal with them justly.

—*Megan Hickman.*

World Missions

Apathy is one of Satan's most effective tools because he can get people—believers especially—to believe it is neutral. A mere sin of omission does not seem nearly as serious as outright rebellion. But let's think of it from the enemy's perspective, somewhat like in *The Screwtape Letters* by C. S. Lewis.

We can imagine Satan telling his servants, "Don't inspire them to rebel in an overt way. No, what would help our cause much more would be to persuade them that someone else would be a better fit for the work; that someone else is more spiritual, more qualified, has more skills and resources at their disposal. Persuade them that conserving their money is the wisest priority. Persuade them that, after all, God understands how busy they are. Persuade them that their children's college education and their own retirement are their first priorities. Only if they have extra left over should they give to missions."

Satan's servants cackle with glee. They know that if they can get a believer to be neutral (ignoring concern for the lost, fearing to be seen as a religious fanatic, making sure they maintain personal security), then that believer, although he or she may belong to Christ eternally, is co-opted into serving Satan's cause.

Apathy is *not* neutral.

Satan has effective arguments he has been using for centuries to prevent God's people from making an impact: "Of course you want to stay near family, in a safe community. To give up your home, financial stability, and future plans—that's really asking too much." Jesus, however, says to go (Matt. 28:19), to die to ourselves and our ambitions (Luke 9:23-24; Gal. 2:20; Phil. 3:7-8), and if necessary, to reject everything else for Him (Matt. 10:37).

"A person's spiritual condition is a private matter," Satan whispers. "Bringing it up means you're not tolerant and loving." But how is it "loving" to ignore people's lost condition while we possess the light of deliverance in Christ's gospel (John 3:16-17; Acts 26:18)?

Satan tells us, "You've got enough problems! Once things get settled, once you get a better job with more money, then you'll have the time, finances, and energy to serve God." But God says that we must offer ourselves as living sacrifices (Rom. 12:1). Living for ourselves is only reasonable if we are still slaves to sin. To believe the above things is to be on the wrong side. When the line is drawn, it is clear which side apathy is on—and it is anything but neutral.

Apathy *is* rebellion.

Does all this sound extreme? God issues a harsh assessment in Philippians 3:19 of those who are religious, but not godly: "whose end is destruction, whose God is their belly, and whose glory is in their shame, who mind earthly things."

By neglecting to submit fully to Christ with everything we have and are, a choice is made (whether consciously or not) to likewise neglect the welfare of the lost souls in the world around us. From the perspective of God, looking down on His people all across this planet, how can that neglect be justified? Let us live in such a way that our love for Christ is clearly evident.

The choice must be made. Will we resolve to take a stand, confessing that "as for me and my house, we will serve the Lord" (Josh. 24:15), or will we remain in apathy?

—*Kimberly Rae.*

The Jewish Aspect

Korah was a descendant of Levi, the third of Jacob's sons, and a first cousin to Moses and Aaron. Korah was born in Egypt during the period that Pharaoh enslaved the Jews. He experienced the Exodus and the journey through the Red Sea. He was among the Israelites as they received the Torah at Mount Sinai (Altein, "Korah: The Rebel of the Bible," chabad.org).

In this week's lesson, Korah attempted to incite a rebellion against Moses. Next week we will see that as a result, the ground swallowed him.

Jews write that Korah was an extremely wealthy and clever individual. His status as a Levite allowed him to participate in the service involving the portable sanctuary that the Jews carried throughout their journey to the Promised Land (Altein). Rabbinical literature claims that Korah possessed great wealth because he discovered one of the treasures that Joseph had hidden in Egypt and that he was one of the two richest men in the world ("Korah," jewishencyclopedia.com).

The Midrash contains stories or legends about what supposedly precipitated the situation behind Korah's uprising. One of these depicts how he tried to undermine Moses by pointing to laws he considered illogical.

One story has Korah focusing first on *tzitzit*—the blue- or purple-dyed strings, or fringes, that Jews are commanded to attach to the corners of their garments. The story relates that Korah prepared 250 cloaks without tzitzit, but dyed all in blue, and gave them to his supporters in protest.

Next, he continued to challenge Moses, asking whether a house filled with Torah scrolls required a mezuzah (a parchment on which the Shema prayer is written) affixed to its door-post. According to the story, Moses said yes, but Korah taunted him, claiming the scrolls inside were better than a scrap by the door (Altein).

Tradition also relates a parable that Korah is said to have told the people: A widow, the mother of two young daughters, had a field. The widow tried to plow the field, but Moses told her not to plow it with an ox and ass together as per the law. She attempted to sow the field, but Moses told her not to sow it with mingled seed as per the law. At the time of harvest, she tried to reap it, but the law required her to leave parts of the field unharvested and to give the priest his share.

The woman sold the field and with the proceeds bought two sheep, but the law obligated her to give the priest the firstborn and the wool from the first shearing. Finally, the young widow stated she could not bear these demands any longer and decided to sacrifice the sheep to the Lord. At that point Aaron claimed the meat as the priest's portion and left her with nothing ("Korah").

The intent of this was to highlight the hardships that Moses and the law created. In rebelling against God's anointed, however, Korah was actually rebelling against God Himself.

Korah died, but his sons survived (Num. 26:11). Tradition holds that initially they followed in his rebellion but soon repented. Because of their repentance, the prophet Samuel arose from Korah's lineage as did the Levites who sang in the temple (Altein). The good that came from Korah's family line despite his bad example shows that God forgives those who are truly repentant.

—*Robin Fitzgerald.*

Guiding the Superintendent

When reading these accounts as closely as we have been during the past ten lessons, we find it more and more incredible that the Israelites doggedly persisted in their stubbornness and pride of heart. They are a microcosm of mankind as a whole, and we too suffer from the same fundamental flaws that they exhibited so incessantly. Their sin is our sin, and through these accounts we see how hopeless we would be without the mighty forgiveness of Jesus Christ.

In this account, we witness yet again an act of rebellion against God's ordained authority. A prominent Levite, Korah, and his cohorts rejected God Himself and His lordship over them. Just as Miriam and Aaron had done earlier (lesson 7), these men accused Moses of lording it over them. The malcontents appear to have forgotten the consequences of that previous ill-fated rebellion. They refused to remember the commandments of the Lord.

DEVOTIONAL OUTLINE

1. Korah's accusations (Num. 16:1-3). In a brazen act of defiance, Korah rallied 250 men to oppose Moses. With the confidence that comes from such numbers, he accused Moses and Aaron of exalting themselves beyond their due. Korah's words made it clear that he considered his cause a righteous one. In reality, he was merely manifesting his own depravity and personal ambition.

Korah's pride had evidently taken a beating when the people had been banished to wander the wilderness, and perhaps he had disagreed with the stoning of the Sabbath breaker (cf. 15:32-36). Korah fell into the trap of allowing bitterness to gain mastery over his heart and mind, fatally clouding his judgment.

2. Korah's condemnation of Moses (Num. 16:4-11). Upon hearing the accusation brought against him by Korah, Moses immediately fell face-first to the ground. He understood the reckless foolishness of the developing power play as well as its most likely consequences. Moses reminded Korah and his followers of their own already important position among the people as Levites. He did not hold back in warning that they had gone too far. Silence is not an option in the presence of those who speak against God. We must humbly confront all such rebellion, standing firmly on our faith in the Lord.

3. Dathan and Abiram's stubbornness (Num. 16:12-14). Dathan and Abiram, two leaders of the rebellion along with Korah, refused to honor Moses' summons to appear before the Lord. They continued to reject the authority that God had given Moses as their leader and prophet. They refused to meet with him, and they gave further vent to their discontent.

CHILDREN'S CORNER

Our children will learn a very important lesson from the account of Korah's rebellion against Moses. Korah, Dathan, and Abiram were jealous of Moses' special standing and authority among the people, even though they themselves had been graciously given prominent status. They chose to challenge Moses' authority in the presence of the Lord Himself. Children should be encouraged to be thankful for what they have and not be jealous of what others have. Humble obedience and diligent service to others, not strife and conflict, is the way to greatness in God's kingdom.

—*Mike Spencer.*

SCRIPTURE LESSON TEXT

NUM. 16:23 And the LORD spake unto Moses, saying,

24 Speak unto the congregation, saying, Get you up from about the tabernacle of Korah, Dathan, and Abiram.

25 And Moses rose up and went unto Dathan and Abiram; and the elders of Israel followed him.

26 And he spake unto the congregation, saying, Depart, I pray you, from the tents of these wicked men, and touch nothing of theirs, lest ye be consumed in all their sins.

27 So they gat up from the tabernacle of Korah, Dathan, and Abiram, on every side: and Dathan and Abiram came out, and stood in the door of their tents, and their wives, and their sons, and their little children.

28 And Moses said, Hereby ye shall know that the LORD hath sent me to do all these works; for I have not *done them* of mine own mind.

29 If these men die the common death of all men, or if they be visited after the visitation of all men; *then* the LORD hath not sent me.

30 But if the LORD make a new thing, and the earth open her mouth, and swallow them up, with all that *appertain* unto them, and they go down quick into the pit; then ye shall understand that these men have provoked the LORD.

31 And it came to pass, as he had made an end of speaking all these words, that the ground clave asunder that *was* under them:

32 And the earth opened her mouth, and swallowed them up, and their houses, and all the men that *appertained* unto Korah, and all *their* goods.

33 They, and all that *appertained* to them, went down alive into the pit, and the earth closed upon them: and they perished from among the congregation.

34 And all Israel that *were* round about them fled at the cry of them: for they said, Lest the earth swallow us up *also*.

35 And there came out a fire from the LORD, and consumed the two hundred and fifty men that offered incense.

NOTES

Judgment on the Rebellion

Lesson Text: Numbers 16:23-35

Related Scriptures: Numbers 16:15-22, 36-50; Psalm 16:1-11

TIME: about 1443 B.C.   PLACE: Desert of Paran

GOLDEN TEXT—"Preserve me, O God: for in thee do I put my trust" (Psalm 16:1).

Introduction

After the blatantly rebellious accusations of Dathan and Abiram, Moses was angry to the point of telling God not to accept any offerings they might bring to Him.

Moses then turned to Korah and told him to make sure he and his 250 men would bring their censers the next day and come before the Lord, along with Aaron.

The glory of God appeared to the congregation, and the Lord spoke to Moses and Aaron, telling them to get away from the people because He was going to consume them (vss. 19-21).

Moses again interceded for the people, asking God not to destroy all the people for the sin of Korah (vs. 22). The Lord would in fact spare the congregation, but Moses knew the rebels had to be judged in order to prevent their rebellion from spreading among the people. Unrepentance would be the demise of the insurrectionists.

LESSON OUTLINE

I. THE LORD WARNS MOSES— Num. 16:23-24

II. MOSES WARNS THE PEOPLE— Num. 16:25-30

III. GOD JUDGES THE REBELS— Num. 16:31-35

Exposition: Verse by Verse

THE LORD WARNS MOSES

NUM. 16:23 And the LORD spake unto Moses, saying,

24 Speak unto the congregation, saying, Get you up from about the tabernacle of Korah, Dathan, and Abiram.

God was clearly angry with Korah, Dathan, Abiram, and the other rebels for rising up not only against Moses and Aaron but against the Lord Himself. God had repeatedly shown the people that Moses was His chosen representative and that He had a unique relationship with Moses.

Numbers 16:23 states that the Lord spoke to Moses. God did not speak to Korah, Dathan, or Abiram. He did not speak to the other 250 men. He did not speak to the elders of Israel or to anyone else in the camp. He spoke to Moses. When it was time for God to speak a message to the people, He did so through Moses. This was no exception, and it further solidified the fact that God was with Moses and had blessed his leadership.

Korah, a Levite of the family of Kohath, and Dathan and Abiram, who were Reubenites, lived in close proximity to each other near the tabernacle on the south side (Num. 2:10; 3:29). Dathan and Abiram had refused to appear before the Lord at the tabernacle with the other 250 men, as Moses had instructed. The Lord knew where they were, however, and would hold them accountable, for their rebellion was not merely against Moses but ultimately against God Himself.

We cannot think that we can hide from the Lord when we sin. It is foolish to assume that if we stay out of church or away from God's people that what we do does not matter. We may not like what our church leaders say, but it is important to understand that they are serving under the authority of God and that we are accountable to the Lord, who called them into leadership over us. It is not wise to rebel against them or try to wrestle authority from them. It is especially foolish to think that we are an authority unto ourselves.

Since the rebel leaders would not go to Moses, Moses would go to them. Answering Moses' request not to kill all the people, God instructed him to tell the people to get away from the places where Korah, Dathan, and Abiram lived. This gave the people ample warning to remove themselves from the judgment of God. Anyone who refused to get away from these three men and their tents would undoubtedly suffer the same divine punishment.

MOSES WARNS THE PEOPLE

25 And Moses rose up and went unto Dathan and Abiram; and the elders of Israel followed him.

26 And he spake unto the congregation, saying, Depart, I pray you, from the tents of these wicked men, and touch nothing of theirs, lest ye be consumed in all their sins.

27 So they gat up from the tabernacle of Korah, Dathan, and Abiram, on every side: and Dathan and Abiram came out, and stood in the door of their tents, and their wives, and their sons, and their little children.

28 And Moses said, Hereby ye shall know that the Lord hath sent me to do all these works; for I have not done them of mine own mind.

29 If these men die the common death of all men, or if they be visited after the visitation of all men; then the Lord hath not sent me.

30 But if the Lord make a new thing, and the earth open her mouth, and swallow them up, with all that appertain unto them, and they go down quick into the pit; then ye shall understand that these men have provoked the Lord.

Moses goes to Korah, Dathan, and Abiram (Num. 16:25-26). {With the elders of Israel in tow, Moses went directly to Dathan and Abiram.}[Q1] Their stubborn refusal to go to him as he had instructed led Moses to go to them. They would not in any way escape the punishment that was going to come upon them. It appears that at some point Korah left the 250 men at the tabernacle (vs. 19) to stand alongside Dathan and Abiram in their defiance.

Perhaps one reason for commanding the rebels to meet with God at the entrance of the tabernacle was to offer them one final chance to repent. As we have already learned, God is slow to anger and abundant in mercy (cf. Num. 14:18), meaning that He does not take pleasure in executing judgment upon anyone (cf. Ezek. 33:11).

Even if a reprieve *was* being offered, however, Dathan and Abiram's refusal to report indicated their refusal to repent. When Moses had to go to them because of their continued rejection of God's word, it sealed their fate. They would not escape the judgment of God and would suffer the dire consequences of rebelling against the Lord. In that rebellion they had led others to rebel as well; they tried to circumvent God's entire plan for leading the Israelites into the Promised Land.

{When Moses and the elders reached Dathan and Abiram, he immediately told all the people to get away from the tents of these men and not touch any of their belongings.}Q2 {These men were under God's wrath, and any contact with them or their possessions put a person at great risk of God's judgment.}Q3

Since these two men, as well as Korah, were well-known, influential leaders among the Israelites (cf. Num. 16:1-2), it is not unreasonable to think that their possessions were substantial. It may have been tempting for the people around them to want to take what they owned and gain personally from the situation. God prevented this by forbidding anyone from even touching what they owned.

Dathan and Abiram appear at their tents (Num. 16:27-28). The people wasted no time in moving away from Korah, Dathan, and Abiram. They knew that these men were wicked and had evil intentions, so they disassociated themselves from them very quickly. The three insurrectionists quickly found that they had no loyalists among the people they were attempting to manipulate.

After the people scattered, Dathan and Abiram came to the door of their tents. They had nowhere to go and no place to hide, as Moses and the elders were right at their front door.

The two men stood defiantly in oppo-sition to Moses, along with their wives and children. Korah probably did the same at his nearby tent. The setting is pathetic. Instead of sending their families to find cover, these men actually brought them out with them. It is one thing to rebel against God, but it is even worse to lead our families to join us.

Moses stood before Dathan and Abiram and boldly declared that God was with him and had sent him to lead Israel out of Egypt and into the Promised Land. The charge made by the rebels against Moses was that he had assumed control on his own volition and that he was no better than anyone else. They believed Moses was leading the people to their demise in the wilderness and claimed he was unfit and incompetent as a leader.

Of course, any charges they made against Moses along these lines was also an accusation against God. God had shown His approval of Moses several times in public demonstrations that were witnessed by everyone. There simply was no excuse now for Korah, Dathan, Abiram, or anyone else to accuse Moses in such a way.

Moses was not afraid to stand before anyone, whether it be three rebels or the entire congregation of Israel, and publicly state that the Lord had sent him to do all the things he had done. The works he spoke of here likely refer to the ten plagues back in Egypt, the parting of the Red Sea, the miraculous provision of quail and manna, and bringing water from a rock. Moses was not claiming to have done any of these exploits by his own power. In fact, his point was that all of them were evidence that God had chosen him and did these acts through the servant He chose.

Moses knew he could not have done even one of these things by himself. He was simply pointing to the past to show that he was appointed by God to lead His people and God used him in miraculous ways. Moses was an instrument in God's plan. In no way was he orchestrating his own agenda. We should remember that Moses had been perfectly content being a shepherd in Midian (cf. Ex. 3:1-4:17). He tried to get out of the job of leading the people, but God would not release him from his calling.

Moses announces a severe test (Num. 16:29-30). Moses' authority had been challenged a number of times before this particular event, and he usually did not offer much in the way of personal self-defense. Here, however, he put forth a test that would either prove or invalidate his divine calling and ministry entirely.

{Moses declared before the people that if Korah, Dathan, and Abiram died as men commonly died—that is, by natural causes—it would mean the Lord had not called him. However, if they died in a very unique way—namely, by the ground suddenly opening up and swallowing them alive and taking them down into "the pit" (Heb. *sheol*)—this would clearly demonstrate that God had sent him and that these men had despised the Lord.}[Q4]

Moses knew the Lord well enough and long enough that he had full assurance that God had sent him and would respond favorably to his voice. There was no sense of insecurity on his part and no wavering in his faith. He knew that God was going to judge these men and that they would die that day in a unique manner that was unmistakably God's judgment.

GOD JUDGES THE REBELS

31 And it came to pass, as he had made an end of speaking all these words, that the ground clave asunder that was under them:

32 And the earth opened her mouth, and swallowed them up, and their houses, and all the men that appertained unto Korah, and all their goods.

33 They, and all that appertained to them, went down alive into the pit, and the earth closed upon them: and they perished from among the congregation.

34 And all Israel that were round about them fled at the cry of them: for they said, Lest the earth swallow us up also.

35 And there came out a fire from the LORD, and consumed the two hundred and fifty men that offered incense.

Deaths of Korah, Dathan, and Abiram (Num. 16:31-32). What happened next is one of the most dramatic events ever recorded in human history. {In vivid demonstration that the Lord was with Moses and had sent him, the ground split apart underneath Korah, Dathan, and Abiram. They fell into the crevice, along with all their possessions and those people who stood with them.}[Q5]

This spectacular event was something Moses was utterly unable to make happen by himself. He did not possess the power to do this simply by waving his hand; it was not some trick. Moses had stated that if the ground opened up and swallowed these men, it would mean that God was with him and he had not assumed his leadership position on his own accord.

By Moses' own word, he said that these men would die by something new, something unexpected that the people had never seen before. This is precisely what occurred, as God heard him and caused the ground to split apart. There should have been no doubt in anyone's mind now that God was with Moses.

Swallowed alive (Num. 16:33-34). Korah, Dathan, and Abiram all fell into the opening in the earth and plunged to their deaths, as evidenced by the statement that they went down into the pit. {"Pit" translates the Hebrew word *sheol*, which refers to the place of the dead.}[Q6] These otherwise healthy men did not die of natural causes but rather by a direct act of God in judgment of them and affirmation of His calling on Moses.

The people of Israel witnessed these men plunge to their deaths as objects of God's divine wrath for orchestrating a rebellion against Him. Their motives and actions were not only an offense against God but also very dangerous to the people. This is made clear by the fact that many of the Israelites later expressed anger with Moses for killing "the people of the Lord" (vs. 41). {So while the Lord's actions might at first appear quite severe to some, we can see why such drastic action on His part was necessary. The rebellion had to be squelched.}Q7

{The Israelites scattered in an effort to find secure ground. Fear and panic set in quickly as everyone fled in an attempt to avoid suffering the same fate as the three rebels and their households.}Q8

{This occurrence cannot be dismissed as a natural event such as an earthquake that coincidentally happened at this particular moment. For one thing, it took place just as Moses had said just minutes before. For another, when the ground breaks apart in an earthquake, it does not repair itself. In this incident, the ground closed back up once the guilty parties had fallen into the opening.}Q9

Death of the 250 (Num. 16:35). {Back at the tabernacle, fire came forth from the Lord and consumed the 250 men who had joined with Korah, Dathan, and Abiram in this insurrection.}Q10 As these men stood with their censers burning incense, God punished them for their part in the rebellion.

These men were seeking priestly status as they burned incense before the Lord. The Lord rejected this offering, for they were seeking personal power instead of trying to please Him.

This does not mean they were unimportant just because they had not been selected to be priests. God established Aaron and his descendants as priests, in part to prevent instances such as this from happening. The priesthood was never something to be aspired to. One had to be elected by God for it, and His election was established by birth. If a man was not a descendant of Aaron, he could not be a priest.

It is a serious mistake to aspire to something God has not called us to or equipped us for. There are no unimportant people in the church; everyone's role is significant. Be content to do what God has called you to do, and you will find that He will bless you immensely.

—Robert Ferguson, Jr.

QUESTIONS

1. Who went with Moses to approach Dathan and Abiram?

2. What did Moses tell the people to do in regard to these two men?

3. What did Moses warn concerning anyone who stood with the rebels or touched any of their belongings?

4. How would the people know that God had sent Moses?

5. What happened to Korah, Dathan, and Abiram immediately after Moses finished speaking?

6. What does the Hebrew word *sheol* refer to?

7. Why was it necessary for God to deal with this rebellion in such a drastic way?

8. How did the people respond when they saw God judge the men?

9. Why can this event not be written off as a natural phenomenon such as an earthquake?

10. What happened to the 250 men who joined Korah in the rebellion?

—Robert Ferguson, Jr.

Preparing to Teach the Lesson

Last week's lesson text told of the rebellion against Moses and Aaron by Korah and 250 other very prominent men of the people of Israel. These men attacked Moses and Aaron, challenging their leadership and questioning their motivations.

Today we will see the divine response to this rebellion in Numbers 16:23-35. The terrible situation described here gives us a unique vantage point on the Lord's character and disposition. We will see the righteousness of God on display, and we will be reminded that God's holiness must be taken seriously.

TODAY'S AIM

Facts: to study the Lord's character and disposition in reference to addressing the sin of rebellion among His people.

Principle: to affirm that God is holy and righteous and is always fair and measured in His response to sin.

Application: to acknowledge God's holiness and righteousness when it comes to matters of divine discipline and to realize that our attitudes and actions are seeds that ultimately will bring forth either good or bad fruit.

INTRODUCING THE LESSON

All of God's attributes are very important and worthy of much study, for they encourage spiritual growth in the life of every believer. God's holiness and righteousness are especially on display in His response to Korah's rebellion in Numbers 16:23-35. His judgment issues from His holiness, or moral purity, and is always righteous—that is, it is in conformity with His own holy nature and character. God's righteousness is not like human righteousness,

which often is adherence to some arbitrary standard of behavior.

We who have put our faith in Christ for salvation have been declared positionally righteous. In practice, we should be growing daily in righteousness, or conformity to God's holy standards, as the Holy Spirit works in us through God's Word.

God's holiness and righteousness teach us important aspects of how we must think and act in order to be in alignment with the Lord's character.

DEVELOPING THE LESSON

Korah's rebellion was a serious affront to the Lord's plan for the nation of Israel. The Lord's response to Korah's rebellion must be viewed in the larger context of the book of Numbers, which includes numerous failures on the part of Israel and their leadership in the wilderness journey to the Promised Land (cf. chaps. 11—15).

1. Warning for the congregation (Num. 16:23-27). God's response to Korah's rebellion begins very simply: "And the Lord spake unto Moses, saying, Speak unto the congregation, saying, Get you up from about the tabernacle of Korah, Dathan, and Abiram" (vss. 23-24). This beginning statement sets the expectation that the ensuing judgment is going to be both sudden and serious.

The divine pronouncement is followed in verses 25-27 by Moses' stern and quick action toward the congregation of Israel, ordering them to move away from the tents of the rebels and to not even touch anything that these men owned. It is important to note that the Lord was determined to judge only those who were deserving of judgment. The Lord is more than fair and is kind to the innocent. His care in protecting others from the fate of Korah, Dathan, and Abiram may indicate that the family members of these men who would perish with them were complicit in their rebellion.

2. Vindication for the leaders (Num. 16:28-30). Moses made an extended statement prefacing that which the Lord was about to do. He wanted the congregation of Israel to really understand what was about to occur. He did not want anyone to think that the calamitous impending events were in any way a coincidence but rather were a divine judgment. In fact, the unique nature of the judgment would affirm it as coming from God alone and vindicating His chosen servants, Moses and Aaron.

3. Judgment of the rebels (Num. 16:31-35). As Moses finished speaking, the divine retribution began; there was no delay whatsoever. The form of judgment was unique; the ground under Korah and his accomplices split open and swallowed all the dissidents and their possessions. They all fell into the chasm, and then the earth closed upon them.

As this divine action concluded, another act of divine judgment occurred. The leaders who aligned themselves with Korah in his rebellion and had gathered at the tabernacle (vss. 16-19) were consumed by a fire from the Lord.

Part of living as the creation of a sovereign God is the realization that our actions reveal who we are. Jesus set forth this principle in Matthew 7:16-18, when He stated, "Ye shall know them by their fruits. Do men gather grapes of thorns, or figs of thistles? Even so every good tree bringeth forth good fruit; but a corrupt tree bringeth forth evil fruit. A good tree cannot bring forth evil fruit, neither can a corrupt tree bring forth good fruit." It is extremely important, therefore, to consider what type of tree we are, as evidenced by the attitudes and actions of our lives. Are we producing good fruit or bad fruit?

ILLUSTRATING THE LESSON

Our attitudes and actions will ultimately bring forth either good or bad fruit in this life and will reveal who we really are—those seeking to please the Lord or those worthy of His condemnation.

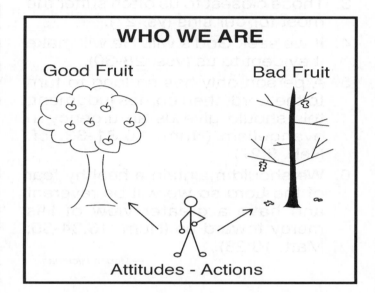

CONCLUDING THE LESSON

The lesson text presents a number of important points regarding the holiness and righteousness of God and how they relate to people in rebellion against Him. We see that the Lord isolates His judgment to those for whom the judgment is intended. We also see a clear exposition so that all understand what is happening and why. And, of course, we see that divine judgment is the very real and righteous outworking of God's holy nature.

ANTICIPATING THE NEXT LESSON

Next week's lesson from Numbers 20:1-13 reinforces the truth that there are consequences for disobedience. It also reminds us that no one is exempt from this divine principle.

—*Nigel C. Black.*

PRACTICAL POINTS

1. When we stand up for what is right, we can trust those who are loyal to the Lord to stand with us (Num. 16:23-25).
2. If we collaborate with sinners, we are likely to become guilty in our actions (vs. 26).
3. Those closest to us often suffer the most for our sins (vs. 27).
4. If we seek God's will, He will make it evident to us (vss. 28-30).
5. A person only has so long to turn to the Lord, then comes judgment; this should give us an urgency in evangelism (Num. 16:31-33; cf. Heb. 9:27).
6. We should maintain a healthy fear of the Lord so we will be reverent and have a greater view of His mercy toward us (Num. 16:34-35; Matt. 10:28).

—Megan Hickman.

RESEARCH AND DISCUSSION

1. Why is it so important to have unified leadership within the church?
2. Can you have close relationships with unbelievers? How can you evangelize people without making them feel like "projects"?
3. Should we attempt to appeal to the world by being like the world? Why or why not?
4. Are natural disasters always judgments from God against wickedness? Why or why not?
5. Have you ever known someone who has died young? How does this affect your motivation to evangelize?

—Megan Hickman.

ILLUSTRATED HIGH POINTS

Touch nothing (Num. 16:26)

Most museums have strict policies that no one is to touch the art. Some museums go as far as requiring that children be accompanied by a parent or guardian at all times.

Moses told the congregation that they should not touch anything that belonged to the people who had sinned by rebelling against the Lord. If they disobeyed, they too would be punished. In this case, of course, the warning against touching was even more serious than in a museum!

Fled at the cry (vs. 34)

Instinctive behavior can help protect both animals and humans from potential danger. If you have ever watched a squirrel, you have probably recognized that they are very cautious creatures. Their vision covers a very wide area, and they are always alert, expecting danger from any direction. Their attentiveness and caution is always evident.

When a person hears a loud sound or a scream, he or she instinctively blinks and flinches away from the source of the commotion. People usually run away from danger without being told to do so. A healthy fear is important. It keeps us safe.

When the Israelites heard the screams and clamor of those involved in Korah's rebellion being swallowed alive by the earth, they fled for their lives from the sovereign wrath of God, knowing that those being judged were beyond all help or hope. Proverbs says that a "fear of the Lord is the beginning of wisdom" (9:10). Though we do not need to fear God's wrath if we have trusted in Christ, we must always recognize that salvation is only due to His great mercy.

—Chelsea Villaseñor.

Golden Text Illuminated

"Preserve me, O God: for in thee do I put my trust" (Psalm 16:1).

The golden text for this week provides a much-needed positive perspective to balance the severity of the judgment recorded in this week's lesson text. It is a prayer of David expressing abiding confidence in the Lord's goodness and provision for His people. Psalm 16 also famously contains lines that were cited by Peter in his sermon as a prophecy of Christ's resurrection (cf. Acts 2:25-31; Ps. 16:8-11).

Korah, Dathan, and Abiram decidedly did not put their trust in the Lord as David did. They were preoccupied with challenging Moses' God-anointed authority over the Hebrews, perhaps because they viewed their punishment—namely, that they had all been condemned to die in the wilderness without ever entering the Promised Land—as an injustice. They also coveted Aaron's priesthood for themselves, since they were also Levites, because they were not content with their more modest roles in serving the tabernacle worship.

In this cause, Korah, Dathan, and Abiram were immovable in their stubborn determination. They refused to cooperate or listen to Moses' warnings against their petitions and his requests that they repent to save their own lives.

The consequence of their persistence in this incorrigible rebellion was that the Lord caused the earth beneath their feet to open up like the yawning maw of some gigantic beast and swallow them all alive—them, their wives, their children, and even their houses with all their belongings.

Not only that, but the 250 men who were employed to offer incense for the rebels were also consumed by fire that came out from the Lord's presence.

As astonishing and disturbing as this judgment was, the Lord's original intent was once again to destroy the entire congregation of the Israelites (cf. Num. 16:20-21). But Moses and Aaron interceded for the people (vs. 22), and only the conspirators themselves were destroyed.

In the New Testament, the Lord's ferocity in defense of His holiness as displayed in Numbers 16 is not diminished, but rather it is vehemently reaffirmed! The writer of Hebrews unflinchingly asserts that, "Our God is a consuming fire" (12:29) and that it is still "a fearful thing to fall into the hands of the living God" (cf. 10:26-31). Paul also reaffirms that Christ will one day return "in flaming fire taking vengeance on them that know not God" (II Thess. 1:8). Peter likewise acknowledges that on that day, "the heavens being on fire shall be dissolved, and the elements shall melt with fervent heat" (II Pet. 3:12). And during the final rebellion, when the enemies of God surround the people of the Lord and their beloved city, fire will come down out of heaven from God and devour them! Same problem; same God; same solution!

The plea for preservation in our golden text is imperative when we consider what it means to be found on the wrong side of redemptive history. Yes, our God is abounding in love, mercy, patience, and forgiveness, but only to those who take refuge in Jesus Christ.

—*John Lody.*

Heart of the Lesson

Learning to trust the Lord can sometimes be a frustrating process. We know that the fact that He does all things for our good (Rom. 8:28) does not mean He will do everything we want. God exalts the humble and humbles the proud, but He does not always do this the way we would like or as quickly as we want. But the more we learn about Him, the more likely we are to trust Him.

Moses had ample opportunity to see God's faithfulness. Even when he was being challenged as the leader of the Israelites, Moses knew that God would affirm his calling.

Moses commands the people (Num. 16:23-27). After conferring with the Lord, Moses had agreed to let Korah and his followers (whom Korah had claimed were holy) come before the Lord and burn incense. God would then reveal who was truly holy among them. A congregation of Israelites gathered with Korah, probably supporters of the rebellion. God did appear, but He did not declare their holiness. He threatened to consume them (vss. 19-21). When they saw the Lord, the congregation realized their mistake and begged for mercy (vs. 22).

Before God judged Korah and his followers, he told Moses to go deal with Dathan and Abiram. Since they had refused to come to him, Moses once again humbled himself, going to their camp to warn their followers. Moses commanded the people to depart from the wicked men and not even to touch anything of theirs. So often we are led astray by associating with the wrong people (I Cor. 15:33); this was also the case with the Israelites. We must be sure to have godly men and women in our lives who will speak truth to us and counteract the world's influence.

The Israelites heeded Moses' warning, leaving only Dathan, Abiram, and their families standing at the doors of their tents.

Moses trusts the Lord (Num. 16:28-30). The Lord was ready to bring judgment on these men, but even in victory, Moses gave glory to the Lord. Moses would not take any credit for his validation as the Israelites' leader.

To make God's will totally clear, the rebels would not die normal deaths (vs. 29). God would use these men to validate Moses' leadership.

God supports Moses (Num. 16:31-35). Right after Moses spoke their judgment, the ground opened up and swallowed Dathan, Abiram, their families, and their supporters. Though the judgment was clearly against the rebels, while the people who stood with Moses were safe, they reacted with terror because they realized the power of the Lord and recognized the sin they had committed by standing with the rebels, only moments before.

We all were once dead in our sins, but we are called by God, and we trust in the work of Jesus and can depend on Him for grace. However, there are many others who are standing on shaky ground, unknowingly awaiting God's judgment. All men are accountable to His law (cf. Rom. 1:20), but they need someone to warn them of the consequences of sin and bring them to Jesus.

When Christ died for our sins, He endured the wrath that we deserved. Now Jesus is our Advocate. We are no longer God's enemies; He is for us (Rom. 5:10; 8:31).

God will affirm us as we walk in His will. Though His plans may not fit our expectations, we can trust His faithful promises and endure persecution in His good and perfect name.

—*Megan Hickman.*

World Missions

Imagine if the choice to attend church this week meant risking your life. Carrying a Bible would make the risk even higher. Imagine that to own a Bible—or even just a page of it—was illegal. To speak of Christ to the wrong ears could result in prison or even death for you and your family.

This is a reality for millions around the world. The cross they carry is heavy indeed.

A story is told of one underground church in China that was invaded by soldiers during a secret service. The soldiers charged in with guns and stood over the terrified congregation.

They said they would kill everyone who would not renounce Jesus Christ. However, if any person there would deny their faith, that person would be free to go, free to live.

How would we feel in such a moment, in such a setting, with guns aimed at us, our children, and the family we love? What would we choose? What would we hope for our children to choose?

As expected, in order to save themselves, some were quick to recant their allegiance to Christ. They ran to freedom. The soldiers gave those who remained another chance. Anyone willing to recant would leave unharmed. Those who would not reject Christ would be shot. More people left.

The core of committed believers remained. They faced the soldiers—faced the death that was coming. It came as a huge shock when the soldiers put down their weapons and smiled. They were believers! They had carried out this charade to make sure they met only with those who were truly committed to Christ and not secret communist spies.

How those true followers must have felt that day! Surely they were relieved to still be alive, but beyond that, what strength of courage it must have given them in the future to know that even when given the hardest test of all, they did not deny Christ, no matter the cost.

The others, though, had shown their true loyalty. They had chosen themselves, their earthly lives, over the Lord.

If persecution were to come to our shores, into our churches, where would we stand? Would we be a part of the group who denied Christ the moment that serving Him became dangerous? Or would we find ourselves in the second group, who at first wanted to stay but in the end gave in to fear and fled? Or would we remain steadfast, unmovable, ready to take up our cross and follow our Saviour, no matter the cost?

We may never face a test like that, but knowing our answer to that paramount question will aid us in answering much lesser questions. If we are committed to being faithful to Christ unto death, we can certainly be faithful if it means the loss of a job, ridicule from others, or any other difficult choice that involves self-sacrifice for Jesus' sake.

If Jesus asks us, we must go, give, serve, love, or abandon ourselves. We must be poured out as living sacrifices. As Romans 12:1 assures us, this is just our "reasonable service." We can follow and obey in complete trust and full joy. Elisabeth Elliot, wife of missionary and martyr Jim Elliot, once said, "Yes to God *always* leads in the end to joy. We can absolutely bank on that" (*Passion and Purity*, Revell). What are you banking on?

—Kimberly Rae.

The Jewish Aspect

A Jewish writer states that although Jews have excelled in many different things, only one sport truly has a claim as being the national sport. Is the national sport soccer? Is the national sport playing with the dreidel? Nope! The Jewish national sport is arguing ("Conversation & Debate," myjewishlearning.com).

The writer is using humor to make an important point. In Judaism, there are only a few topics in which you cannot ask questions. Jewish scholars and leaders encourage questions and debate to get to truth.

Over the centuries, rabbis have debated various topics and included the debates in their texts. For example, the Mishnah uses the language of the dispute as its mode of expression (Spritzer, "Valuing Debate and Conversation," myjewishlearning.com). In the Talmud, Jews raise argumentation to an art form; the Talmud itself is a collection of thousands upon thousands of arguments among rabbis.

Hillel and Shammai were two leading sages alive just prior to the time of Jesus. They founded opposing schools of Jewish thought: the House of Hillel and the House of Shammai. These schools debated many areas of Jewish life, and these debates shaped Judaism.

Rabbis generally believe arguments are good. For example, Rabbi Tzvi Freeman suggests that you count the words of the Torah to discover what lies at the center. He states that at the center lies the story of Moses and Aaron arguing. Freeman points out in addition that Moses argued with God and that Abraham argued with God about His judgment on Sodom and Gomorrah ("Why Can't the Rabbis Agree on Anything: The Jewish Obsession with Arguments," chabad.org).

This week's Scripture lesson describes the result of Korah's argument against Moses. As punishment against Korah's error, the Lord caused the earth to open its mouth and swallow him.

Knowing that Jewish culture encourages the art of argument, some Jews question why God viewed Korah differently from other men throughout history who engaged in the art of argument. Most rabbis agree that debate is a crucial component of Torah study and understanding. So why were Korah's actions so problematic?

The Pirkei Avot (5:17) states that "Any controversy that is for the sake of Heaven shall in the end be resolved. A controversy that is not for the sake of Heaven shall not be resolved" (Kravitz and Olitzky, *Pirke Avot*, URJ Press). Most rabbis agree that the problem with Korah's argument was that it was not for the sake of heaven.

Jews believe arguments for the sake of bettering life for the Jewish people have merit. However, they believe arguments to gain power, attain personal wealth, or promote division are sinful (Simonds, "An Argument with Intention," reformjudaism.org). Korah tried to disguise his power play as a holy action. Yet his intentions were far from holy as he attempted to divide Israel and rebel against God (Simonds).

As Christians, we must heed the lesson of Korah. Scriptural discussions for better understanding can prove helpful, but power plays that harm others and divide the body of Christ are sinful. God does not expect us to be mindless followers, but He does demand respect and honor. When we have questions, we must approach the Lord with humility.

—Robin Fitzgerald.

Guiding the Superintendent

Once again, we are confronted with a fearful judgment on the sins of the people of Israel. The Lord threatened once again to punish the people's sins in a mighty and terrifying manner. And once again, Moses interceded effectually on behalf of the nation (Num. 16:22), even though they had rejected both him and God. Moses succeeded in his intercession, and the three leaders of the rebellion were set apart to face judgment. The people were warned to move away from the rebels so as not to be caught up in their punishment.

There are several themes in this account that we should learn from. One is that pride in self will always lead to destruction. Another is that success in recruiting great numbers to one's cause is by no means a sign that the cause is right. We must always respect authority from God when speaking against any perceived injustice. We must always remember what the Lord has done for us, especially during uncertain times.

DEVOTIONAL OUTLINE

1. God speaks (Num. 16:23-24). After threatening to consume the entire congregation of the people, God commanded Moses to move the people away from the tents of Korah, Dathan, and Abiram. God does not tolerate rebellion to continue in His holy community. He was building a holy nation, a people to be set apart for Himself.

How many of us have sacrificed the joy of knowing God's blessing for the sake of mere momentary gratification? We owe so much to God, and He calls for our allegiance in return.

2. Moses warns and challenges (Num. 16:25-30). The people were about to learn yet again a very important lesson. God will not countenance rebellion against His sovereignly chosen leaders—in any form, or from anybody.

As Moses spoke to the people, he issued a challenge to them regarding his own leadership. If they witnessed the deaths of these rebels in spectacular fashion, then they would know that the Lord had indeed chosen him to lead them. But if the rebels died in an ordinary manner—of natural causes over the course of time—then it meant that his leadership was illegitimate.

3. Judgment falls (Num. 16:31-35). Moses' confidence is astonishing. His faith in God is inspiring. God will answer us if we ask Him in faith and full confidence in His ability to accomplish His sovereign will. God did indeed do as Moses prophesied. The rebels and their families were completely swallowed up by a gaping maw in the earth, along with all their belongings. Almost immediately after that, the 250 rebellious Levites outside the tabernacle were instantly consumed by fire from the Lord. We learn here of the horrific consequences that rebellion brings.

Today, it is popular to "speak truth to power." Although injustice and corruption in high places must be challenged (and many of God's prophets did so), it should always be done humbly and prayerfully, with respect to the authority God has set in place.

CHILDREN'S CORNER

The fearful judgments recounted in this week's lesson may conjure disturbing images and feelings for children. Encourage them to focus on the fact that God is faithful to protect His chosen servants from those who rebel or seek to oppose them. Examples of authority for children to respect include their parents, their pastor, and their teachers.

—*Mike Spencer.*

SCRIPTURE LESSON TEXT

NUM. 20:1 Then came the children of Israel, *even* the whole congregation, into the desert of Zin in the first month: and the people abode in Kadesh; and Miriam died there, and was buried there.

2 And there was no water for the congregation: and they gathered themselves together against Moses and against Aaron.

3 And the people chode with Moses, and spake, saying, Would God that we had died when our brethren died before the LORD!

4 And why have ye brought up the congregation of the LORD into this wilderness, that we and our cattle should die there?

5 And wherefore have ye made us to come up out of Egypt, to bring us in unto this evil place? it *is* no place of seed, or of figs, or of vines, or of pomegranates; neither *is* there any water to drink.

6 And Moses and Aaron went from the presence of the assembly unto the door of the tabernacle of the congregation, and they fell upon their faces: and the glory of the LORD appeared unto them.

7 And the LORD spake unto Moses, saying,

8 Take the rod, and gather thou the assembly together, thou, and Aaron thy brother, and speak ye unto the rock before their eyes; and it shall give forth his water, and thou shalt bring forth to them water out of the rock: so thou shalt give the congregation and their beasts drink.

9 And Moses took the rod from before the LORD, as he commanded him.

10 And Moses and Aaron gathered the congregation together before the rock, and he said unto them, Hear now, ye rebels; must we fetch you water out of this rock?

11 And Moses lifted up his hand, and with his rod he smote the rock twice: and the water came out abundantly, and the congregation drank, and their beasts *also*.

12 And the LORD spake unto Moses and Aaron, Because ye believed me not, to sanctify me in the eyes of the children of Israel, therefore ye shall not bring this congregation into the land which I have given them.

13 This *is* the water of Meribah; because the children of Israel strove with the LORD, and he was sanctified in them.

NOTES

Water from the Rock

Lesson Text: Numbers 20:1-13

Related Scriptures: Exodus 15:22-27; Deuteronomy 1:37-40; 32:48-53; Numbers 20:24-29; Psalm 95:1-11

TIME: about 1405 B.C.   PLACE: Kadesh

GOLDEN TEXT—"Speak ye unto the rock before their eyes; and it shall give forth his water, and thou shalt bring forth to them water out of the rock" (Numbers 20:8).

Introduction

Failure to obey God always has consequences, regardless of how faithful others may perceive us to be. A lifetime of faithfulness does not give us a pass to indulge in occasional disobedience.

Failure to obey God does not mean that He no longer loves us. However, disobedience does invite discipline. In this week's lesson, we will see that this was true even for Moses, for God held him to the same standard He held every member of the nation of Israel.

Moses was a divinely called and equipped leader who had a unique relationship with God. As such, he especially was expected to carefully obey everything God commanded him. Moses was not immune from being disciplined for disobeying God's instructions. As great a man as he was, he was not God's equal in any way. Like us, he was expected to be an obedient servant of the Lord who simply and fully did what God called him to do. It is a privilege to serve the Lord, and it is imperative that we serve Him diligently.

LESSON OUTLINE

I. NATIONAL SADNESS—
Num. 20:1

II. NATIONAL CRISIS—
Num. 20:2-9

III. PERSONAL DISOBEDIENCE—
Num. 20:10-13

Exposition: Verse by Verse

NATIONAL SADNESS

NUM. 20:1 Then came the children of Israel, even the whole congregation, into the desert of Zin in the first month: and the people abode in Kadesh; and Miriam died there, and was buried there.

{The children of Israel were nearing the end of their wilderness wanderings. They had come to the wilderness of Zin. This was the first area inspected by the twelve spies and was just north of Kadesh (cf. 13:21, 26), where the people were now once again encamped after four decades of wandering.}^Q1

It had been a long time since the negative report of the ten rebellious spies set off a calamitous turn of events that led to the years of wandering through the wilderness. The generation that turned against God had now nearly all died off in the wilderness, and the new generation would soon take possession of the Promised Land. The death of Aaron at the end of this chapter is further indication that we are at the end of the forty-year sojourn (20:27-28).

A sad moment for Israel came as they stood on the brink of the wilderness of Zin at Kadesh when Miriam, the sister of Moses, died. Her obituary is admittedly quite simple, but it was undoubtedly a profound moment.

Miriam was a leader in Israel (cf. Mic. 6:4). {She was the sister of Moses, the divinely chosen leader and intercessor of Israel, and of Aaron, Israel's first high priest. She was also a songstress and prophetess (cf. Ex. 15:20-21).}^Q2 Even as a youth she showed great compassion and courage when she was assigned to look out for her baby brother Moses, whom their mother placed in a basket and set adrift on the river. When he was found by Pharaoh's daughter, Miriam arranged for his mother to serve as his nurse (cf. 2:1-10).

The death of Miriam shows us that there is no favoritism with God. When God said that those who were twenty and older at the time of the earlier rebellion at Kadesh would die in the wilderness, Miriam was not excluded (cf. Num. 14:28-30). Despite being a leader and the sister of Israel's two most influential men, she would never see the Promised Land.

Miriam's experience is a reminder that while in Christ we are saved from the eternal penalty of sin, our sinful actions can still carry temporal consequences. Miriam was a genuine follower of the Lord, but there were consequences for her rebellion against Moses (cf. 12:1-5). Her opposition to God's chosen leader could not be overlooked. Following the Lord does not mean we are somehow unaccountable for our actions; it means we are all the more accountable for what we do. Moses would soon face this truth in his own life.

NATIONAL CRISIS

2 And there was no water for the congregation: and they gathered themselves together against Moses and against Aaron.

3 And the people chode with Moses, and spake, saying, Would God that we had died when our brethren died before the Lord!

4 And why have ye brought up the congregation of the Lord into this wilderness, that we and our cattle should die there?

5 And wherefore have ye made us to come up out of Egypt, to bring us in unto this evil place? it is no place of seed, or of figs, or of vines, or of pomegranates; neither is there any water to drink.

6 And Moses and Aaron went from the presence of the assembly unto the door of the tabernacle of the congregation, and they fell upon their faces: and the glory of the Lord appeared unto them.

7 And the Lord spake unto Moses, saying,

8 Take the rod, and gather thou the assembly together, thou, and Aaron thy brother, and speak ye unto the rock before their eyes; and it shall give forth his water, and thou shalt bring forth to them water out of the rock: so thou shalt give the congregation and their beasts drink.

9 And Moses took the rod from before the Lord, as he commanded him.

Out of water again (Num. 20:2-3). The Zin wilderness was a dry place where water was scarce. {Now, in the familiar setting at Kadesh, they found the water supply there dried up as well.}Q3 This was a problem they had faced almost forty years earlier, {and their reaction this time was the same as it had been then. They met the situation with anger and unbelief, despite the precedent God had set for them many years before by providing water from the rock at Rephidim (cf. Ex. 17:1-7).}Q4

{The people raised their voices against Moses and Aaron in rage and stated that it would have been better for them to have died along with their brothers before the Lord.}Q5 This may refer specifically to those who died in Korah's revolt (Num. 16:32, 35), though others had died in God's judgments along the way (cf. 11:33; 14:36-37; 16:49). God had repeatedly spared the nation as a whole because of Moses' intercession (cf. Ex. 32:9-14; Num. 14:11-20; 16:20-22), yet, tragically, here they were again provoking the Lord and complaining against the man (Moses) who was constantly praying for them.

It is absolutely striking that the people were saying that being killed like Korah and other rebels was preferable to standing on the brink of entering the Promised Land. The Israelites never showed a substantial, ongoing faith in the Lord that He would see them through their hardships and do what He had promised. It is important to always trust in the Lord, regardless of what our circumstances might tell us.

An old accusation renewed (Num. 20:4-5). {The people asked Moses why he brought them into a wilderness that would surely end up being their graveyard.}Q6 What good was the Promised Land to them if they died before taking possession of it?

The people were so certain that they and their livestock were going to die that they could see no other possible outcome. They never asked Moses to pray for them. They never sought God's intervention. They looked only at the situation and then assumed the worst.

Let us be clear about one thing. The need for water was very real. Everywhere they looked was arid. There was no visible water supply around them. There was no water to drink, and they desperately needed it. Nothing written here should be taken to diminish the need the Israelites had. However, the one thing they lacked besides water was the one thing that would carry them through: faith. The severity of the problem was no excuse for not seeking and trusting God.

The people referred to the wilderness of Zin as an "evil," or bad, place (vs. 5). Again, they expressed their desire to have stayed in Egypt, which they did not acknowledge was evil in spite of the many generations of slavery they had endured there. It is stunning that they trusted in the previous slave drivers, known for their cruelty, to provide for them but did not trust God, who was abundantly merciful to them.

When the Israelites looked around at the surroundings of Zin, they saw no fruit or water. There was nothing from the land to eat or drink. What they failed to realize was that Zin was a stopping place, not a dwelling place. God did not intend to leave them there. It was necessary, however, for them to pass through.

If we want to get to where God is leading us, we must be prepared to go through a few valleys and deserts. There are valuable lessons to be learned in these places. We learn to trust God and cling closely to Him in the desert. He will provide for us and care for us, and we can rest assured that He will bring us through. The desert is a temporary place, and God will not abandon us there. He will give us water where there is no water and food where there is no food. He will care for our every need.

Moses and Aaron fall before the Lord (Num. 20:6-7). After hearing the people grumble against them once again, Moses and Aaron turned from the assembled crowd to the entrance of the tabernacle. There, they fell on their faces before the Lord as they had done numerous times before. How wonderful it would have been if the entire congregation had joined them in falling before the Lord in faith rather than complain in despair.

To be on our faces before the Lord is to be in a place of reverent submission. Moses and Aaron knew they were helpless without God, and they simply fell before Him. Before they could say a word, the glory of the Lord appeared, and God spoke to them.

God instructs Moses and Aaron (Num. 20:8-9). God told Moses to take the rod, or staff, he had and hold it in his hand while speaking to the rock that was before the people. The staff was a symbol of authority Moses had used on numerous occasions to effect God's miracles (cf. Ex. 4:17; 7:19-20; 14:15-22). It was not to be used for anything in this instance except to show authority.

The next instruction was to gather the people. The provision of water from the Lord was going to be demonstrated in front of them so they would see that it was once again God working through Moses to provide for the people.

{The final command was then for Moses and Aaron to tell the rock to bring forth water.}^{Q7} This order was different from the one given at Rephidim, where Moses was told to strike the rock with his staff (Ex. 17:6). This time he was told to simply speak to the rock without striking it. When he did so, God would bring forth enough water from the rock to provide for all the people, as well as their livestock. Moses took the staff as God commanded him and set out to care for the needs of the people.

PERSONAL DISOBEDIENCE

10 And Moses and Aaron gathered the congregation together before the rock, and he said unto them, Hear now, ye rebels; must we fetch you water out of this rock?

11 And Moses lifted up his hand, and with his rod he smote the rock twice: and the water came out abundantly, and the congregation drank, and their beasts also.

12 And the LORD spake unto Moses and Aaron, Because ye believed me not, to sanctify me in the eyes of the children of Israel, therefore ye shall not bring this congregation into the land which I have given them.

13 This is the water of Meribah; because the children of Israel strove with the LORD, and he was sanctified in them.

Moses' anger burns hot (Num. 20:10-11). {Moses and Aaron gathered the people together at the rock, and then Moses had an uncharacteristic outburst of anger. His frustration boiled over, and he no longer contained his resentment toward the people.}^{Q8}

{Calling the people rebels, Moses included himself along with God as one who would bring forth water. Notice that nowhere did God instruct Moses to speak to the people. Rather, He told him to speak to the rock.}^{Q9} God was perfectly capable of dealing with the people in their rebellion; His purpose for Moses was to provide for the people, not lecture them or rebuke them.

Moses' pride got the best of him as he talked down to the people in anger. Infuriated with their incessant insubordination, he took his staff and twice struck the rock with it. God had told him to strike the rock before, at Rephidim, but here He told Moses simply to speak to it. Moses took matters into his own hands, though, and hit the rock instead.

Water came immediately gushing out of the rock, and the people drank to their full. They also had plenty to give to their livestock. Despite His servant's pride and disobedience, God still provided for His people. The Lord's provision did not depend on the people's perfection. The children of Israel were rebellious, and Moses was angry and prideful in this instance, yet God took care of them anyway.

This does not mean, however, that the way we live is unimportant. Disobedience brings heavy consequences that can be avoided altogether if we simply do as God tells us. However, His love for us is not based on how well or consistently we act. It is reassuring to us that although the people of Israel were ungrateful and Moses was arrogant, God still remained faithful to His word and cared for His people.

Moses and Aaron are punished (Num. 20:12-13). God was angry with Moses and Aaron because they did not represent Him appropriately before the people.

Some have asserted that Moses was prevented from entering the Promised Land merely because he struck the rock instead of speaking to it. {That was the outward act of disobedience, to be sure, but God was more concerned with the motive behind it. Moses apparently did not *believe* God was going to do what He promised and achieve His purpose in this instance apart from using Moses' staff and rebuke, so he angrily struck the rock.}Q10

Acting out of anger almost always leads to more problems, because the anger of man does not produce the righteousness of God (Jas. 1:20). Moses' attitude was the root problem in this case, not simply the fact that he hit the rock.

Because of their unbelief, God declared that neither Moses nor Aaron would enter the Promised Land. Just as the older generation of Israelites that left Egypt would not receive this blessing of God, neither would the two leaders.

The water here was named Meribah, which means "quarreling." The people quarreled with the Lord, yet the Lord showed them that He is still holy. Their continued ingratitude did not keep Him from doing as He had promised. God keeps His word because He is holy, not because we are good.

Moses is an example for us today of the importance of daily, disciplined living and the need for constant reliance upon the Holy Spirit. Through many crises, Moses demonstrated unwavering faith in God and love for the people. Here, he showed neither, and it cost him. Let us follow the Lord in faith and love, serving Him and others every day.
—*Robert Ferguson, Jr.*

QUESTIONS

1. How long had the Israelites been on their wilderness journey when they came into the "desert of Zin" (Num. 20:1)?

2. Why was the death of Miriam so significant?

3. What crisis did the Israelites face at Kadesh?

4. How did the people react to this crisis?

5. What did the people say they would have preferred?

6. What familiar accusation did the people bring against Moses?

7. What did God tell Moses and Aaron to do to provide water?

8. In what uncharacteristic way did Moses react?

9. How did Moses transgress in his words to the people?

10. What was God most concerned about with Moses' disobedience?
—*Robert Ferguson, Jr.*

Preparing to Teach the Lesson

Our lessons this quarter in Leviticus and Numbers have been very helpful in teaching us about God's character and how we can prevail in the trials of life. Throughout our studies, we have seen the faithfulness of God in contrast to the doubt and depravity of man through Israel. As we look to pass the tests we face in life, we need to learn from both: we must emulate God's character while also learning from Israel's mistakes. Our last lesson this quarter brings us to Numbers 20, the story of God providing water from the rock. Like so many of our lessons, it is a story of both divine blessing and human failure.

TODAY'S AIM

Facts: to observe once again God's faithfulness to a people who were largely faithless.

Principle: to remind us that the Lord can be trusted to provide what is needed in any and every circumstance we encounter.

Application: to grow in our faith by reviewing God's faithful dealings with Moses and His people, even when both failed the Lord.

INTRODUCING THE LESSON

When Israel triumphantly passed through the Rea Sea, they left a life of harsh Egyptian slavery behind them forever. Although at that moment it would have been easy to assume that Israel's problems were over, we have seen this quarter that for God's people, trouble was unrelenting. What should have been a short journey from Egypt to Canaan turned into a grueling forty-year trek through the wilderness.

Throughout this quarter, we have seen instance after instance of the people of Israel failing the Lord as they faced various trials. Yes, times were difficult, and no one should minimize the severity of Israel's struggles in the hostile environment of the Sinai Peninsula. However, after reading the narratives of Leviticus and Numbers, we must concur that the Israelites were themselves the initiators of the majority of their problems; they were their own worst enemy.

In Numbers 20:1-13, we encounter one of the more curious passages in the Old Testament. When we read this episode without the benefit of the larger literary context, it is very difficult to understand why God would react to Moses in such a way. However, when we realize how this incident is actually the culmination of many previous situations recorded in the biblical record, the narrative becomes easier to understand.

DEVELOPING THE LESSON

1. The people's complaint (Num. 20:1-6). In verse 1, we enter our narrative with a context-setting statement: "Then came . . . the whole congregation, into the desert of Zin in the first month: and the people abode in Kadesh; and Miriam died there, and was buried there." We are told the month but not the year, but it was apparently near the end of their wilderness travels, and the generation of those who had left Egypt were dying off.

As we continue in the story, we learn that a natural difficulty of journeying in the wilderness arose once again—there was a water shortage. But with the natural problem there arose yet another spiritual problem—the people began to grumble again. They began to ask unhelpful questions, accusing Moses of bringing them out of Egypt only to let them die in this desolate place. Commendably, Moses and Aaron responded rightly by falling down before the Lord at the door of the tabernacle, where God's presence was manifested.

2. The Lord's command (Num. 20:7-8). Instead of punishing the complaining and ungrateful people, the Lord issued a command to Moses that, when followed, would provide the water the people needed. The means of providing the water was miraculous and very intentional in its design. The Lord told Moses, "Take the rod, and gather thou the assembly together, thou, and Aaron thy brother, and speak ye unto the rock before their eyes; and it shall give forth his water" (vs. 8).

3. Failure and consequences (Num. 20:9-13). Moses and Aaron moved forward in the execution of the Lord's plan, and initially it seemed as if things would go well. However, in anger Moses spoke harshly to the people, which seemed to indicate that the bringing forth of water was his doing rather than God's, then struck the rock twice with his staff rather than simply speaking to it as the Lord had ordered. While the Lord provided water from the rock, Moses' actions stand out as an act of disobedience to the command the Lord had just given.

The episode concludes with verses 12-13, where the Lord pronounced a severe judgment upon both Moses and Aaron. He stated, "Because ye believed me not, to sanctify me in the eyes of the children of Israel, therefore ye shall not bring this congregation into the land which I have given them" (vs. 12). Although it is not explained in the narrative itself how Moses' actions revealed unbelief, what he and Aaron did distracted Israel from the glory that was due to the Lord Himself. This was an especially serious offense for the leaders of God's people and warranted His judgment: they would not accompany the nation into the Promised Land. Sometimes the only way to learn something is through failure.

It should not have to be this way, but unfortunately we are not always open to learning through less painful means.

ILLUSTRATING THE LESSON

Sin has consequences. However, human failure does not make God any less faithful to His people.

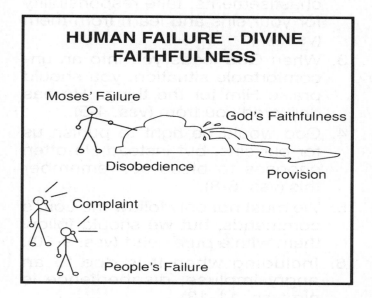

HUMAN FAILURE - DIVINE FAITHFULNESS

Moses' Failure

God's Faithfulness

Disobedience

Provision

Complaint

People's Failure

CONCLUDING THE LESSON

Numbers 20:1-13 is the conclusion of multiple narrative accounts this quarter that teach God's faithfulness in the face of human doubt. The congregation of Israel failed the Lord; the leadership of Israel failed; Moses and Aaron and Miriam failed.

Through it all, the Lord remained faithful to His people and the promises He had made to them. The very fact that God's people would still be allowed to enter the Promised Land was itself an amazing testimony to the Lord's grace, mercy, and patience.

ANTICIPATING THE NEXT LESSON

Our new quarter begins with a lesson that gives us insight into Jesus' mission on earth by comparing the preparation for His birth with the preparation for His death.

—*Nigel C. Black.*

PRACTICAL POINTS

1. Use your testimony to witness to your children so they do not make the same mistakes as you (Num. 20:1-2).
2. Do not blame the Lord for His chastisements; take responsibility for your sins and learn from them (vs. 3).
3. When God leads you into an uncomfortable situation, you should praise Him for the things He has delivered you from (vss. 4-5).
4. God would be right to punish us for our sins, but instead He often chooses to bless us; remember this (vss. 6-8).
5. We must not only follow the Lord's commands, but we should follow them with a pure heart (vss. 9-10).
6. Including when it is due to an angry impulse, disobedience is sin (vss. 11-13).

—Megan Hickman.

RESEARCH AND DISCUSSION

1. Why is it that we often look back fondly at the sins of our past? What does this say about our hearts?
2. How can complaining shape the way we feel about God (cf. Phil. 2:14-15)? Why do you think it is such a culturally prevalent sin?
3. Does it seem fair to you that we can sin through emotions? How does this show the impossibility of following God's law?
4. How do we often not realize that we are striving with the Lord when we fight with other people in our lives?

—Megan Hickman.

ILLUSTRATED HIGH POINTS

There was no water (Num. 20:2)

Water is vital for all living things.

Sometimes safe drinking water becomes unavailable. The Flint, Michigan, water crisis began in 2014. Inefficient water treatment allowed lead to contaminate the drinking water of over one hundred thousand people. There was no water safe enough to drink in the city system.

The Israelites thought they were going to die of thirst in the desert. They were so concerned with their physical needs that they forgot all about their spiritual needs.

We must remember that Christ is our source of Living Water.

Into this wilderness (vs. 4)

The wilderness can be a dangerous place. But many people enjoy being in the wilderness. They enjoy outdoor activities such as hiking, camping, hunting, or fishing. People who participate in these outdoor activities should know just how they need to prepare for them in order to be safe.

For example, people who go camping need to have some form of shelter, such as a tent or RV. They also need to pack clothing that is appropriate for the weather they will be encountering and bring an appropriate supply of food and water. A first aid kit is always essential. People who hunt or fish can obtain food in the wilderness if necessary, but they often bring provisions along as well.

God provided the Israelites with everything they needed in the wilderness—food, water, and shelter. Even though they had whatever they needed, they were often ungrateful and complained about God's provision.

We should always be thankful and content with whatever God provides.

—Chelsea Villaseñor.

Golden Text Illuminated

"Speak ye unto the rock before their eyes; and it shall give forth his water, and thou shalt bring forth to them water out of the rock" (Numbers 20:8).

Here we go again; the favorite song of the Israelites in Exodus and Numbers goes something like this: "Why have you brought us into this wilderness to die? Were there no graves in Egypt, that you brought us into this wilderness to die? Oh, how we wish we were still back in Egypt, where we had plenty of food and drink for the asking!"

No matter how often or how severely they were punished for complaining against Moses and about the Lord's provision for them, their attitudes never seemed to reform, and they continued to sing this same doleful dirge whenever adversity occurred.

This time, after the people finished their lament, Moses and Aaron knew what was likely to come next and dashed immediately to the door of the tabernacle, where they fell on their faces to intercede for the complaining people. The Lord Himself also seemed to anticipate the next step in this all-too-familiar drama. The Lord's glory immediately appeared to Moses and Aaron in response to their pleas.

But the Lord said nothing about any punishment for the complaining people! Perhaps by now He was just so used to their annoying complaints that He decided to skip the judgment part and go straight to providing what they desired. But more likely this was intended as a test for Moses and Aaron. Would they follow the Lord's instructions explicitly to the last detail, or would they use this occasion to exalt themselves, chiding the people as payback for the people chiding them?

Rather than merely speaking to the rock, as the Lord had commanded, Moses called the people "rebels" (vs. 10), arrogated credit for the miracle to himself, and angrily struck the rock with his staff. Aaron was complicit in this act. Water did indeed come forth abundantly from the rock, and the people probably never took notice of any impropriety in their eagerness to quench their thirst.

But the Lord immediately spoke to Moses and Aaron and pronounced a bitter judgment on their impudence: because they did not trust the Lord and did not give Him the glory for this miracle before the people, neither of them would lead the people into the Promised Land. They would both die before the Israelites entered their inheritance.

It is a sad realization that none of the three siblings, Moses, Aaron, or Miriam, who were instrumental in freeing the Hebrews from Egyptian slavery, ever personally experienced the expected fruit of their labors.

So, what are we to make of this rather sour-tasting episode? Was Moses and Aaron's offense really deserving of such a bitter penalty? Or was the Lord just nitpicking? What spiritual wisdom can we glean from this sad drama?

First, remember that the longer we have served the Lord faithfully, the more faithfulness God expects from us. Jesus put it thus: "Unto whomsoever much is given, of him shall be much required" (Luke 12:48). May we remember that our faithful service should never be viewed as license to disobey or arrogate God's glory to ourselves.

—*John Lody.*

Heart of the Lesson

It was not the first time the Israelites had found themselves in the desert without water. In Exodus 17, the Lord had affirmed Moses' leadership by giving him water from a rock for the people. However, the account of the Lord's faithfulness does not seem to have been handed down to the next generation, and the Israelites once again murmured against the Lord. But even more notably, today we will see Moses' rash reaction to this familiar situation, which cost him dearly.

The people's peril (Num. 20:1-5). The introduction to this chapter marks the fortieth year of the Israelites' wandering. The death of Miriam reveals the end of an age and another chance for God's people to enter the Promised Land. But as stated above, the Lord's faithfulness had been forgotten among the people.

Readers of the book of Numbers should be struck with the familiarity of this situation. The Israelites need water, complain to Moses, and blame the Lord for taking them into the wilderness to die. They even compare the desert to the riches of Egypt. The parallels to the story in Exodus 17 are darkly instructive.

How important it is to continually declare the goodness and faithfulness of the Lord to the next generation! If we do not learn from our mistakes and instruct our children appropriately, they will be prone to the same weaknesses.

The Lord's instructions (Num. 20:6-8). Once again, Moses sought the power of the Lord. Both Moses and Aaron knew that the people needed intercession for their complaining. Once again, God was faithful to provide, promising to bring water from a rock. All Moses had to do was speak to the rock.

God's mercy toward the Israelites should amaze us. It should give us great comfort to know that even when we commit the same sins repeatedly, God is patient with us, wanting us to repent. He is slow to anger and abounds in steadfast love (Ps. 103:8).

God's blessing and judgment (Num. 20:9-13). As Moses approached the rock to display God's works to the people, his language conveys exasperation: "Hear now, ye rebels; must we fetch you water out of this rock?" In his frustration, Moses did not give glory to the Lord for the work he was about to perform. His unthinking attitude regarding the miracle could have jeopardized the Israelites' chances for water. Yet when Moses disobeyed the Lord's instructions by striking the rock instead of speaking to it, the promised provision came anyway.

But Moses' actions were not without consequences. Because of his disobedience to the Lord, he would not lead the Israelites into the Promised Land.

Moses, above all others, knew the cost of disobeying God. But in his anger, he did not revere the Lord as he should have. As we grow in our faith, we gain more knowledge about how to honor God. We are judged on the condition of our hearts toward Him, even if our disobedience does not seem severe to the outside world. When Moses carelessly claimed authority over the miracle and struck the rock, he let his frustration with the Israelites become more important than serving God.

In spite of Moses' sin, God still used him to bless His people. When we do not perfectly submit to God, He is still merciful to us and uses us for His work anyway, but there are always consequences. We must check our motives to ensure we are following the Lord wholeheartedly.

—*Megan Hickman.*

World Missions

Bringing water from a rock is a picture of what God does with a hardened human heart when He fills it with the living water of Christ's gospel through the Holy Spirit. Christ, our Rock and spiritual foundation, pours forth the living water of salvation, making us alive with Him (I Cor. 10:4).

At the Bible correspondence school for Source of Light International in Madison, Georgia, over half the students taking the courses are prisoners. Prisoners are a mission field ready for harvest and thirsty for living water.

Here are excerpts from one prisoner's letter:

"I was a drug addict, alcoholic, and a very mean person, spending my life chasing the world. I would as soon hit you in the face as speak to you! I had a lot of anger and hate in me! My addictions, fighting, and thieving caused me to spend a lot of time in county jails and prison!

"I had a grudge against the world, and I showed it daily! I stayed high on cocaine and alcohol to numb the rage in me, or so I thought! Oh, how wrong I was! As my addictions got worse, I started stealing from family, friends, stores, wherever or whomever to get money to get my next high!

"Well that ended me up in prison . . . the Lord was trying to get my attention then! But I wasn't ready. I rejected Him!! I was released and went back to the same thing—drugs and liquor!

"My habits were getting worse and I didn't have the money to support them. I started embezzling money from the company I was working for. I knew it was wrong, but my addictions had a death grip on me. Well that got me 67–93 months in the Department of Corrections!! Again, Jesus was right there trying to get my attention. I wasn't ready and rejected Him again. . . .

"I was at rock bottom and had no earthly idea how to get up and out of the hole I was in. . . . I was laying in my rack one night and started to pray to God for help, guidance, and love, because I had none of these in my life. I asked the Lord to come into my life and save me, to be my Lord and Savior!! . . . I wasn't fighting, running, or rejecting Him anymore. . . .

"It took 39 years for me to finally accept Jesus Christ! He was there beside me the whole time and I chose to ignore Him, but He didn't [ignore] me!! I know and realize that my Lord was doing my prison time right beside me the whole time. . . . He saved my life in PRISON of all places. Jesus Christ is everywhere.

"I still have 32 months left to serve, but I am as free as I can be because of my Lord's love and grace. I'm attending church, reading my Bible, and praying to the Lord, things I never did. I am so grateful that I let go of the world and accepted Jesus Christ as my Lord and Savior. He has transformed my heart and life so much. All the anger, rage, addictions, and ignorance is gone. He has filled me with His love and grace, changed me from the inside out. . . .

"I still slip and fall, but Christ is right there to pick me up, dust me off, and lead me again. This is not a love you can ever get from the world. Anyone who doesn't know Christ needs to come to Him and experience the true love, peace, and freedom that you can only get from Him. . . . I'm so thankful and blessed! I love you, Jesus Christ! Thank you for setting me FREE!!"

—Kimberly Rae.

The Jewish Aspect

Be'erah shel Miriam ("Miriam's well") is the name of the spring that Jewish people believe miraculously provided water for the Israelites throughout the forty years they traveled in the wilderness. Jews believe it accompanied the people as they wandered (Shurpin, "Miriam's Well: Unravelling the Mystery," chabad.org).

Some commentators believe Miriam's gift was water because symbolically she represented the quality of adaptation; water adjusts to its surroundings. For example, it will naturally assume the shape of the container into which it flows. Writers state that Miriam too could adapt her faith and steadfastness to God's will under all circumstances (Reich, "Miriam's Well," torah.org)

As mentioned previously, Miriam was born during a hard time in Jewish history. When she was a young girl, Pharaoh decreed the murder of all male babies; yet rabbis believe Miriam persuaded her parents to have faith and remain together. Because she adapted to the oppression and suffering and remained strong in her faith, they believe God provided the Israelite people with the miraculous water in the desert on her behalf (Reich).

The Bible tells us that the congregation of Israel arrived at the desert of Zin, where Miriam died. At the same time, the congregation had no water, so they assembled against Moses and Aaron. Because of the timing of Miriam's death and the water shortage, the sages in the Talmud believed that for the previous forty years the water source was due to Miriam (Shurpin). In this week's Scripture lesson, the people find themselves without water. Rabbis believe Miriam's well ceased to produce water after she died.

The Talmud states that the Israelites had three gifts in the desert. One gift was the well of water, attributed to Miriam. The second gift was the pillar of cloud, attributed to Aaron. And the third gift was manna, attributed to Moses (Hattin, "Miriam's Well," etzion.org).

With the absence of the water, God instructed Moses to get the people water by speaking to the rock. Instead, Moses, gripped by anger, struck the rock twice. Rashi, an influential Jewish commentator stated in the Talmud that Miriam's well was a water-flowing rock that rolled alongside of Israel wherever it went. He claims that this was the rock Moses struck. He explains that Miriam's well had not actually run dry but that Moses did not *want* to draw forth any water for Israel because he was in mourning for his sister. In his grief, he had finally had enough of the people's murmurings.

According to Rashi, Moses was so upset over Miriam's death that he could not perform his duties as leader (Taanit 9a). Another rabbi surmises that Moses had not maintained the proper emotional state necessary to mediate between God and Israel (Schorsch, "Miriam's Death," jtsa.edu). It was this intentional neglect of his role that prevented Moses from entering the Promised Land.

Moses, Aaron, and Miriam held central roles in Jewish history. Although each of them demonstrated their humanity by making mistakes, God still used them to advance his plan. The stories of their lives (even apart from the legendary elements attached over the centuries) teach us that God uses imperfect people to do the miraculous. The lives of Moses, Aaron, and Miriam should inspire us to follow after God's plan.

—*Robin Fitzgerald.*

Guiding the Superintendent

Prior to this lesson text, God had provided another miraculous sign for the people; He did this specifically to put an end to their grumbling and complaining (Num. 17:1-12). He caused Aaron's staff, alone among all those belonging to other tribal leaders, to bud with almonds. This proved that the Lord had chosen Aaron and his descendants for the high priesthood.

Yet the people were again quick to forget their amazement at this demonstration of the power of the Lord. This time their complaints led even Moses astray, and he himself was prevented by the Lord from entering the Promised Land.

We learn in this lesson the pernicious way in which sin creeps into the lives of a congregation and how easily a people forget that which they once highly valued. We are reminded to keep the Lord and His holiness ever before us so that we do not take Him for granted.

DEVOTIONAL OUTLINE

1. The people complain (Num. 20:1-9). We find the Israelites in the desert of Zin. Miriam, Moses' sister, had recently died. Water was scarce, so once again the people came together to complain to Moses and Aaron. They once again went through their usual routine of wishing they had died rather than follow Moses. They again accused Moses of leading them to their deaths. They complained about the fruitlessness of the land. In short, they once again allowed their fears to master them.

Fearing swift judgment on the complaining, Moses and Aaron fell on their faces before the Lord. But then a surprising thing happened: God indeed appeared, but He merely ordered Moses and Aaron to provide water for the people. He told Moses to speak to a nearby rock and that water would spring from it, enough to sustain all the people and their livestock. But there was no mention of the judgment that Moses expected!

2. Moses strikes the rock (Num. 20:10-13). At the rock, Moses took it upon himself to chastise the people for their discontentment, calling them rebels. He also spoke as if he himself were miraculously producing the water. Then he angrily struck the rock with his staff instead of merely speaking to it as God had commanded.

In his anger over the Lord's apparent decision not to punish the people for their ingratitude, Moses failed to give Him the glory for the provision of water. For this reason, Moses and Aaron were disqualified from entering the Promised Land.

Jesus said, "Unto whomsoever much is given, of him shall be much required" (Luke 12:48). No servant of God had ever been entrusted with more authority and responsibility than Moses. He fell into the trap of assuming that his long and faithful service to the Lord entitled him to be selective in his obedience. The idea that faithfulness to God somehow gives us a free pass to sin, even occasionally, is a fatal one. Sin is sin. Thankfully, Christ suffered and died to pay for each one!

CHILDREN'S CORNER

Children will learn from this account that even if they serve God long and faithfully, they do not earn any right to sin. Thinking that we can go soft on sin shows that we are relying on works, for we are ignoring the truth that all sin is deadly: Christ Himself died to pay for each and every sin we ever commit!

—*Mike Spencer.*

and sent him packing. God then directed Abraham to return to the place called Bethel, where he had built his first altar to God. There he renewed his faith.

That is what we must do when we fail. We renew our faith. We confess, return to God, then continue to learn and grow. Where else can we go (cf. John 6:68)? Our confidence is that God will receive us. We are His children. Our sins and failures do not change that. God is going to be true to us no matter how faithless we have been or for however long we continue to wander.

Our failures often bring hard lessons. We may carry some baggage with us as we seek to move past them. There are consequences. But we should never doubt God's forgiveness and His love for us as His children. I have encountered many people who seem to think they have ruined their relationship with God because of some sin. They should read the lessons we have this quarter, or better yet, read the whole Bible! God does not cast off His children. Thankfully, His grace is sufficient for our failures.

The experience of learning that God is still with us, that He desires to teach and guide us even after our failures, often results in significant spiritual growth. As we grow in our understanding of the mercy of God, our spirits are encouraged and our hearts soar. Sometimes our failures can be our greatest teachers because we learn how good God is.

Donald Grey Barnhouse, a great preacher of the twentieth century, in his commentary *Genesis: A Devotional Exposition* (Zondervan), put it this way: "All Christians get out of the will of God at times and many remain out for long periods. . . . Jacob had to return from Padan-Aram, Moses wandered for forty years in Midian, David defiled himself with lust and blood, Peter denied the Lord with oaths and cursings, Thomas was loud in his doubting. . . . Faith is not a mushroom that grows overnight in damp soil; it is an oak tree that grows for a thousand years under the blast of the wind and rain." Amen.

God is gracious with us, even in our failures. Let us not give up because we have failed. Let us return to the God who loves us, who sent His Son to redeem us, and who claims us as His own.

How Can We Grow in Our Faith?

JEFFERY J. VANGOETHEM

In the first article this quarter, I noted the many failures we see in the life of the nation of Israel following the Exodus from Egypt. As they began their walk with God, their faith failed at many points, whether it was rebelling against Moses' leadership, grumbling against God's provision, or simply wanting to return to Egypt without completing the divine mission God had given them. Their faith needed to grow.

Somehow their confidence in God's provision and the availability of His mighty power often seemed to escape them, despite the miracles they had seen Him do. Still, God was patient. Even after the faithlessness of the spies who went into the land, God said to Moses, "I have pardoned according to thy word" (Num. 14:20). He was patient with them. God gives time for us to grow more mighty in our faith. How can we grow our faith? How can we get past faithless responses in life? What does it mean for faith to grow? Let us explore this.

The first key, of course, is to receive the Word of God. Faith is confidence that God will perform what He has promised in His Word. So we have to be in His Word. As we seek to believe and pray, here are some helpful practices through which God promises to grow us:

1. Spend ample time with God and His Word. It is hard to fuel our faith if we never stop to "fill up" on God and His Word. The Bible says, "So then faith cometh by hearing, and hearing by the word of God" (Rom. 10:17). Faith is driven by God's Word.

2. Narrow your focus. The writer of Hebrews spoke of "every weight" and the "sin which doth so easily beset us" (12:1). Sometimes we have to shed some things to grow spiritually. Would you ever see a track athlete compete with weights in his hands? Of course not! Can we ask the question, What might be hindering me in my spiritual growth? Ask God to show you what you can do to focus on Christ.

3. Get more desperate for God. The poor father of the demon-possessed boy of Mark 9 was desperate for Jesus to help him. But he sensed he did not have much faith, so he asked the Lord, "Lord, I believe; help thou my unbelief" (vs. 24). That was a good prayer. I am going to say more about prayer in a moment, but let us remember to honestly confess to God that we need help to grow in our faith. The first step of prayer is transparency with God.

4. Join forces with other Christians. I have always been amazed by that first story of the church in the upper room in Jerusalem after the Lord returned to heaven. Jesus had instructed His followers to wait for the Holy Spirit to come. They gathered to wait, not really knowing what to do. They had been told to preach the gospel to the ends of the earth, but they had no idea how to go about doing that. So they waited on God, praying together. Acts 1:14 emphasizes that they remained together. It was a group effort.

Our spiritual growth is stimulated and encouraged by time spent with others who seek to grow in faith as we do. Are we seeking out others to help our faith grow?

5. Pray consistently. Along with the Word, it is prayer that also makes our faith grow. As we receive the Word into our hearts, prayer energizes faith. As we meditate on God's Word and pray His promises back to Him, our faith grows. Praying God's promises does not remind Him what He has promised us; He never forgets. Instead, it helps us remember the Lord's faithfulness and goodness toward us.

The Bible says that "faith is the substance of things hoped for, the evidence of things not seen" (Heb. 11:1). The Word, prayer, and faith go together. Are we diligently seeking to pray God's promises? As our faith grows, our stability also grows (cf. Ps. 1:3). Our trust in God becomes stronger, and we gain confidence that He hears us when we pray. This is how we become like Elijah and other great people of the faith (cf. Jas. 5:17-18).

As we persevere in the life of prayer, we begin to see spiritual growth. We begin to delight more in God. We become more spiritually minded. We experience the help and assistance of the Holy Spirit. Our hearts grow warmer toward God and we become more confident in Him and more dependent on Him. Wonderful answers to prayer come when we stick with it. It is exciting to grow stronger in faith!

It may seem trite that I am just saying, "Read your Bible and pray more!" But yes, that is what I am saying! It remains the tested path to growing faith. Only, we must not give up, because God does not give up on us. As God eventually brought the Israelites through their season of difficulty into the Promised Land, He will teach us His will and way and show us mighty answers to prayer, even occasions of great deliverance.

Each and every one of us can aspire to become mighty in faith as we grow in the Word and in prayer. The great prayer teacher Andrew Murray issued a challenge with these words: "Men of all ages have prayed. . . . As they pleaded with God for the removal of the unknown obstacles, and in that preserving supplication were brought into a state of utter brokenness and helplessness, of entire resignation to Him, of union with His will, and of faith that could take hold of Him. . . . As God conquered them, they conquered God. As God prevails over us, we prevail with God" (*The Ministry of Intercession*, Aneko). The Word and prayer bring power as we grow more and more mighty in faith.

TOPICS FOR NEXT QUARTER

PARAGRAPHS ON PLACES AND PEOPLE

WILDERNESS OF PARAN

The wilderness of Paran (Num. 13:3) is a desert area of the Sinai Peninsula north of the Gulf of Aqaba. The Israelites camped here during their forty-year wanderings with Moses. It was the launching point for the Israelite spies to scout the land of Canaan.

It is believed that the area is the same as the "wilderness of Beersheba" mentioned in Genesis 21:14. It was here that Sarah's Egyptian bondservant, Hagar, was languishing with Ishmael, the son she had with Abraham. The angel of God came to their aid, and told Hagar the Lord would make a great nation of her son.

WATERS OF MERIBAH

This site was in a wilderness area located in the Desert of Zin, through which the Israelites traveled during their forty-year wanderings. It was here that the people complained against Moses and Aaron, asking them why they had led them out of Egypt into a dry and barren land to die (Num. 20:3-5).

The Lord told Moses, along with Aaron, to take up his staff and speak to a rock before the whole congregation. God would bring forth water from the rock for the people.

In his frustration, Moses struck the rock twice with his staff, disregarding the Lord's instructions. Because of this disobedient action, Moses would not be allowed to enter the Promised Land.

MIRIAM

Miriam, a prophetess of the Old Testament, was the sister of Aaron and Moses. She may be best known for leading the Israelite women in song and dance in praise to the Lord for His deliverance of the people through the Red Sea (Ex. 15:20-21).

Born into slavery with her family in Egypt, it was Miriam (although not specifically named in Scripture) who kept an eye on Moses' ark of bulrushes when it was placed along the banks of the Nile. When the ark was discovered by Pharaoh's daughter, Miriam approached the princess and arranged for Moses' mother, Jochebed, to nurse the infant Moses.

We learn in Numbers 20:1 that Miriam died in the Desert of Zin during the wilderness wanderings and was buried there.

CALEB

We read about Caleb, son of Jephunneh from the tribe of Judah, in Numbers 13. He was one of the twelve Israelite spies sent out by Moses from the wilderness of Paran to scout the land of Canaan and its people. These spies were to assess the might of the people and the potential of the land.

The twelve spies returned forty days later and reported to Moses and Aaron that Canaan was a land that "floweth with milk and honey" (vs. 27). Ten of the spies thought the people would be too mighty to conquer, but Caleb stood before the people and told them they should immediately conquer and possess the land because the Lord would be with them. He was rewarded for his faithful report many years later during the conquest of the land (Josh. 14:6-15).

—Dan Holland.

Daily Bible Readings for Home Study and Worship

(Readings are for the week previous to the lesson topics.)

1. September 5.   Ordination of Aaron and His Sons

M — Sacrifices and Offerings. Lev. 8:14-36.
T — Consecration of Priests. Exod. 29:1-9.
W — A Pleasing Aroma. Exod. 29:10-18.
T — A Wave Offering. Exod. 29:19-26.
F — A Regular Sacrifice. Exod. 29:38-46.
S — Draw Near to God. Heb. 10:19-25.
S — Moses Follows God's Commands. Lev. 8:1-13.

2. September 12.   Death of Nadab and Abihu

M — The Duty of Teaching. Lev. 10:8-11.
T — Eli's Sons Displease God. I Sam. 2:12-17.
W — The Death of Eli's Sons. I Sam. 4:11-17.
T — Achan Displeases the Lord. Josh. 7:1-20.
F — Ananias and Sapphira Displease God. Acts 5:1-11.
S — Serve God with Fear. Ps. 2:10-12.
S — Honor God's Awesome Holiness. Lev. 10:1-7.

3. September 19.   The Day of Atonement

M — Offerings for Atonement. Num. 29:7-11.
T — A Sacred Assembly. Lev. 23:26-32.
W — Christ Our Atonement. Isa. 53:4-6.
T — Sacrifice Once for All. Heb. 10:4-9.
F — Enter the Holy Place. Heb. 10:11-22.
S — Righteousness Through Faith. Rom. 3:21-26.
S — Aaron Enters the Sanctuary. Lev. 16:1-16.

4. September 26.   A Blasphemer Stoned

M — Worship God. Exod. 20:1-8.
T — Do Not Worship False Gods. Deut. 13:6-18.
W — The Arrogant Envied. Ps. 73:1-17.
T — The Arrogant Ruined. Ps. 73:18-28.
F — Recognizing Our Maker. Isa. 45:9-12.
S — Blaspheming the Holy Spirit. Matt. 12:30-32.
S — Ultimate Penalty for Blasphemy. Lev. 24:10-23.

5. October 3.   Complaints About Manna

M — Manna and Quail. Exod. 16:1-8.
T — Praise God for Provision. Ps. 34:1-22.
W — Ask for Needs. Matt. 6:9-13.
T — Spiritual Provision. Eph. 6:10-18.
F — Jesus Feeds the People. Mark 8:1-9.
S — A Warning from Israel's History. I Cor. 10:1-6.
S — Meat to Eat. Num. 11:4-6, 10-23.

6. October 10.   God Sends Quail and Plague

M — The Israelites' Craving Met. Exod. 16:9-13.
T — God Will Judge Wickedness. Ps. 1:1-6.
W — God's Care. Ps. 105:37-41.
T — Israel's Sin Against God. Ps. 78:18-31.
F — The Gospel Advances Despite Strife. Phil. 1:15-18.
S — Israel's Unfaithfulness. Ezek. 39:21-24.
S — God's Judgment. Num. 11:24-35.

7. October 17.   Miriam and Aaron Oppose Moses

M — Judgment upon Uzziah. II Chron. 26:16-21.
T — Judgment upon Moses. Deut. 34:5-12.
W — Seeing God's Glory. Exod. 33:12-23.
T — Jesus Greater than Moses. Heb. 3:1-6.
F — Blessing of Blamelessness. Ps. 119:1-8.
S — Purity in the Camp. Num. 5:1-14.
S — Response to Opposition. Num. 12:1-6.

8. October 24.   The Mission of Twelve Spies

M — Israel Moves On. Deut. 1:1-8.
T — Leaders Appointed. Deut. 1:9-18.
W — Spies Sent Out. Deut. 1:19-25.
T — God Is Great. Ps. 106:1-5.
F — Israel's Unbelief. Ps. 106:6-25.
S — Israel an Example to Us. I Cor. 10:11-13.
S — Exploring the Promised Land. Num. 13:1-3, 17-20, 25-33.

9. October 31.   Rebellion of the People

M — The Bronze Snake. Num. 21:4-9.
T — Give Thanks. Ps. 118:1-9.
W — God Is Worthy of Praise. Ps. 96:1-11.
T — Do Not Rebel. Heb. 3:8-16.
F — Always Thank God. Eph. 5:15-20.
S — God Desires Praise. I Chron. 16:23-36.
S — The Israelites Grumble—Again. Num. 14:1-12.

10. November 7.   Moses' Prayer and God's Answer

M — God Did Not Desert Israel. Neh. 9:16-21.
T — God Responds to Prayer. Ps. 102:1-28.
W — God Is Great. Ps. 145:1-7.
T — God Is Compassionate. Ps. 145:8-13.
F — God Watches Over His People. Ps. 145:14-21.
S — Jesus Faces Unbelief. John 12:37-40.
S — God Forgives. Num. 14:13-24.

11. November 14.   Korah's Rebellion

M — Anger and Pleas. Num. 16:15-22.
T — Love and Obey God. Deut. 11:1-7.
W — Gift of Leadership. Rom. 12:3-8.
T — Christ Is Our Leader. Isa. 55:1-7.
F — God's Leadership of Israel. II Chron. 13:10-12.
S — Give God the Glory. Ps. 29:1-11.
S — Attack on God's Appointed Leaders. Num. 16:1-14.

12. November 21.   Judgment on the Rebellion

M — The Plague. Num. 16:36-50.
T — God Our Refuge. Ps. 16:1-11.
W — Strength in God. Isa. 40:28-31.
T — More than Conquerors. Rom. 8:28-39.
F — Preserved Until His Coming. I Pet. 1:3-5.
S — Believers Kept Safe. Jude 1:24-25.
S — Korah's Demise. Num. 16:23-35.

13. November 28.   Water from the Rock

M — Bitter Waters Made Sweet. Exod. 15:22-27.
T — Moses Incurs Punishment. Deut. 1:37-40.
W — The Death of Aaron. Num. 20:24-29.
T — The Death of Moses. Deut. 32:48-52.
F — Hard Hearts. Ps. 95:1-11.
S — God Rescues Us. Ps. 66:8-12.
S — The Waters of Meribah. Num. 20:1-13.

REVIEW

What have you learned this quarter?

Can you answer these questions?

Faith on Trial

UNIT I: Learning God's Holiness

September 5

Ordination of Aaron and His Sons

1. What was the significance of the public washing of Aaron and his sons?
2. What was the ephod, and what was included in its composition?
3. What was attached to the breastplate of the high priest, and with what was the breastplate associated?
4. What purpose did the Urim and Thummim serve?
5. What does oil sometimes represent in Scripture?

September 12

Death of Nadab and Abihu

1. What was unacceptable about the fire that the two sons of Aaron brought before the Lord?
2. What did Moses immediately tell Aaron after the deaths of his two sons?
3. Who did Moses call on to remove the corpses of Nadab and Abihu, and why did he choose these men?
4. What was Aaron forbidden to do under these circumstance?
5. Why could Aaron, Eleazar, and Ithamar not leave the tabernacle?

September 19

The Day of Atonement

1. What occasion prompted God to give instructions for the Day of Atonement?
2. What sacrifices was Aaron to offer to the Lord for himself on the Day of Atonement?
3. What animal was to be presented as a sin offering for the people?
4. What is a key difference between the priesthood of Jesus and the priesthood of Aaron?
5. How did the sacrifice of the goat in particular point to Jesus?

September 26

A Blasphemer Stoned

1. What nationality was the man who is discussed in Leviticus 24:10?
2. Of what sin was this man guilty?
3. What did the people do with the man after he cursed God?
4. Who was responsible for carrying out the final punishment God commanded?

UNIT II: Seeing God's Faithfulness

October 3

Complaints about Manna

1. What was the specific complaint of the people at the start of this passage?
2. What did Moses' distress cause him to question?
3. Why did Moses ask the Lord to take his life?
4. What hard lesson would God teach in meeting the people's desire for meat?
5. What did Moses' reply to the Lord reflect?

October 10

God Sends Quail and Plague

1. What was the immediate result of the Spirit's coming upon the seventy elders?
2. Why did Joshua want Moses to stop Eldad and Medad from prophesying?
3. How did God bring quail into the Israelite camp?

4. What indicates how many quail came into the camp?
5. Why did God send a plague on the people?

October 17
Miriam and Aaron Oppose Moses
1. What did God do immediately in response to Miriam and Aaron's words against Moses?
2. How did God say He typically spoke with prophets?
3. How did God say He spoke with Moses?
4. In what way did God punish Miriam?
5. How did God answer Moses' prayer on behalf of Miriam?

October 24
The Mission of Twelve Spies
1. How many men were chosen to spy out the land of Canaan?
2. What two important purposes did Moses give for the mission of the spies?
3. What report did they give regarding the land itself?
4. What report did the majority of spies give concerning the people in the land?
5. How did Caleb's report contradict that of the majority?

UNIT III: Taking God Seriously
October 31
Rebellion of the People
1. What did the Israelites do after they heard the spies' reports?
2. Where did the people decide they would go?
3. How did Moses and Aaron react to the people's rebellious plan?
4. What did the people threaten to do to Joshua and Caleb?
5. What did God say He would do to the Israelites?

November 7
Moses' Prayer and God's Answer
1. How did Moses want God to display His great power?
2. On what basis did Moses appeal to God to pardon the people?
3. What judgment did the Lord pronounce on the rebels?
4. What two people were exempted from God's judgment?

November 14
Korah's Rebellion
1. What two tribes were involved in the rebellion against Moses and Aaron?
2. What did the rebels accuse Moses of doing?
3. What privileges did Korah and the other Levites already enjoy?
4. What did the Levites have against Aaron, and what role were they seeking?

November 21
Judgment on the Rebellion
1. Who went with Moses to approach Dathan and Abiram?
2. How would the people know that God had sent Moses?
3. What happened to Korah, Dathan, and Abiram immediately after Moses finished speaking?
4. What happened to the 250 men who joined Korah in the rebellion?

November 28
Water from the Rock
1. Why was the death of Miriam so significant?
2. What crisis did the Israelites face at Kadesh?
3. What did God tell Moses and Aaron to do to provide water?
4. How did Moses transgress in his words to the people?
5. What was God most concerned about with Moses' disobedience?